THE
LIVING WORD

A THEOLOGICAL STUDY OF
PREACHING AND THE CHURCH

◆

GUSTAF WINGREN

Professor of Systematic Theology
in the University of Lund

Wipf and Stock Publishers
EUGENE, OREGON

Translated by Victor C. Pogue
from the Swedish
PREDIKAN

Wipf and Stock Publishers
199 West 8th Avenue, Suite 3
Eugene, Oregon 97401

The Living Word
A Theological Study of Preaching and the Church
By Wingren, Gustaf
Copyright©1960 Kedidjan, Anna
ISBN: 1-57910-942-X
Publication date 4/24/2002
Previously published by SCM Press, LTD., 1960

THE LIVING WORD

CONTENTS

PREFACE

FOR more than one reason I am glad to write a preface to this book. I have enjoyed the privilege of the author's friendship for more than a decade and have participated with him in ecumenical conversations in England and abroad, across the North Sea, across the Channel and across the Atlantic. I have learnt much from him and have found his approach to the great theological questions of our day both stimulating and congenial.

In this book we meet with a Continental viewpoint less familiar to us but not less important than those other European influences which we style 'Dialectical' or 'Existentialist'. In the past, great teachers like Aulén and Nygren have convinced us that from Sweden there is much that we may thankfully receive; today Gustaf Wingren upholds the standard of excellence in the field of Systematic Theology which we expect to find in Lund. He has become one of the leading theologians of the whole ecumenical movement, and this book is one of the most significant Lutheran contributions to ecumenical understanding.

It is a book about preaching, but it does not deal with the techniques of the preacher's art; it deals with the more fundamental theological issues involved in the very act of preaching. What does the preacher (and his congregation) think that he is doing when he is preaching? Does he know that he is handling the Word by which in this age Almighty God rules his world? The light which this book throws upon such questions as these is derived from the Bible, and this is why the author speaks to us ecumenically, illuminating for us so many urgent theological issues concerning the Church's understanding of her own existence and of her mission in the world of today.

Moreover, this book is ecumenical because it speaks from one Christian tradition to others, 'from faith to faith'. It is personal and challenging, and it presents the great theological issues which it raises as matters of personal faith and obedience. It challenges not only the preacher but the hearer, not only the minister but the congregation. 'The preacher is one among others in a whole people of priests.' He

dares to preach, not because he is certain of himself, but because he is
certain that Christ is Lord, his own Lord. The congregation listens to
the preaching because it is the place where the certainty of Christ's
Lordship dwells. Preaching is the deed by which both the preacher
and the congregation affirm the fact which calls the Church into being,
that Christ is Lord. Gustaf Wingren's book will help us to understand
this truth afresh.

ALAN RICHARDSON

PUBLISHER'S NOTE

The original Swedish edition of this book contains many more footnotes referring in detail to Scandinavian, Continental and British theological literature. With the author's consent, these notes have been omitted, for three reasons. (1) The difficulty of translating worthily a Swedish book of this size and importance has meant a delay in the appearance of this English language edition, and consequently many of the original references are somewhat dated. (2) It is hoped that readers with linguistic equipment will be persuaded by this edition to secure for themselves the fuller original or the German translation, published in 1955. (3) There is also the factor of cost.

The phrasing of the chapter titles, and the divisions of the chapters into sections, are new features of this edition, approved by the author.

Biblical quotations are normally taken from the Revised Standard Version.

I

THE WORD AND MEN

1. The Word is to be preached, and men are to listen

THE place and function of preaching are best seen in relation to two major entities—the Word that is in the Bible, and the people who have come together. The task the preacher faces is that of bringing about a meeting between the Word and men, of establishing a bond between the passage in the Bible and the congregation. To come to the main argument of the present work, it may be said here on the very first page that in this meeting there comes about that for which both Word and men were destined. *The Word* exists to be made known; only when it is preached is its objective content fully disclosed. Man was created in the beginning by the creative Word, and destined to live by that which comes from the mouth of God. Men understand themselves aright and receive true human life in the hearing of God's Word. The Word reaches the objective for which it was sent out only when it effects an entrance into men. Man reaches the spring out of which he can draw human life only when the Word of the Creator comes to him.

This twofold thesis about the Word and men is not self-apparent. On the contrary, it needs to be properly established if it is to end by being strong enough to counteract the false opposing view which prevails widely today.

According to this interpretation of the Word of the Bible, it is by impartial examination, as little related to the preaching of the Word as possible, that the objective meaning of the text is established.[1] From this view it follows logically that what is unique and constitutive in

---

[1] Of course, from one point of view there is a measure of truth in this. The exegete must regard topical preaching as something which can distract him from attempting to elucidate the objective meaning of the Word. He must be engaged in *observation*, just as the scientist is when he investigates the setting and meaning of a thing. But just as the concept 'nourishment' implies that nourishment is given to men and is partaken of, so it is implied in the very existence of Scripture given in history that it shall be preached and listened to as a summons. That the Bible is kerygmatic in character is the conclusion reached by the exegete who works in a purely historical manner. Hence it follows that the preaching of Biblical passages adds nothing new or alien to them. What is subjective is not

preaching is its possession of a personal, subjective element. According to this school of thought, it is this personal, subjective element which makes preaching preaching. Hence it follows that the end towards which homiletics continually tends is the preacher—*his* openness to the Word, *his* contact with the times, *his* relation to God and *his* struggles. There is no possibility of escape from this totally unfruitful concentration on the preacher so long as there is this false basic assumption that preaching goes beyond a fully objective treatment of the Biblical passage in order that it may give a subjective colouring to what is to be read there.

If we consider the widely held view of the other entity, men, for whose sake the Word is preached, there, of course, we come up against the corresponding phenomenon. Man is thought of as a being whose existence is in himself, who is precisely as much man whether he accepts the Word or does not. If he does accept it something 'religious' is considered to have taken place, something which he himself could have managed without and still have retained his humanity. This 'religious' addition to the purely human corresponds exactly with the subjective, personal factor in the priest, which according to this same false basic conception is what constitutes preaching.

Throughout our whole treatment of this subject we shall oppose the mistaken conception of preaching that we have just outlined. From continually fresh points of view we shall come to perceive that the Word of Scripture which confronts us cries out to be preached, and that the Word's inmost being is laid bare where it is preached. In the same way men as men are intended for God's Word. They derive their life from the Word.

But describing preaching by showing its relation to the Word and men hardly makes such deep fundamental significance as we have suggested apparent. The simplest and most obvious meaning is that which lies on the surface. What is basic for preaching is the occurrence of two things: a word to proclaim, and one or several men to whom it can be proclaimed. It is contrary to the meaning of the word to restrict the term 'preaching' to the proclamation which takes place in the regular service of worship, set within the framework of a liturgy. Sermons which the New Testament reports—for example Peter's sermons in the earlier chapters of the Acts of the Apostles, which are the fundamental type of the Christian *kerygma*—are not always in a setting of worship. Never-

preaching but *bad* preaching, preaching that does not penetrate to the actual meaning of the passage.

theless, indispensable to preaching are the Word which is set forth and men before whom it is set forth. Petition, praise and intercession need not be heard by any man to be what they are. Research, learned exposition and biography are all descriptive literature, with no inherent necessity to be written *for* somebody. Propaganda is indeed directed at somebody and expects results in its hearers, but it does not by nature carry a message, a word about something that has taken place. So one might pass in review one type after another and find that preaching stands out unique and distinct from every other type—except one.

Suppose an important event has taken place, for example that an enemy has been beaten, and that someone is sent to those who are concerned in the event, say the inhabitants of a country or town, to tell them the news. It is of the essence of the news that it should be told to a body of people. So far as literary type is concerned there is no difference between such a message and a sermon. This is, however, really a confirmation of our own definition of preaching. To differentiate between a message and a sermon is not easy, for the difference is a vague and an elusive one. In the New Testament the words *kerygma* and *euangelion* contain a summary of the Christian message, and both these terms are derived from the same sphere: they are terms used of a herald or a courier. When Jesus and the Early Church wanted to describe in a word or two the nature of what should be preached they did not use wholly new terms, but expressions with deep roots and everyday usage, expressions which were already charged with a definite significance. Preaching is the news brought by a messenger. We shall deal with this aspect of preaching in much greater detail in what follows.

The place of preaching, then, is indicated by the double factor that a word is spoken to listening men. In the usual morning service in the Lutheran tradition this is further indicated by the use of a prescribed lectionary, that the passage is read from the pulpit itself and after it the sermon, the exposition of the passage, begins. In the pews men sit and wait for the Word. This simple picture, repeated Sunday by Sunday, is a good illustration of the nature of preaching, of all preaching without exception, the bringing of the entrusted message to those who are within call of the Word. But it is profitless to raise the mechanical question whether every sermon must have a text or not. When a missionary tells about Christ for the first time to a group that has come together by chance in an African or Asian village, it is not likely that he will begin by reading the Scriptures. But if the Gospel is set forth all the marks of preaching are present. The message to men after the first Pentecost, addressed to Jews in the first place, since they were nearest at hand, reaches the African or Asian village today through missionary preaching. If this preaching does not contain the Word of the Gospel, if it is not the message about Christ's work, about God's acts, but just talk about 'Christianity' as the most valuable, most advanced religion, then it may well be asked whether it is really preaching at all. Religious lectures about 'Christianity' are to be found even in Swedish morning services and, in spite of their beginning with a passage of Scripture, it is doubtful whether they should really be called sermons. The important question is not whether there is a passage as the starting point but whether what the preacher says as a whole is a *kerygma* or not. Once the carrying of a message is seen as the important thing, then the preacher will be glad to have a passage of Scripture prescribed and not to have to select it himself. It is, however, wrong to make that the indispensable sign of preaching. The truly Biblical perspective is much deeper: the Word is supremely God's creative Word, and this creative Word is flesh in Christ. Where Christ is preached there the Word is preached.

2. Theology's recovery of the Biblical proclamation

The problems on which we have just touched have, however, been matters of controversy in homiletical literature, and this is a suitable point at which to deal with them further.

It is agreed that preaching in some way is connected with the prominent place which the spoken word held in ancient Israel. If by preaching is meant exposition of Scripture, of the passage, then in that technical sense preaching did not begin before the post-Exilic period. Probably Judaism and Christianity—as a result of the influence of common cultic patterns—are alone among religions in this, that they place the freely offered message so much in the centre. The reading of a passage of Scripture, which characterized the synagogue service, is a sign of the bond with Judaism. In the history of homiletics the majority of those who formulated theories about preaching laid stress on the indispensability of a passage of Scripture for evangelical preaching, and had good historical basis for so doing. But certain important individuals have argued stoutly that it is both right and possible to preach without a passage. In our day Helmuth Schreiner in his comprehensive work, *Die Verkündigung des Wortes Gottes* (2 vols., 1936), has sought to settle the dispute by making a distinction between 'proclamation' and 'sermon'. In his view a 'sermon' is tied in two ways, partly to the service and partly to the passage of Scripture. 'Proclamation' is the wider concept, in which there is room for that which neither has liturgical setting nor is exposition of a passage. A linguistic distinction like that in itself seldom means much; all depends upon what concrete cases are included in each group. In this case Schreiner gives us an example of a 'proclamation' that is not a 'sermon', and not exposition, the missionary preaching in the Acts of the Apostles. Since the Petrine *kerygma* in the earlier part of the Acts is of basic importance for our treatment in what follows, we must tarry for a while with the problem that is presented here.

It must be said first of all that the original *kerygma*, of which information is provided in the first half of Acts, is clearly and obviously exposition of Scripture. Central to what is proclaimed is an event, the death and resurrection of Christ, and the message has its full meaning as a message only because of the fact that these events are set forth as the 'fulfilment of the Scriptures' (Acts 2.17, 25; 3.18, 24; 10.43 and many others). If we give up the somewhat mechanical view according to which exposition of Scripture is only found where a passage is first read out and then followed by an exposition, and instead pay attention to the factual content of what is spoken, then we may say that many such major portions as the Petrine speeches of Acts are in substance and content wholly expositions of Scripture. Still more important from the same fundamental point of view is the fact that the message about the fulfilment of the Old Testament prophecies in the death and resurrection of Jesus which was declared orally by the apostles, according to the Acts, is the *kerygma* which is found all through the collection of writings known as the New Testament and that each group of writings in the New Testament, whatever its own particular type, has this common *kerygma*. This means that if we take the New Testament in the written form in which we have it today and ask the question what its fundamental message is, what (to use a good hermeneutical term) its general scope is, the answer is identical with the brief summary given at the beginning of Acts: this Jesus, who was crucified, God has made to be Lord (Acts 2.36); the Prince of life who was insulted in Jerusalem, God has raised from the dead (Acts 3.15). The sermons in Acts are exposition of the Old Testament and, further, they are the very beginning of the New Testament's message about its fulfilment.

The *kerygma* in Acts, then, is exposition of certain Old Testament passages. This *kerygma*, however, is undeniably missionary preaching as Schreiner indicates. It is possible that the preaching we are told about

B

in the New Testament gives us no information at all about the preaching that took place within the congregation. C. H. Dodd appears to make a marked distinction between *kerygma* and *didache*. 'Teaching', *didache*, was built on the *kerygma* and was given to the Church members or to those who were about to become such. The *kerygma*, on the contrary, was itself missionary preaching, in Dodd's phrase 'the public proclamation of Christianity to the non-Christian world'. It is surprising that Dodd, who in the whole New Testament sees the manifestation of one and the same oft-repeated *kerygma*, can be tempted by such a distinction. The Epistles that preach the *kerygma* most clearly, for example I Peter and others like it, were sent to Christian *congregations* in trouble. All four Gospels show by their construction and proportions that for them the death and resurrection were the central part of Christ's ministry. It may, of course, be said that the New Testament as a whole is missionary writing, just as the Church is missionary. But in that case the liking for mechanical distinctions must give way, and the Christian life, both in its beginnings and its continuation, must be seen as *life from the Word*, as a continual returning to the one Gospel, to the Word about Christ. It is false intellectualism to separate those who belong to the Church from the missionary *kerygma*. That is considered possible only because of the idea in the background that once anyone has heard the Gospel he ought to go on gradually to something else. In fact the message of Christ's death and resurrection has as its most prominent objective that we who hear it should die and rise again and, since our own will refuses to submit itself to this living process, the word about Christ is always new, unexpected and fresh even to the day of our death. To apply the one *kerygma* to all the situations of life, to 'instruct' so that it conquers, overturns and builds up, certainly demands new *formulae*. There are marked differences even within the New Testament; the one *kerygma* is still there, however, in the midst of the differences, yes, even because of them. It is of the utmost importance that the New Testament's unity does not consist in expressions that are repeated in unchanging words in book after book.[1] The living breath of the *kerygma* is change. The moment that change departs, the deep unity of the message will have gone.

As we shall see later, the kernel of the *kerygma* of the Early Church is not to be found only in the New Testament but in the Bible as a whole.

[1] Equally important is the fact that the common message was derived from different parts of the Old Testament—for example, Ps. 22 and 69, the Servant Songs of Deutero-Isaiah, which constituted the Holy Scripture of the Christian community and were certainly read at worship.

There is a noticeable similarity between the view of the unity of the Scriptures towards which exegetes today are moving and the basic view of the content of the Scriptures on which the reformers, Luther especially, insisted in all their work. Not least in English exegesis and Biblical theology are traits found which point right back to the message of the Reformation. Moreover, an effort is being made to come to grips with the problem of 'communication'—with the task, that is, of passing on the Gospel to the world of today without making use of the help which the Reformation can undoubtedly offer. Biblical students in non-Lutheran countries who see the New Testament *kerygma* as centring on the fact of the death and resurrection of Christ may very well be unaware that in using these twin terms, death and resurrection, they have penetrated to the very core of Luther's theology, to the centre around which all that Luther says revolves, as a wheel on its axle. That applies not only to Luther himself but generally to the whole Lutheran Reformation as it was carried through in several European countries in the sixteenth century. The Reformation principle for preaching was very clear and simple: 'to preach' means to convey the content of the Scriptures to listeners, to say that which the Bible itself is saying. God speaks in the Bible, and when the Bible is proclaimed God speaks to men from the pulpit. God's Word is Christ. So when the Gospel sounds forth it is the living Christ come down among men who listen in faith. If the effort of the modern Biblical theologians is in the right direction, then Luther's preaching in the years when the Reformation was beginning stands forth as an unusually pure declaration of the New Testament *kerygma*. Moreover, this sixteenth-century preaching is, in its basic form and type, quite definitely congregational preaching. The Early Christian *kerygma* of Christ's work in death and resurrection has demonstrated, as no other factor in human history has, that it holds the power of renewing the Sunday preaching. In analysing the essential nature of preaching it is impossible to overlook that. The message of the cross and the resurrection is the main pillar, not only of missionary preaching, but of preaching in general.

The Lutheran assertion that we have just now mentioned, that preaching, in so far as it is Biblical preaching, is God's own speech to men, is very difficult to maintain in practice. Instead it is very easy to slip into the idea that preaching is only speech *about* God. Such a slip, once made, gradually alters the picture of God, so that he becomes the far-off deistic God who is remote from the preached word and is only spoken about as we speak about someone who is absent. It does not help to say of

God that he is God the Creator, and is near to those who are in distress, if the word of the preacher is not his *converse* with the men who are assembled there. God is creative and near simply by speaking his Word. Conversation, in its turn, does not take place through any sort of psychologically studied approach on the part of the preacher, but exclusively as, without artifice, the sermon elucidates the meaning of the passage as a word to the listening people. In homiletics, this view of preaching has been more difficult to *maintain* than might have been thought. Where success has come its way and it looks like being victorious its success is due, in the main, to the study of Luther and Biblical theology. Exchange of materials and points of view has been going on for some decades now between practical theology, and especially homiletics, on the one side and systematic and exegetical theology on the other. During the 1920s and the first part of the 1930s it was perhaps most of all systematic theology (for example, Barthian theology in Germany) which was the active partner as over against homiletics. In later years it seems to be exegetes—who in the course of time have been developing into Biblical theologians—who have largely come to set the pace, not least in Sweden and England. In addition the positions taken up by homiletics —arising from the actual problems of preaching—have for their part exercised a very wholesome influence on systematic and exegetical work. This influence has raised questions for theological science which, to its loss, it earlier avoided, but with which it is now being gradually driven to deal—not that thereby it becomes less scientific but, on the contrary, more so. Both exegetical and systematic theology have been led to a deeper understanding of their object, the Bible and the Christian message. A co-operation seems to be developing which is promoted best by concentrating on those questions that lie on the common boundaries of the special disciplines, while remaining fully conscious of the end we have in view.

3. The purpose of this book in the theological task

This work is meant to be a contribution of that nature to the ongoing debate on the problem. We are, accordingly, setting out to analyse preaching, the *kerygma*, the Christian message, in order to discover its essential nature. Ours is not a historical task, in the sense that we are trying to provide a picture of the Early Church proclamation, or of the preaching of the Reformation. In dealing with the problems set us in what follows we shall, of course, touch on historical matters, especially those concerning the Bible, the Ancient Church and the Reformation. But what we are really concerned about is the inner nature of preaching. What does it *mean* to preach? What is the *content* of preaching? To answer such questions correctly we turn to our sources, first and foremost to the Bible but also to those who laid bare for their contemporaries the Word of the Bible and especially to those who did that in the classic ages of the Church's history, for example in the first Christian centuries and in the age of the Reformation.[1] In discussing the rich material we shall strive, as far as possible, to maintain contact with what is happening in other realms in theological literature, since it is just the meeting between the actual tendencies in different disciplines that is of such great significance for the question of preaching and that may, presumably, enable progress to be made. Here, then, systematics, exegesis, study of Luther, homiletics and even patristics can meet together and contribute to the solution of a single problem—a theological problem—the problem of what preaching essentially is, of what makes it unique.

But if the basis for our study of preaching is thus somewhat broad and of wide theological character, it must, on the other hand, be immediately pointed out that our intention is to analyse what *preaching* essentially is, nothing more. With that our task is ended; we are not going on to provide a treatise on theology as a theology of the Word, a kerygmatic theology, a Scriptural theology or anything of that nature. It is preaching, that alone, which is to be discussed, and when the meaning and content of preaching has been determined then, for the time being, our task is ended.[2] No doubt questions about the task and method of theology should also be given fresh consideration and to some extent this has already been done, so that it can plainly be seen that the discussion is moving in the direction of such concepts as the Word, proclamation, *kerygma*. Tendencies are very much the same in such different countries as Scandinavia, England, Germany and Switzer-

[1] The periods whose expositors have most to teach us in this respect are those ages when the Biblical message had to contend against teachings which, in their content, were foreign and inimical to Christianity, when the Gospel was preached in a situation where it had been actively distorted. Thus the early anti-Gnostic period and the controversies of the Reformation stand out as the most instructive ages of Church history. The periods when all are agreed about the truth of the Bible unfailingly distract attention from the message and instead begin to focus attention on the question who they are who take Christianity seriously, who among these nominal Christians are the true Christians.

[2] The last section of this book is, accordingly, dominated by questions about the Scriptures, the Christian year and the faith in Christ implied in that—questions towards which the whole, in a certain sense, tends. The specific problem of what preaching is does not constitute a springboard from which one can leap to greater and more general matters, but is itself a terminus.

land. Just because that is so, it is all the more important to insist that the investigation we have now begun be restricted to the less demanding task of analysing the concept of preaching itself, so as clearly to demarcate the field of discussion that is to be ours. But as an introduction it is legitimate to indicate the wider theological problem, at the same time as it is pushed aside—or at any rate left for the future.

Approached from several different points of view, the old saying that it is the 'primacy of the Word' that differentiates the Reformation from Rome seems to gain fresh confirmation. The Word cannot be reckoned under any other category, whether under the teaching ministry of the Church or as a common conception of life, without thereby losing the standing that it has in Luther. If the right interpretation of the Word is that which is given by the Church then the primacy belongs to the Church and not to the Word. But the Word is first since Christ is first; so that the incarnate Word may sound forth he sends out his apostles—that is the correct order. There it is the Word which directs, the Word which fashions. Otherwise it becomes itself subject to direction and being fashioned. Similarly the Word is deprived of its position when theology begins with a clearly defined view of life involving certain fundamental questions to which the Bible and other Christian documents have got to give an answer. In this case the fundamental questions are provided without reference to the Word. The claim that the Word makes, however, implies that it has the right to formulate these questions itself. The Word loses part of its content when it is made to reply to questions other than those that spring from the Word itself. Since, then, the Word must be the starting point and the centre, there is much which indicates that, in determining the task of theology, we must, more consciously than heretofore, collect the threads about the concept of the Word, so that we may then look at other entities *from that viewpoint*. It is in this way that we should approach not only the Reformation but also the Early Church and, above all, the Bible.

A place for theology is provided through this fact alone, that it is a science, a science like other sciences. With the Enlightenment religion came to be regarded as a moment in, a part of, the life of culture, and Christianity came to be regarded as a religion. About the same time theology began to be looked on as a science in the technical sense—a science among others, with 'Christianity' as its object. Luther knew nothing of this 'science'. As *doctor biblicus* he studied the Word and spoke the Word to the men of his day, but there was no difference in essence between the exposition he gave in his lectures and what he delivered from the pulpit. Neither in the one place nor the other was it for Luther a question of 'religion' in the Enlightenment's understanding of the word, or of the cultivation of a certain part of human culture. At all times and in all places, it was a matter of *God's* Word *to* us. In recent theology certain definite tendencies have been revealed, and efforts made towards returning in this direction, with the desire of obliterating the distinction between preaching and theological science. Certainly Karl Barth, for example, has at times inclined towards such a view of theology. In that case theology at once turns into preaching or a science that aids preaching. Such a programme for theology merits detailed discussion. So far as Barth is concerned there is good reason to criticize the manner in which he carries out his programme. The fact is that in the Barthian theology 'the Word of God' is so conceived as to its content, that the Biblical message has sometimes real difficulty in making itself known. That, however, is a different matter, and the programme is not thereby invalidated. An examination of the programme can only take place as part of a thorough-going analysis of the methodology of theology. This task has been attempted in Sweden with an interest and thoroughness scarcely paralleled elsewhere and has been given a wide setting within the philosophy of religion—reference to the work of A. Nygren and R. Bring alone suffices.[1]

The essential nature of preaching can, however, be considered by itself. In this connexion it is not necessary to discuss theories of the philosophy of religion, or to determine the presuppositions of scientific work. No one has insisted on such a setting for preaching; compared with theology, preaching is a relatively independent entity, which can be made the subject of a systematic theological analysis. In saying all this we have defined the limitations of our task. Possibly all that remains to be mentioned in advance is that such very practical questions as the construction of a sermon, its delivery and such like obviously do not fall within our field.[2] Homiletics as a part of practical theology has its own

[1] See the present author's *Theology in Conflict: Nygren, Barth, Bultmann* (ET, 1958).
[2] It may possibly be useful to state definitely that we have not said that all that is written or said in the work of the Church must be preaching. The teaching function of the Church cannot be fully accommodated within the sphere of preaching; special forms are needed for the work of study and education. The same applies to the Church's duty to take action in certain cases in matters concerning the life of the community. It is often unfortunate to make use of preaching for such a purpose: that is clearly a misuse of preaching. For these tasks other vehicles are necessary. These are only two examples; others could be given. To avoid misunderstanding let it be emphasized that our positive handling of preaching does not for a moment involve a negative valuation of such ecclesiastical activity as does not come directly within the sphere of preach-

specific problems which are not theological in nature—just as exegesis as a philological discipline has its own special questions in which systematic theologians have no voice. What we are dealing with here is the problem of the essential theological nature of preaching. Because of the nature of the subject it cannot be treated simply as part of systematic theology; our understanding of preaching must be continually confronted with the ideas which are in the air in other disciplines, for the basis of preaching is the Word of the Scriptures and preaching is a continuing function in the actual life of the Church today. However, confronted by all these questions we shall confine ourselves throughout to such points of view as have a bearing on systematic theology, although they lie within the scope of other disciplines.

ing. On the other hand, it is clear that preaching must include both theoretical instruction about concrete historical events and appropriate references to questions relating to the community when the passage appointed for the day calls for that—to come back again to the two examples above. The important thing is that the passage in question, the part of the Bible appointed, and nothing else, shall regulate preaching and that the Word shall be spoken to those who are present. It is always primarily with those who are present that the Word is concerned. As soon as those who are absent become the people mainly in mind the kerygmatic character has gone, because in the meeting between the Word and men lies the essence of preaching.

II

THE ESCAPE FROM FALSE DILEMMAS

1. The congregation is in the Bible

As the function of preaching is to effect a meeting between the Word and men, as we have argued above, so the dilemma of preaching is that this *meeting* does not take place, and a wrong antithesis arises. *Either* preaching is concerned with the Word, the objective element, *or* with men, the subjective element. Whichever alternative is chosen the message is sacrificed. Preaching suffers most damage when this useless antithesis is created, and the damage is not repaired until the antithesis is scrapped. As that is one of the main purposes of this work, we are now devoting a section to describing the dilemma that this antithesis occasions, and the barrenness of the false situation that emerges from it.

In the Bible men, as hearers, are not additions to the naked Word spoken into empty space. That, however, is just the presupposition when division into objective and subjective is made. It is argued that first there is the Word, which loses nothing of its essential nature when it is neither spoken to, nor heard by, anyone, but rather belongs to a timelessly objective sphere and has its being in itself alone. Next, men are made to appear on the scene and in them the subjective element consisting in human appropriation and application of the Word. Where that mode of thought holds sway the usual reaction against any criticism is the anti-liberal reaction typical of today. According to the anti-liberals, anyone who upsets their scheme is denying that the Word is fully objective. In a word, he is enveloped in 'subjectivity'. Here the dilemma is a real one—there are only two choices. A third never appears above the horizon—indeed, cannot possibly be contemplated. The one hopeful aspect of such a situation, which is largely that of Protestantism today, is the instinctive acceptance of a foreign body alongside the Bible towards which the Bible, united with it in some way, always reaches out. For the Bible is just the third possibility, and the alien body implies that the Bible speaks, and so puts an end to these unbiblical distinctions.

The scarlet thread that runs through the Bible is God and his people.

As A. Fridrichsen has expressed it, 'God is the one pole in the power circuit, his people the other.' When a word is spoken which involves nobody as a hearer, that is not automatically meaningless talk; indeed many examples of such words are to be found, not least in the history of the teaching ministry of the Church. But such is not the word of the Bible. There, both under the old covenant and the new, we unfailingly find a chosen people. To think of the Bible, and not to think at the same time of Israel and the Church, is to omit from the Bible its character as message. The Bible does not acquire that character because we preach its Word, but already possesses it as a historic fact, and having that character it preaches. Our preaching, then, is just the Bible's own preaching—the passage to be expounded already has that meaning— and as God's people belong to the Bible's preaching, so the congregation belongs to ours. Hearers do not just come on the scene in a secondary way when the sermon begins, but that group was already there from the very first moment that the thought of preaching entered the preacher's mind. They were present in the sermon from the beginning not because the preacher felt a missionary interest in them, or had a personal knowledge of his public, but rather *because* they were there in the passage itself. The preacher, on first reading the prescribed passage, found there words, sentences, promises, admonitions belonging to God's people, which had been the water of life to them long before he was born and which will still be the same when his day is done. Now the Word is here in order that by means of a particular sermon it may speak to this congregation which has come to listen and which thereby reveals itself as the congregation of the Word.[1]

It may prove difficult, in the face of a particular congregation there in the pews, to maintain faith's conviction that these particular men are present because the Word has called them, but in essence the difficulty is of the same nature as that of believing that the passage is God's own Word. Here, indeed, there are not two difficulties but one, that of holding fast to the faith that God really speaks to us. If we attempt to isolate faith in the Word from the meeting between the Word and men, then

---

[1] There are, of course, sermons where men are not present from the first because there are bad sermons, sermons which do not set forth the Word. The main point which must be driven home is that the weakness of such bad sermons lies in the fact that the passage is never given its rightful place; the weakness is not that while the passage is correctly expounded the exposition is 'lifeless', 'uninspiring', etc. etc. If the passage is clearly and fully expounded the preaching is good. When the Bible lies open on the preacher's desk and the preparation of the sermon is about to begin, the worshippers have already come in; the passage contains these people since it is God's Word to his people.

faith in the Word immediately becomes spasmodic and stamped with Docetism. It is no longer faith in the message of the Word, but in its superhuman authority. Accordingly, the passage read becomes the objective entity because of its superhuman origin, whereas men come to Church for many reasons, some of them very superficial, some deeper and more pious. Such are the convictions that become inescapable when that view of the origin of Scripture is adopted. But, on the contrary, it is really the case that the Word and men belong together. When, on Sunday, the Word meets its congregation nothing new takes place in the history of the Word, for it was given from the first to a people of God. We might put it like this: before the Word was written down, it was spoken to a gainsaying Israel and to disciples who did not understand, but both groups were *chosen* by that God who spoke the Word. We can explain the origin of the entire Scriptures in the same relative way as we can explain why people come to church—or why the minister attempts to preach a good sermon. It is misleading to try and cut away the human element so as to arrive at a point where the Word is entirely divine, without any human admixture. Such an effort implies that God can be found and grasped beyond the human sphere whereas, as Luther says, the true God lies in the straw of the manger. From human mouths are heard the voice and tones of God, 'not the voice that speaks from heaven above, but that which is down in the midst of men'.[1]

2. Christ's conquest is for the congregation

It is, however, impossible to conserve the unity between the Word and men unless it is kept clearly in mind that men are prisoners of the devil. Otherwise the unity is a thought consciously retained for a brief hour, but forgotten as soon as the concrete problems of preaching loom up. These problems are then dealt with as if the Word and men stood opposed to each other as objective and subjective elements. That this antithesis should appear self-evident is due to the prevailing superficial concept of sin, according to which man listens to the Word and, though he 'has' sin, is none the less man. Now comes the news to which the Word accords major importance, that Christ has accomplished our redemption through his death and resurrection. That is the objective element, and it becomes subjective as soon as I take the Word of the Bible seriously and the depravity of sin begins to be rooted out as a result. Sin is here regarded as an individual attribute—though, of course

[1] *WA* 17(I), 224.5-7.

I think that I might be a light and have a story to tell but whose story and whose light is it? It is not my story it is God's story and God's light.

- you don't take and you don't receive, you *are* it

   You are *in* the Word

all 'have' it since their hearts are depraved. But in the New Testament
sin is a power under which the human race is imprisoned. It is not just
that all are wholly sinful, but that all are 'slaves' of sin (John 8.34),
'captive to the law of sin' (Rom. 7.23), enslaved by the devil, and 'the
devil has sinned from the beginning' (I John 3.8). Christ's death and
resurrection, of which the *kerygma* tells, are the contest with the Devil
and the victory over him; Christ came into the world 'to destroy . . . the
devil' (Heb. 2.14), 'to destroy the works of the devil' (I John 3.8).
Consequently the distinction between subjective and objective loses its
meaning, for the *kerygma* implies that when we speak of Christ's death
and resurrection—that unique, objective event, far back in time and
distant in space—we speak of an event in the life of man, an event that
happened to the man sitting listening in the pew. We are talking about
him when we talk about *Christ.* We do not first speak of the objective
event and then try to find a way of applying it to men, for in the *kerygma*
concerning Christ's death and resurrection man is already present; the
hearer is there in the passage when the minister opens the New Testament.

If this truth is to be kept in sight, the relation between Christ, the
world of men and Satan must be clearly visualized, as is the case in
Luke 11.21 f.: when a strong man, guarding his house, is overcome by
a stronger and conquered, an event takes place in which his household
is involved; they are affected by the struggle that is going on, and all is
utterly changed for them when victory has been won. The strong one is
Satan, the stronger is Christ, and the household is the human race. The
Gospel is called the Gospel, *besora*, 'good tidings', because it is news of
victory brought to those who are freed by it. The background to the
New Testament usage is Deutero-Isaiah's reference to a 'herald of good
tidings' who announces to God's people the victory the Creator has won
through Cyrus (Isa. 40.9; 41.27; 52.7—this last verse is quoted in Rom.
10.14 f., a fundamental passage of the New Testament, in which the
content of the *kerygma*, the Gospel, the Word, is set forth). If a tyrant
rules a household, then in the night when the tormentor is overpowered
and bound something happens to those held in tyranny. It is not only
in the life of him who conquers the Evil One that something happens,
but also in the lives of those who are held in bondage, even if at that
time they should chance to be in bed asleep. News of the night's events
is more than the story of the conqueror's achievement; when the prisoners hear the tidings they hear of something that involves themselves and
the speaker has no need of clever devices to apply the news personally

to the listeners. The listeners know that in telling of the night's achievement, which happened in the listeners' absence and without their knowledge, he is speaking of an objective event which happened in their own
lives. So the listeners hear from the mouth of the messenger the turning
point of their own existence being described, that is to say—if we may
continue to use this unfortunate terminology—they hear the subjective
element being set forth. Such news of victory is the Early Church's
message about Christ; hence its surprising simplicity and its concentration upon a definite outward event, Jesus' death and resurrection.
In his death and resurrection is the victory over the enemy of the human
race. So the news of the death and resurrection becomes the main content of the message that is ordained to reach the whole human race
through preaching.[1]   _self help

There is a 'subjective' preaching which is concerned with the religious
life of the hearers and takes care of it. Such preaching does not regard
its task as the bringing of a communication, a message, to those who have
come, but as caring for their religious life. There is also an 'objective'
preaching which sets forth the facts of the redemption which God has
wrought, which took place in Christ: that is done, all is clear—now you
have only to believe it.[2] Such preaching is regarded as bringing men
something which they have not already got. What is brought in the
Word is conceived of as something divine and supernatural, superhuman, which in the Church is to be added to the human, and sink into
the human as a transcendent body sinks down on the immanent. Super-
ficially, these two types of preaching are mutual enemies, but they grow
together from the same root and support each other superbly. The more
'subjective' the former becomes, and the more it dissolves everything
into pious emotions, so much the more 'objective' and the more massive
does the latter become, so much the more authoritative its teachings,
which have got to be believed, and its ecclesiastical usages which have
got to be observed. Just as in the former religion is conceived as essentially a cultivation of the human, so in the latter the Word and the
Church are conceived as essentially a coercion of the human, as some
miraculous anti-human command with which a capricious and power-

[1] World mission is a necessary consequence of the resurrection of Christ,
since it was the enemy of the whole human race who was defeated in the resurrection. Just as the old covenant could prophesy about redemption without
accomplishing it, so in the Old Testament certain foreshadowings of universalism keep appearing, though universalism did not become actual before Pentecost.
[2] The Satisfaction theory in the doctrine of redemption of Lutheran orthodoxy
often demanded such preaching, which in the first place is objective and then
—in order to apply it—subjective.

you cannot separate humans from the Word

thirsty God has, for some inconceivable reason, bound up redemption. Neither the one nor the other has a *kerygma* or a Gospel. Both live in a mental atmosphere where there is no real place for a message in the real, that is, the New Testament, sense of the word.

Bound up with this is another matter which is most important for what follows. What is to be accomplished by preaching in the world of men is viewed quite differently according to the point of view adopted. 'Subjective' preaching sets out to serve the cause of the cultivation of the mind and the building up of character, that is, it tries to develop religious personalities. 'Objective' preaching, on the contrary, is unique in trying to bring to the world of men something that that world lacks, something that cannot be developed or produced from what is human. Consequently the 'objective' type tends to establish its own Christian and ecclesiastical style of life, to generate out of the given revelation something specifically Christian for the shaping of life. Here again, to all appearance, the two types are antagonistic, but as usual, they really have a common root. For both of them it is more or less foreign to think of ordinary loyalty at work, the service of others, as that for which man needs to be set free. That, however, is how Luther looks at the matter: he deduces no ethic out of Christian doctrine, but plunges right into human life as it is and finds that all evil in the world comes from our own sin, from our slavery. We have no need of being fashioned into something or other: we only need to be set free, and then to take the place that is ours in our usual calling. Slavery simply means that we cannot be men, but when freed from the clutches of the Evil One we can be men again, we have reached the goal, we are redeemed. The Church of the first Christian centuries shared this conception of ethics, as is especially evident in the theology of Irenaeus.[1] The fundamental view of the Early Church and of the Reformation on this may be briefly summarized in the expression, 'the restored life of man'. If we think of the *kerygma* against its background of man's slavery under the Devil this way of looking at things becomes natural: the message of Christ's cross and resurrection restores the enslaved, that is, it gives man his natural life and thus redeems him. Subjective and objective preaching are alike in this that they have got to make something out of man's life, either a 'personality' or a 'churchman'—to be just a man seems too tame. A characteristic action of Jesus as a healer, to which the Gospels bear witness, is his sending of those whom he had healed back home again to their everyday life. Christ looses the bonds of the prisoners and

[1] See the present author's *Man and the Incarnation* (ET, 1959).

bids them return to that place in the life of the community to which they belong.[1]

It is characteristic of the present theological situation that a liberal period has been followed in our time by an anti-liberal reaction. The conflict between subjective and objective preaching is a reflection in the life of the Church of a conflict between two all-embracing theological systems which face the same dilemma as preaching. The chief representative of the anti-liberal reaction is Karl Barth. Examination of his theology leads to the quite definite conclusion that for Barth God and man are opposed to each other, and the question with which he is faced is where the emphasis is to be placed. Liberal theology, against which Barth reacted, emphasized man's significance and put him at the centre. Barth's alternative is to emphasize God's significance and to put him at the centre. Negatively it is of fundamental importance that Satan and sin play a very uncertain and minor role in Barth's theological system. Thus in no way is the approach of the theology that preceded it corrected, but instead the speculative antithesis between man and God remains unchanged. From that important consequences have followed for Barth's choice of his central idea, 'the Word of God', for the meaning of 'the Word' and, consequently, for the preaching that has flourished in the wake of dialectical theology. As God's Word, something absolute in a world of relatives, the Word possesses a transcendent element which is not to be imprisoned in the historically given Scriptures. Biblical witness is that which 'points' away from itself to 'God on high'. Barth sees the incarnation in the same light: the human in Christ reflects and calls to mind the divine; even in the incarnate Redeemer the cleavage between God and man remains practically unbridged. It is striking that time and again in his writings Barth reiterates his criticism, most consistent and clear, of Luther's doctrine of the unity of human and divine in Christ, the doctrine of *communicatio idiomatum*. He who does that rejects not only liberal, humanistic religion but also the most central conviction of Luther's original reformed theology. The entire Lutheran conception of the Word and preaching is only to be understood in the light of belief in God's becoming man in Christ, which is dogmatically expressed in the doctrine of the *communicatio idiomatum*.

The meaning of the *communicatio idiomatum* remains obscure until it is seen against the background of man's subjection to the Devil. God

[1] Mark 1.44; 2.11; 5.19, 34; 8.26; Luke 7.15. To be put in one's place as a healthy limb in the body is to belong to the fellowship of the Church in contrast to the fellowship of a sect. The fellowship of the saints becomes real in work and service for others in this world.

and man do not stand opposed to each other as two incompatible and parallel forms of being, but God and the Devil stand opposed as enemies. Man is God's creation who has been brought into captivity to the enemy of God. Christ's task is to enter human life, destroy Satanic might and free man. Christ's humanity is no limitation of the majesty of God, as Barth argues. Christ's humanity is the conqueror's—*God's*—presence on the field of battle where Satan is to be laid low in the conqueror's death and resurrection and forced to let go his grip on men.[1] Luther holds the very same view about the outward text of the Scriptures and about preaching: in what is outward and human we are close to the divine majesty whose work is to overcome the Devil and set men free. Preaching is not opposed to the human as human.[2] But all preaching must enter the fray against the power of Satan. The Devil 'trembles with fear' before the Gospel of the forgiveness of sins which snatches men out of his grasp. A preacher who so conceives the task of preaching has no use for the terms 'subjective' and 'objective', for he stands above the speculative antithesis between divine and human, transcendent and immanent, to which such terms but give expression. Men and Christ belong together. Since we have been incorporated in Christ's body, that is our true life and our freedom, at the same time as it is the building up of the Church of God.

3. 'Edification' builds up the congregation in Christ

'Edification' is a fundamental term in homiletics. All homiletical circles agree with the general statement that preaching should aim at edification. Problems arise and divisions show themselves when a definition of edification is sought for. Agreement about the general statement is, of course, due to the fact that it is a quotation from the New Testament: all that is said should, according to St Paul, be 'building up the the Church' (I Cor. 14.12; cf. vv. 4, 5, 17, 26, and Rom. 14.19). E. Vielhauer may well be right when he argues that the term 'edification', 'building up', in the New Testament *always* refers to a fellowship and

---

[1] God's honour expresses itself in God's accomplishing his work, that is in humbling himself to rescue men and slay the enemy. Had God remained on high, that for Luther would not have implied preservation of his majesty but its abandonment. He who clings to the man Jesus clings to God's true majesty.

[2] It is quite another matter that the Word stands opposed to us as sinful men. The collision is a sign of the old man's crucifixion and the resurrection of the new man, that is to say of the actualization of the *kerygma*, for the *kerygma* has to do with death and resurrection.

never once to the private religious life of an individual.[1] Our speech and our common life together, cult and ethic, come under the same category through the demand that 'all shall edify'. Word and action both serve towards one end, the edification of the Church so that it may be unbroken and united in Christ. At a very early date the New Testament term 'edification' lost the central place it must have had in the Pauline churches. This change took place in the course of the first few Christian centuries. It can scarcely be maintained that the Reformation repaired the damage thus wrought.[2] The term came into its own again under Pietism, to an appreciable extent, but by that time the landslide towards individualism has already taken place: the conception of the Church is shattered; the *ecclesia* is a collection of several individuals, and common worship is meant to 'edify' the individual. Now at the moment when the individual becomes central, feeling necessarily takes the same place: a person is 'edified' when he feels he is, and—as a natural consequence—he gives up worship when that feeling does not come. But if we start out from the Early Christian conception of fellowship, deadness of feeling on the part of an individual worshipper cannot destroy edification, the edification of the *congregation*. On the other hand to abandon the worship of the congregation with pious egocentricity means setting edification aside and breaking up the fellowship.

In relation to what we are discussing, however, the conception for which we were arguing before is much more important, that man is made free in the congregation: he is not equipped with a supernature but he becomes man. The renaissance of the idea of the Church in modern theology seems unfortunately to bring semi-Roman ideas in its train, so that the Church comes to be looked on as something superior to the natural life, something that has come down to earth, which is now a sort of overlay on the natural sphere. All such ideas of an overnature lead us away from the Early Christian idea of the Church as the new humanity. In a world where evil destroys God's creation humanity as it was destined to be by the Creator comes to clear focus in one place, in the congregation whose head is Christ, the conqueror of the enemy of man. The practice of setting the Church *over against* man has little foundation in the New Testament, and just as little in the Reformation. That, nevertheless, this way of looking at things is so common

---

[1] *Homiletiska principfragor*, I (1911), pp. 24 f.

[2] We have something to learn in this connexion from the theology of the Early Church, whose ideas on growth are closely bound up with its ideas on 'edification'. Note the connexion between 'growth' and 'edification' in Eph. 2.20 f. and 4.16. In Irenaeus, as in no other, such Biblical ideas are central.

C

today—that the question of the Church's *authority* is more important than the question of the content of the message—must be due to the fact that an anti-liberal reaction is going on. The idea that *man* is opposed by the Church, and flourishes when freed from its clutches, is rejected —but is then simply inverted. But there is hardly any matter in which we can arrive at the truth by inverting a lie.[1] The way to find out the truth is not to react against liberalism but to investigate how men thought in the days when the Word was the rock on which they built. Of all ecclesiastical complaints and longing backward glances, the most unfruitful is the yearning after the unfortunate periods when the Church held power over men. Better to wish ourselves back in the days when the Church knew what it had to preach and kept its message pure, even if those days did not coincide with days of good fortune but rather of martyrdom! If we go back to those days—that is, the days of the *Gospel* —we shall find there coherence between the Church and man rather than opposition. The practice of setting objective realities as blocks in opposition to man is not met with at all. Luther, for example, who likes to talk of baptism and the Lord's Supper as stronger supports for faith than the Word alone, does not lay the main emphasis on the fact that the sacraments are more massive or more tangible than the Word, but rather on the fact that a man in doubt can lose touch with the Word and believe that the Gospel is for others, not for him. On the other hand, the doubter himself has been baptized, he himself eats the bread and drinks the wine with his own mouth; and therefore he must say, 'I am here; this is happening to me.'[2] As the 'subject' thus becomes involved in the 'objective' facts redemption is secured. The sacraments are thus a witness to the fact that divine and human are not streams that flow side by side but rather belong together.[3]

In preaching the Word is addressed to all who have assembled. The individual who sits in the congregation has no experience of something happening to him as an individual; he can, in a sense, escape contact

[1] One of the real dangers of our time is that Karl Barth, without a doubt the most influential contemporary theologian, has, to a large extent, fallen victim to such a simple inversion of a false position, an inversion of the humanism of the nineteenth century.

[2] Cf. Luther, *WA* 2, 693.21-24: 'What does it avail that you can picture to yourself and believe that the death, the sin and the hell of others were overcome in Christ, if you do not also believe that your death, your sin and your hell were overcome there and washed away and so destroyed?'

[3] Both baptism and the Lord's Supper have their centre in the crucified and risen Christ and both incorporate man into the death and resurrection as something which happened to him. In the theology of Irenaeus the same tendency to make this linkage is, if possible, even stronger.

with the Word in a way that is never possible in baptism and the Lord's Supper. The preached Word is both Gospel and law. Both must strike home to man so that death and resurrection which are the kernel of the *kerygma* can take place in him. But the possibility of hearing only the law and allowing the Gospel to pass to others—and that is where doubt begins—arises more readily where the Word is preached to a large number of people than when in baptism the summons of the Gospel actively embraces me or when, in the Lord's Supper, it nourishes me. The problem on which we have touched, the problem of the Word which is not received, has given rise to lively debate in the history of dogma about the relation between the Word and the Spirit. It may well be the reality of this fact that makes it difficult to abandon the conceptual scheme of 'objective' and 'subjective'. The idea of a special gift of the Spirit, an outpouring of the Spirit on some while others listen to the naked Word, seems to solve our problem: they who receive the Spirit receive the Word, they who do not receive the Spirit do not receive the Word. The 'objective' fact is the same in both cases but the 'inner situation' is different: in one case natural reason alone is present, in the other faith is given by the Spirit. If it is along these lines that the problem is to be solved, the implication clearly is that the Spirit is given apart from the Word and not in it. If the Spirit is given in the Word there is no need for the roundabout road of a special outpouring, for Spirit and Word are one. So it is in Luther.

Thus we have an illustration of the difficulty of holding fast in concrete cases to the conviction that God himself, that Christ, is in the Word. We begin by thinking of the Word as in itself lifeless, powerless, and wondering whence life comes, and end by believing that we have got an answer when we have posited an outpouring of the Spirit apart from the Word. To ask why the fate of the Word can be so different in different cases, and why it can be so unsuccessful when it is preached on earth, is in reality the same as to ask why so few believed on Christ when he came into the world and why the multitude crucified him. If that is explained by supposing that there was a special outpouring of the Spirit on those who believed, then it becomes obvious that the really divine work is conceived as something of an unseen, spiritual nature, while Christ himself becomes just something external and powerless; he releases reactions which have their source elsewhere.

What gives rise to this erroneous conception is that from the very first God and man have been set in opposition to one another. So dead hearing is understandably regarded as something *human*, while faith implies a special outpouring *of the Spirit*. But if the fact really is that the Word is in conflict with the power of Satan, just as Christ came into the life of man 'to destroy the works of the Devil' under whom man was oppressed, then unbelief is not just an intellectual attitude on a purely human level but is something diabolical, and faith simply means that the Word's true content destroys its caricature. The Spirit is the Spirit that is in the Word, that is to say, in Christ, God's Spirit, who judges and makes alive. In unbelief sin rules, in belief Christ rules. The Word is never inactive: as Luther declares, if it does not bring life and forgiveness then it brings death and judgement. The contrast is not between God and man, with a tendency to split into higher and lower values, but between grace and judgement, Gospel and law, since all that God does in his Word is in conflict with Satan, both what he does with his 'left hand' and what he does with his 'right hand'; man cannot escape the Word, he is always subject to it, never superior to it. In unbelief he is not human but depraved, torn away from his humanity and condemned by the law. In faith he draws life from the Gospel. Then for the first time he becomes man.

III

THE BIBLE AS MESSAGE

1. The Bible's unity is found when it is preached

THE Bible is the book of the acts of God. Making use of a title taken
from the Bible itself, it might be called 'The Book of the Wars of the
Lord' (Num. 21.14). One God is spoken of in all of the Bible and
throughout it all that one God is faced with opposition. On the first few
pages is the story of how such opposition arose in the lives of the first
man and woman (Gen. 3). On the last page (Rev. 22), that opposition
is still not quite at an end, but the abiding expectation is there that he
shall come who has the power to annihilate the last remnant of opposition. Between beginning and end lies a history, a series of actions,
which are depicted in the Bible and which the Bible writers describe
and interpret. These actions have a common character throughout the
whole Bible: the one God is continually busy crushing the opposition
that rises against him. The transition from the Old Testament to the
New Testament involves no change in this respect other than that there
the struggle passes into its final stage. Important, however, as this
characteristic of the Bible is, the fact to which we just now made reference is equally important—that on the last page of the Bible the struggle
is not yet over; the final victory is still the object of expectation and
hope when the last page of the Bible has been written. That means
that the history which the Bible describes continues when the end
of the Bible has been reached. The end to which the Book of Revelation looks forward has still not come. Since the chain of actions in the
Bible is the onslaught that the true God makes on the opposition that
rises against him—that is, is conflict, warfare—the delay of the final
victory is certainly a significant fact, so far as the unity of the Bible is
concerned.

A series of actions that result in the breaking down of opposition
achieves its full meaning and coherence in the destruction of that
opposition. If one breaks into the series at any point and looks backward
from that point on all that has gone before he will not be able to under-

stand the full meaning and coherence of what he sees.[1] Since the breaking down of the opposition, of which the Bible speaks, was even then an
object of faith and hope, it is clear that the unity of the Bible is an
interpretation of faith. It is hopeless to treat it as something which has
to be proved in a fully convincing way as a scientific fact. On the contrary, we must begin with the contrary conviction. If the Bible is a
complete literary entity of the far past, wholly passive and dead, it has
no unity. On that way of looking at things we must not enquire about
its unity, but, instead, about its separate parts. It is owing to prosaic,
historical and philological work on the different passages that we have
gained knowledge of the Bible and that its individual words have something to say to us. Even the knowledge that the unity of the Bible consists in something other than literary unity is a gift that we have been
given by exegetes, working in strictly scientific ways. Indeed even the
knowledge which provides the starting point for the directly opposite
view has been given to us by detailed exegesis, form criticism, etc.[2]

If the New Testament—indeed the Bible generally—is *kerygma*, then,
as a matter of fact, its very text preaches: it announces the acts of the
Lord, it proclaims the living God and says that his hand is now on us
and it promises that his kingdom shall come. Here we have to do with
an activity that starts from the pages of the Bible and moves towards us.
This activity is a moment in the great unity that we have mentioned
before, the series of acts that is described in the Bible and has been
going on since the last page in the Bible was written down. To the
history of redemption belongs the preaching of the Bible's message;
that point of time, the time for preaching, is just our point of time, the
present day. The Bible itself preaches. He who preaches the Bible
reproduces its own content. But the preaching carries a message of victory and promises the coming of the kingdom; that belongs, as we have
seen, to the concept of preaching. Preaching binds together what God

[1] If the Bible is regarded as a document of a historical era that is finished, it
has no unity. The question is whether it belongs to the nature of historical science
to regard the Bible in that way. When it does so view the Bible, it nearly always
provides more illuminating and usable material for preaching than when it for-
gets detailed work and concerns itself with more general problems, for preaching
is not meant to deal with the nature of the Bible, its unity, etc., etc.—that is a
theological task—but should expound the Scriptures and allow the different
passages to speak in their own limited way. The Word is God's voice to which
man can only listen. It is God's action with those who have come together to
listen. Any exegetical work which provides concrete information about the
passage in question gives preaching its message.
[2] Form criticism of the Gospels has done away with the idea of the Gospels
as biographies of Jesus and left in its place small pieces, *pericopes*, which from
the first bare witness to Christ, and thus were, from the beginning, proclamation.

did in the past and what is yet to be. Preaching holds together the whole series of acts in the form of a message, a promise, a summons. But this series, so held together, is the unity of the Bible. In this way the Bible finds its unity when it preaches and is preached. If preaching is suppressed, then the book of God's acts falls apart as into *disjecta membra*. We shall return later to the consideration of this unique unity that the Word of the Bible possesses in preaching. The key position of preaching in this respect is bound up with the unique nature of Christ's victory of which the Bible tells. The victory has been won, but is not yet apparent to all eyes—and will be visible to all the world only at the *Parousia*. Between the victory that has been won and Christ's coming again, the victory is to be preached to the whole world. 'And this gospel of the kingdom will be preached throughout the whole world, as a testimony to all nations; and then the end will come' (Matt. 24.14; cf. Mark 13.10). Preaching is itself a part of that series of acts which the Bible depicts and which ends in the resurrection of the dead. For the moment let us forget this wider context which takes in our own time in an activity that starts out from the Bible. For the moment let us look at the Bible alone, concentrate our attention upon the fact that again and again it tells of acts that God did and does. We come across, that is to say, fragments of series of acts which it gives the historian trouble to bind into a unity, if he is not to start preaching.

The acts of God of which the Scriptures tell are acts with his people, with Israel. But before the account of Israel's call, before Abraham was called and promised the land there was a prehistory, and it dealt not specially with Israel but with all mankind (Gen. 1-11). This all-embracing history of humanity contains the accounts of the fall and the other stories of the transgressions of God's will, the story of Cain, 'the wickedness of man' (Gen. 6.5), the sin of Noah's sons and the tower of Babel. Then comes the call of Abraham. The choice of Israel, that is to say, takes place against the background of man's depravity. But just at that point where the original universalistic history and the more restricted series of events of election meet, a unique bond is to be seen. When Abraham is chosen a special history between God and a particular race begins, but just where this begins the promise is given, 'and by you *all the families of the earth* will bless themselves' (Gen. 12.3). The very object of the call, the very purpose of the restriction, is set forth even in Genesis as a return to the universalist breadth that is sacrificed in the call of Abraham. In the Old Testament, however, there is scarcely a word after this about mankind's relation to God. In the Old Testament

Israel holds the stage, and so long as that is the case all is seen from inside Israel. No one who speaks in the Old Testament speaks from outside Israel.[1] All speak on the basis of God's special creative activity with Israel, the call of Abraham, the delivery from Egypt. Only very seldom does anyone call to mind that God created the whole world. It is a striking fact that when references to the creation of the world become more plentiful, the end of Israel as a people is already showing on the horizon. The breadth of universalism can come only when Israel is shattered.[2]

Prehistory is a part of the history of humanity which ends somewhat blindly. It is cut short and replaced by a much longer part which deals with Israel, and that too ends blindly. There stands humanity, and over it arches the rainbow in the sky, the last sign of the covenant that the Lord made before he concentrated his attention on Israel (Gen. 9.8-17). There too, incomparably later in time, stands Israel with its land devastated, its freedom lost, but its hope undimmed—the last we hear of the people until a new series of acts begins with the birth in Bethlehem. In the New Testament the Jews are in the same way antagonistic, and in like manner without understanding, as were the heathen when Israel was chosen. In both cases it is a matter of a disobedient and, consequently, God-forsaken remnant by the side of a new mighty series of events which rolls victoriously onward. New Testament history, however, is not complete in itself but awaits its coming completion. It is interesting to note how often a New Testament book ends with the statement that they preached or with a command to preach (Matt. 28.19 f.; Mark 16.20; Acts 28.30 f.; Rom. 16.25 f.). The fact that preaching is now going on implies an expectation of that which is to come.[3] That mode of thought was still maintained in the Early Church: missionary proclamation at once melts into the events of the last times and binds together the resurrection of Christ and the consequent resurrection of those who believe in him and of all the dead. It is of the greatest

---

[1] Even the accounts of creation in Gen. 1-2 are projections of Israel's experiences. C. H. Dodd, *The Bible Today* (1947), p. 113, says of Gen. 1: 'Its writer has projected upon the universe that which he has learned from God's dealings with Israel.' These stories are, of course, also relatively late.

[2] Only in the New Testament is reference made regularly to the creation and not exclusively to deliverance from the Red Sea; only there is the universal power of Satan seen clearly as the enemy and not the particular peoples who fought against Israel; only there is redemption the possession of all men.

[3] When in Acts 1.6 the apostles ask if the kingdom is at this time to be restored to Israel, the only answer that Christ gives is the command to go out and witness in Jerusalem, in Judaea, in Samaria and to the uttermost ends of the earth. From the Christian point of view question and answer form a unity.

THE BIBLE AS MESSAGE

importance so far as the New Testament is concerned that a foreign
mission, that is a mission beyond Israel's frontiers, did not take place
before the resurrection of Christ and Pentecost—when the enemy was
beaten and the Spirit given. Up to that time Jesus and the Twelve—and
the Seventy as well—live in the narrow compass of Israel. The limitation
in God's dealings with men that took place when Israel was chosen,
remained, in the main, unbroken until Christ's resurrection. When this
limitation was disrupted under the pressure of powerful inner movements in the days of the apostles, Paul recalled the promise that was
given to Abraham, the father of the race, at the time when the universal
history of humanity ended, and the limitation began: 'By you all the
families of the earth will bless themselves' (Gal. 3.8; cf. Gen. 12.3).

Do we not catch a glimpse of a straight line here? A historian could
scarcely agree to that. He knows that 'prehistory', which we have treated
in an obscure and naive way as chronologically before Israel's history,
was, in fact, written down at a late stage in Israel's history. The problem
reminds us of another, that of the relation between Jesus and Paul.
There it is a case of the Synoptics' picture of Jesus, on the one side,
and Paul's belief in Christ, on the other. A historian knows that Paul's
letters are the earliest Christian documents and that all four Gospels
are, considered as writings, relatively late. In spite of that the question
is raised how Jesus' Gospel of the kingdom could change into Paul's
Gospel about Christ. To that it is answered that Paul's Gospel of the
cross and resurrection is the new form that the Gospel of the kingdom
has taken after Easter and Pentecost. A new situation has arisen; a new
event has come into the Gospel and given it a partly new content. It
must be asked what reason a historian can give for the thesis that the
kingdom promised by Jesus reached its fulfilment in his death and
resurrection which are described at the end of the Gospels. Would it
not be more correct to say that Jesus hoped for something of whose
fulfilment we know nothing?[1]

If this cautious position is scientifically correct the New Testament
falls asunder into two parts. In other words, he who sees the New
Testament as a unity is already a believer—he has linked up two series
of events, one that leads up to Christ's death and resurrection and one

[1] Paul, in common with other New Testament writers, has certainly a definite
conviction about the fulfilment of Jesus' words in his own death and resurrection, but that surely is no reason why a historian should adopt the same conviction. All the New Testament writers regard the Old Testament expectations
as having reached their fulfilment in Jesus' death and resurrection, but about
this a historian generally takes the line that it is a New Testament interpretation
of the Old Testament based on faith.

that follows the death and resurrection. But this link binding the two chains snaps in bits for him who does not believe in the death and resurrection. If then, an element of faith has slipped into New Testament exegesis one may wonder why it must be excluded when it is the unity of the Bible that is in question, or why in the New Testament, and only there, 'belief' is to be entered, and accounted for as belief, in a sharp contrast with 'historical science'. It is not usual to call attention to the fact that the unity of the New Testament is an interpretation of faith. But there is no essential difference between the unity of the New Testament and the unity of the Bible. It must be correct to regard the unity as open to dispute in both cases. That a difference is often made nowadays between the two cases is possibly due to the fact that in the theological faculties all the writings of the New Testament fall under one discipline, while a corresponding discipline for the Biblical writings as a whole is not usual.[1]

Assume that it is allowable to adopt the same method in dealing with the whole Bible as is adopted without objection in the case of the New Testament, and then the whole Bible from Genesis to Revelation can be regarded as a unity. In that case it would be taken for granted that the first question to be asked is not about when a book was written, but that the subject matter of the book will be the starting point. Then it would be natural to begin with prehistory in Genesis and afterwards take the events in this order: the choice of Israel and its struggles, its decline as a people, the life of Jesus, his death and resurrection, the preaching of the apostles and, as a last item, the events which the Apocalypse describes as future, and which have not yet begun.

2. The Bible's theme is the conflict of God and the Devil

The first thing in prehistory is that God is the Creator, he who calls all into existence and issues his orders: life comes from the Word of God.[2] Then sin emerges. In the form of 'the serpent' there comes on the scene that same inexplicable opposition to God which for us is represented by 'the Devil'. Creation and sin, taken together, describe the human situation. The earlier chapters in Genesis describe how wave

[1] In this respect there is an important difference between us and the time of the Reformation. Luther was *Doctor der Heiligen Schrift* (Professor of the Holy Scriptures), *doctor biblicus*, not Professor of the New Testament.

[2] For this section, reference may be made especially to J. Pedersen, *Israel* (vols. 1-2, 1926; vols. 3-4, 1947), and W. Eichrodt, *Theology of the OT* (ET, 1960); and, in Swedish, Ivan Engnell, *Gamla testament* (2 vols., 1945-47).

upon wave of depravity breaks over God's world, and how God's will
stands out against this onslaught. That period ends in the choice of
Abraham and the promise of the land. With that prehistory is at an end,
and Israel's history is beginning. Of that history the Exodus is the
foundation stone and indeed, in its way, is a sort of creation story. At
the peaks of the history which Israel enjoyed as a people, the memory
of the rescue from Egypt held the centre of attention. The creation of
the world was not so often called to mind; it was not the subject of
preaching to the nation.[1] It is very intimately connected with this that
the major prophets do not speak of a 'devil', of a universal power of evil.
Satan cannot be an actuality for thought so long as Israel exists. While
Israel is a power, and armed combat with the surrounding nations is
going on, these nations take the place of sin. Pharaoh is the original of
the 'enemies'. When Israel's army shatters the opposing might of the
neighbouring peoples creation is restored and the Exodus repeated. The
conflict between God and Satan can take no other form at this stage of
the history of God's redemption of mankind. Essentially, the event is
God's conflict with the Devil; basically it is a history where humanity is
present and in which the original and universal sin of man is being
driven out; but that can as little be said in advance as before his death
Jesus can preach the Pauline Gospel. In the Bible the rule stands that
God's acts must actually take place before new terms can be coined.

The new transforming event is the defeat, enslavement and ignominy
of Israel and Judah. Creation, Satan and sin find a bigger place in the
thought of Judaism than in the prophets. The major task of the prophets
was to proclaim God's judgements against Israel itself, not just against
the neighbouring peoples but against their own people. In that way the
meaning of 'enemy' was deepened to mean 'sin'. God's justice is something that can persist, though the nation perish. Indeed it even demands
that the disobedient nation should be defeated and punished. As long
as such thoughts are only spoken by the mouth of the prophets they do
not succeed in destroying the concentration on Israel. But they do
succeed in laying the foundation on which hope can build in the day
when outward history brings death and misfortune to Israel. Even ruin
itself can be a source of consolation. The coming of ruin is the victory
of the Lord: he is carrying out his designs, and by his Suffering Servant

[1] The central place of the Exodus is bound up with the fact that the account
of it formed the central point of the feast of the Passover which was celebrated
yearly. For this reason it is an important fact that a new meaning is given to the
Passover in the New Testament. On the other hand, creation has the same
meaning throughout the whole Bible.

he will reach all peoples and bring his original intention to bless in Abraham 'all the families of the earth' (Gen. 12.3) nearer to completion through the shattering of his people than he could when they were whole and entire. The God who by his Word through the mouth of the prophets had said that he would kill and that he would thereafter give life again—this God has already accomplished his death-bringing work. So a remnant of living Jews has now to wait for his life-giving work. Eschatology comes to be cultivated again, and is brought into relation with two other Jewish elements, the conception of Satan and the thought of creation. All three together are, in the new situation, identical respectively with the king's assumption of power, 'the enemies' and the Exodus from Egypt in the old situation. The fall of the nation remodels the armoury of ideas, and the vocabulary is filled with terms that are at home in the New Testament and which Jesus soon has on his lips. But, at the same time, the movement went in another direction. Through the shattering of the nation we are back in the chaos of mankind that prevailed before the call of Abraham. The series of events with Israel as its centre grows ripe for its ending, ripe to pass into that which, from the beginning, was God's objective for it: the history of mankind.

In Jesus prehistory begins anew. In his thought the demons come together into a unified power, with Satan as their chief. The old 'enemies' who were divided out among Israel's neighbours in the days—now past —of the chosen people again come together, and everywhere he feels the presence of one universal power of evil in the need of the sick, in the guilt of the tempted.[1] Conquering 'the prince of the evil spirits' means establishing God's rule for ever. When this takes place, God has again become the God of the whole world. His Word which creates and gives life, is once more the word for the whole world which must be preached to the ends of the earth. But till that moment when the divine victory has been won the restriction remains; the limitation to the house of Israel remains in force. Only after the resurrection are the apostles sent out. God's raising up his Servant Jesus out of the grave is the greatest, and the last, of the many mighty acts by which God raised up people in Israel. He was always the God who struck down and who healed, who raised up and 'awakened' out of defeat. Now at last he lifts up the whole race of man from death, which has held the field since the 'serpent' was

---

[1] It is not wholly without significance that the demons, seen from the point of view of the history of religions, are linked in Judaism with the gods of the heathen peoples, that is, of 'the enemies'. It is these enemy powers, unified in the Satanic kingdom, whom Jesus fights in every action. To some extent, therefore, it is the reshaping of a primitive cultic struggle.

victorious. But if Christ conquered at Easter how then can the Apocalypse describe as still in the *future* the conflict in which 'the dragon,
that ancient serpent, who is the Devil and Satan' is conquered and
brought to nought (Rev. 20.2-10)? The New Testament fulfilment is
divided into two stages, two phases separated in time, one that has
already taken place and one yet to come. The last and most radically
new item in the series of the acts of God that binds together the end
and the beginning of the Bible and which is the end and sum and unity
of all the acts described within the covers of the Bible is Christ's resurrection and ascension. But the really final event is the future that the
Apocalypse promises. If that end does not come, then Israel's conflict
and Christ's conflict have *not* brought God's created world back to the
purity it had before sin entered. If that end does not come then 'prehistory' continues to be a torso which ends blindly and is succeeded by
a specifically religious, particularized Israelitish history and now by
church history. Only the last judgement is, in the strictest meaning,
humanity's history as Gen. 1-11 is. At the last day the chain of events
of the Bible is complete and comes to an end.[1]

Between that which, for the witness of the New Testament about
Christ's acts, is the end and the complete end there is a gap. Christ's
work culminated in the resurrection and ascension; the resurrection of
humanity from the dead and the judgement lie in the future. Between
the former and the latter lies an empty space of waiting. It is in this
gap, this empty space, that *preaching* sends forth its voice. For this
reason the *Spirit* is poured out: 'But you shall receive power when the
Holy Spirit has come upon you; and ye shall be my witnesses . . . to the
end of the earth' (Acts 1.8).[2] There is no empty space here, no gap—

---

[1] A. G. Hebert, *Scripture and the Faith* (1947), pp. 23 ff., treats Gen. 1-11 as
a foreword and Gen. 12 ff. as an introduction to 'the main story', which begins
with the Exodus. That is due to a tendency, common in High Church circles,
to treat the Church as the end and meaning of the history of redemption. The
Bible itself, however, begins with the creation and ends with the Eternal City
in which there is no temple (Rev. 21.22); it begins with humanity and ends with
humanity. If we end with the Church then, essentially, our faith remains
narrowly confined to Israel, and men are regarded as existing in order that they
may subordinate themselves to the Church. The Early Church believed the
opposite—that the Church is Christ's coming to men in order to loose the bonds
of those who are in prison and let them go free. A Church that sees itself as the
end automatically adopts the same attitude towards those without as the Jews
had to their heathen neighbours. A Church that knows itself to be on pilgrimage
cannot view its own existence *vis à vis* those without otherwise than as Christ
viewed his *vis à vis* those still without then. 'The Son of man also came not to
be served, but to serve, and to give his life as a ransom for many' (Mark 10.45).

[2] According to the Israelitish conception—and this holds for the Bible generally—the Spirit and the Word belong together from the first. The word of the
mouth and the garb of the Spirit belong together (Ps. 33.6; 147.18; Isa. 34.16).

that only exists for those who regard preaching as a word of man *about* a divine act of long ago. Preaching means taking one's place in the midst of the mighty series of events that binds the beginning of creation in prehistory with the resurrection of the dead in eternity, to take God's Word, the source and spring of life, and speak it forth to men who cannot free themselves from the hold of the enemy. Where the Word is, there is *God*, involved in his duel with Satan that has been going on since prehistory and will come to an end when man is freed. The unity and the unbroken connexion of the series of events that the Bible describes lies in preaching *as a present event*. There is no other 'unity of the Bible'.[1]

3. The Bible's realism

It clearly appears from what has been already said that Christ, in his death and resurrection, is the centre of the message that the Bible as a whole proclaims. What is central in a message about a battle is naturally the news of victory. Further attention must be focused on that aspect of the matter later. But just now something else must be stressed. What makes the content of the Bible a message to us is that we in our lives have the same enemy to fight against as the Bible speaks of and Christ conquered. The moment that inner connexion between the Bible and us grows dim the Bible loses its character as message. There in the far past is the Bible with its world of thought and here are we in ours; how are two so different worlds to be brought together? In such a situation the main problem comes to be the authority of the Bible. If anyone is harassed by sin, he immediately asks about the message he hears because

The theological meaning of the relation between the Spirit and the Word becomes clearer when this primitive Oriental mode of thought is kept in mind: the Spirit's union with the outward word, God's activity in his Word.

[1] Perhaps it should be made quite clear that in the interpretation of the Biblical unity which has been given above, it is not presupposed that the Old Testament contains prophecies that are fulfilled in the New Testament, nor that it contains elements that should be interpreted allegorically, nor yet that the Old Testament, in a timeless way, contains the truth of redemption and that Christ only came to open the locked box. What is important, rather, is the following. (a) The Bible tells of ordinary, factual history which has the characteristic of a conflict. (b) The conflict has not reached its end with the end of the Bible. (c) To the continuation of that conflict preaching belongs as the present stage of God's redemptive action in history. (d) To preach or to hear someone preach is to take one's place within the long chain of Biblical acts; to give up preaching, on the contrary, is to drop the link from the chain which clips the present part to the part that precedes preaching—and a chain with a missing link is no longer whole, is not a 'unity'. (e) The conflict of Biblical history will be unfinished even when preaching comes to an end; it will only be complete in the resurrection of the dead and the last judgement.

the message describes his own need and the way out of it. But if the earth is a neutral place, free of all conflict, in which on one side are men who think freely and are masters of their own destiny and on the other side are books of various kinds, it must be a source of surprise that the Bible has any right to exercise control over men. Only in such a situation do questions about the inspiration of the Bible and the origin of the Canon become theologically important.[1] He for whom the message of the Bible is vital will not contest the belief that God directed the events that resulted in the writing of the books of the Bible and the work that in time resulted in their being collected into one. The whole history of redemption is just a simple course of events in which God is at work. Why should he become a passive God in the origin of the books? But the unexpressed conception basic to any theological system that makes the question of inspiration, or of the Canon, a *vital* concern must definitely be challenged. There is no possibility of attaining a right view of the Bible as long as such problems are dominant. The central realities of the Bible are suppressed until these problems become unimportant.[2] When the origin of the books and their collection is the important matter there results a completely unbiblical picture of God as someone far distant from us who sent his revelation down to us in a case, the Bible.

It is not true that what we find in the Bible derives its authority from the way the Bible has come into existence. It is rather the case that the

[1] It is a very important fact that Luther, who was occupied all his life with the text of the Bible and had the task of opposing that Word to the authorities which had been growing up for almost a thousand years, was uninterested in the question of the inspiration of the Bible and, without any embarrassment, could talk about how poorly the Biblical authors order and relate the historical material. Luther resembles a man who is awaiting a sentence of death, but instead hears his acquittal being read aloud. Such a man is eager for the news that is to be made known to him and that will decide whether he is to live or die. It is the decision that is vital to him, and even if he observes that, for example, a place name or something like that which is mentioned in the announcement is incorrect he will pay no attention to it. He who is irritated by such a thing must be unharassed and sure of himself.

[2] Though believers in the theory of verbal inspiration must necessarily change over to the belief that the *words* of the Bible are not literally inspired, the question still continues to be of importance. In getting rid of the problem one does not make the words of less significance, because the centre of the Bible is *Christ* and the words are the humanity of Christ in which the *Spirit* dwells. It is the question about Christ that is important and primary: he is the Living One, and it is his life that is brought to us by the outward word. If we begin with inspiration, then without desiring it we arrive at a Christ who is remote and shut up in a Biblical box, whose life is derivative, whose holiness springs from the prior holiness of the Biblical word. In the former case the word is the Word of the living God in the present; in the latter the word is a divine record of what God said long ago.

books of the Bible deal with the most important series of events that can
be made known at all to men and for that reason the Bible has an importance possessed by no other book. Since the Lord of the Bible is
Christ, the same thing may be expressed in this way—the Bible is an
incomparable book because it gives us Christ. On the other hand, we
make facts stand on their head when we say that Christ is important
because he is spoken of in the Bible, which is of supernatural origin.
Faith can well endure that those who decided on the contents of the
Canon hesitated and disputed about certain books; it can endure that
the books of the Bible show traces of different sources and that questions
of authorship are uncertain, that legendary elements are to be detected,
and that insertions and omissions in the text come to light on examination. All these are peripheral to the fixed and secure centre, which lies
in the historical course of events itself, lies in the conflict, and, therefore,
last of all in Christ's death and resurrection.[1] If Christ has not really
risen from the dead our faith is vain and 'then is our preaching in vain'
(I Cor. 15.14), for there is no resurrection of the dead and the Bible is
just a source of information about religion. We propose to consider the
question about factuality later on when discussing the *kerygma*. It suffices at this point to emphasize where the centre of gravity lies. It lies
in the full reality and factuality of the history of redemption and not in
any special character of sanctity in the origin of the Bible as a book.

Since, then, the centre of gravity lies in what *happened*, any piece of
exegesis which sets out simply and solely to lay bare the historical truth
is of positive value for preaching. That is to be especially stressed in
dealing with the exegesis of the Old Testament. So far as the New Testament is concerned, it has often and rightly been insisted how important
a correct understanding of the text and its literal meaning is. On the
contrary, when it is the Old Testament that is being dealt with, the
assumption is readily made that there is a difference between our present
life of faith and the historical meaning of the Old Testament. The
historical meaning is made to refer to Israel who once heard the Old
Testament Word, while we, who hear that word in the time of its fulfil-

---

[1] The question immediately arises if it does not make it easier to grasp what
is central, the message, when it is seen clearly that the historical conditions for
the origin of the Bible were the same as those affecting other books. By these
historical observations the attention of readers of the Bible and of preachers
is focused in the right direction: here, right in the midst of this Biblical world
something must have happened—what was it? Past generations, believing in
verbal inspiration, found it more difficult; these could scarcely fail to adopt a
specially religious attitude of mind as they listened to the Bible's words, that is
to say, they shut out the power of the Scriptures and instead expected power
from their own piety.

ment, live upon the meaning the Old Testament gets from the New Testament, which is other than the historical. In some cases that sort of reasoning may hit on the truth. But it cannot represent a satisfactory solution of the problem, for according to this view the purely historical exegesis of the Old Testament has no immediate significance for our present-day Christian preaching. Actually, such exegesis has positive significance. It penetrates deeper into the passages of the Old Testament, and gives the preacher better stuff than can be provided by typological exegesis which decides beforehand that every text of the Old Testament must refer to Christ. The explanation for this is not that the exegete has in hidden ways been influenced by the Christian point of view, but that he has penetrated to the real event about which the Old Testament bears witness; an event that belongs to our own lives.

The Old Testament is a history of *humanity's* liberation, humanity's conflict, in the destiny of a single people, a conflict to get free of sin, a conflict that is won in Christ's death and resurrection. In my present life the same conflict is taking place, because I am a man and belong to the humanity whose struggle goes on in Israel. My freedom depends on my continuing in the struggle till victory is achieved, that is, it depends on my incorporation into Christ's death and resurrection. That is the objective I have not yet reached (Phil. 3.9-12). Just now, perhaps, Jacob's struggle at the brook Jabbok is the beginning on which I am engaged.[1] The *whole* story which the Bible relates is, in its expanse from creation till the resurrection, 'the story of Everyman'. To understand this Biblical history, even when it is only a matter of a tiny fragment of it, means understanding ourselves, and thus the Word of the Bible comes to be a word that says something to us in the *actual* situation in which we find ourselves, not in some pious and constructed situation. To be in the battle into which ordinary life in its impious and savage ways flings us is to be shaped by the hands of God, as Israel was. Only the *historical* meaning of the Old Testament makes that clear to us. Flight from the historical meaning is flight from our own humanity and from Christ's humanity. It is the construction of a special religious upper storey above the life of man, of such great capacity that no message can be heard there.

[1] About this episode in the life of Jacob (Gen. 32.22 ff.) it should be noted that the religio-historical theories that find its background in a story of the god of the river or the night do not deprive the passage of its ability to speak to us, but increase it. There was a struggle, too, which the people of Israel had to wage to be Israel, and to win through to greater clarity of faith in God. Thus the passage comes all the closer to us who have also heathenism in our background and idols in our origins.

D

IV

CHRIST THE LORD OF
THE SCRIPTURES

1. The Scriptures proclaim a conflict and a victory

THE centre of the New Testament is the news of Christ, and the centre of the news about Christ is the news of his death and resurrection. And this news is the resolution of the conflict that dominates all Israel's history. The Old Testament Scriptures as a whole point forward to something that is to happen and has not yet happened.[1] The New Testament Scriptures just as clearly look back on something that has happened and that has definitely put an end to all waiting on something else. Christ rises up as Lord on the frontier between these two sets of writings. It is incorrect to reckon Christ as belonging only to the New Testament, and shut him out from the Old. It is equally incorrect to think of the Old Testament alone as Holy Scripture containing Christ, and the New Testament as a mere appendix about the fulfilment. In both cases Christ is locked up in a book and is not Lord. But Christ is Lord of the Scriptures, and they are his servants, the bearers of *his* life. By their very attitude—looking forward and backward—they put themselves below him and set *him* in the centre.[2]

Our plan is to examine first the *kerygma* that unites the New Testament Scriptures. After that we shall learn that the same *kerygma* is the centre and basic message of the whole Bible. This is because the New Testament *kerygma* is news of a victory, that is, of victory in the conflict

[1] Respect for the sources should be sufficient to counteract the temptation to an Old Testament exegete to work out an 'Old Testament theology' from certain religious expressions that are found in the books of the Old Testament. The sources loudly call out: 'What we believe in is not to be found within the covers of the Old Testament.' Two 'theologies' can be based on the Old Testament, one that puts the Christ of Bethlehem in the centre and one that ends in expectation of a Messiah who will one day come, that is to say, one clearly Christian and one clearly Jewish. There is no third, for the messianic theme is the main theme of the Old Testament.

[2] It is an entirely different matter that Christ, when he comes, is a man among men, and a servant who gives his life (Phil. 2.5-11). That belongs to the nature of his rule in which the first is the servant of all (Mark 10.44). Jesus' position as Lord is not weakened thereby, but strengthened. It is by taking the place ordained for Israel as the Suffering Servant that Jesus becomes Lord.

that is the theme of the Bible as a whole. To say that Christ is Lord of all the Biblical writings is just another way of saying that he is Victor in the war that the different writings describe in various ways.

The most important sources for the Early Christian *kerygma*, with its singular concentration on the death and resurrection, are the four Gospels. They describe the activity of Jesus, spread out over a long period, in such a way that, regarded as historical documents about this activity, they lack proportion, balance and meaning. In Mark and John the Passion narratives including the story of the resurrection dominate, in marked degree, all else. Even Matthew and Luke allow the death and resurrection to have disproportionate space. Only in the case of these events, the advance towards death and the events of Easter, are day and hour indicated. We do not even know what time of the year it was when Jesus was born. With the exception of the death and resurrection— events that take up two or three days, about which there existed really connected accounts from the first—the Gospels consist of single pearls, strung together without any chronological order that is natural or original. To use such material to describe Jesus' inner development, his life's story, is a task which historically instructed people could only be tempted to undertake in a perverse age. In times of clearsightedness such attempts are never made at all. But the same material that is so meagre from a biographical point of view is seen to be well proportioned and well balanced when it is looked at from the point of view which, quite clearly, is that of the material itself—namely, that what was important, what was decisive, for hearers and readers was Christ's death and resurrection. We do not need to guess at such a presupposition on the part of the Gospels nor to conjure it out of the air—it is clearly stated in so many words in the other New Testament writings.

The earlier speeches in Acts unveil the main items in the *kerygma* that was proclaimed immediately after Pentecost. There can scarcely be any doubt at all that the death and resurrection were its centre. 'This Jesus . . . you crucified. . . . But God raised him up, having loosed the pangs of death' (Acts 2.23 f.). ' . . . . God has made him both Lord and Christ, this Jesus whom you crucified' (2.36). ' . . . And killed the Author of life, whom God raised from the dead' (3.36). 'The God of our fathers raised Jesus, whom you killed by hanging him on a tree' (5.30). 'They put him to death by hanging him on a tree; but God raised him on the third day' (10.39 f.; cf. 4.10; 13.26-41; 17.3). Paul received the same message and, in his turn, passed it on to others: ' . . . that Christ died for our sins in accordance with the scriptures, that he was buried, that he was raised on the third day in accordance with the scriptures' (I Cor. 15.3 f.; cf. Phil. 2.5-11). An examination of Paul's theology makes it clear that it is faith in Christ as the crucified and risen One which constituted the element that bound it together. Another New Testament writing which, in a most striking way, centres on Christ's sufferings and subsequent glory is the First Epistle of Peter (for example, 1.11, 19, 21). Hebrews is yet another (9.12, 24). The message which the Apocalypse brings, and on which it bases its hopes for the future, has the same structure (e.g. chap. 19). The New Testament as a whole, though employing varying expressions, proclaims one single message; no writing or group of writings essential to the New Testament departs from the remainder, in the question of what the message is and what its centre.

Such a message degenerates into a purely theoretical dogma, which is laid down authoritatively to be accepted and believed, when sight is lost of the background which in the New Testament is taken for granted and doubted by nobody—the background of a universal enslavement affecting the whole race of man. The *kerygma* is unintelligible without this background, and will remain so until recognition of this background becomes the atmosphere that men breathe—that is, until it comes to be that man's enslavement is understood without reflection and is the point from which all thought sets out. It is profitless to add further to the authoritatively declared dogma of Christ's death and resurrection the dogma of the existence of the Devil as something which 'must be believed'. We have seen that in Ancient Israel the opposition between God and Satan lay unrecognized and hidden in the opposition between Israel and the surrounding peoples. Our human life today is humanity's struggle for release from the grip of the tyrant. That is, it is Israel's history; and with us, too, the struggle between God and Satan is camouflaged under social and political differences, marital troubles, labour

---

[1] The strength of Luther's exposition of the Bible consists in this, that the whole life of man is unveiled and is seen to be such as the Scriptures describe it, so that Christ's death and resurrection have to do with the affairs of everyday life. Luther's teaching about vocation is a central point in this respect. See the present author's *The Christian's Calling* (ET, 1958). Such concretion adds nothing new to the Word: on the contrary the kernel of the Word is hidden until I see that the Word is talking about something where I already am, and not about something to which in a religious act I may rise. In the Gospels Christ releases men from Satan's power, but that takes place by his healing of their sicknesses. 'Belief' in the Gospels is often clearly belief in the power of Jesus to help in a definite need in which the sufferer finds himself. Examples are Mark 5.36; 9.23 f.; 11.23 f.; Matt. 8.5-13; 9.28 f.; 15.28; Luke 1.45; 5.19 f.; 8.25 f.; John 11.40. Abraham is the father of the faithful. He believed in the promise that he would have a son, and by so doing he believed in Christ (Rom. 4.17 ff.).

difficulties, nervous illnesses and sicknesses.[1] Just as little as one can think docetically about God can one think docetically about the Devil if he is to keep his eye on him and resist him. God is in humanity, not beyond what is human, and Satan is in the affairs of everyday, not outside them in some specially religious affairs—for such special spheres exist only in the dreams of certain theologians. It is the task of preaching to speak about God and the Satanic power in such a way that everyone listening can detect the point in his own life where the battle is being waged and where he is enslaved and bound.[1] We shall return to this on several occasions in what follows. At this point we have to make clear that when the New Testament puts Christ's death and resurrection in the centre, that is bound up with the conviction that there the enemy of humanity was beaten.

Eschatological language—for example, an expression like 'the coming of the kingdom of God'—easily loses its connexion in our thought with a situation where *conflict* is going on. The situation before the breaking in of the kingdom is unqualified—that is, is marked only by the absence of what is to come. But in the eschatological tradition the coming of the Kingdom is regarded as identical with the catastrophe and the collapse of the enemy. The name of the enemy varies in the New Testament— Satan, the Devil, sin, death, etc.—but his dominion is the same. We simply go astray if we split up these entities, as if they did not all together constitute one single entity.[2] When Jesus heals the sick and drives out evil spirits, Satan's dominion is departing and God's kingdom is coming (Matt. 12.22-29). All Christ's activity is therefore a conflict with the Devil (Acts 10.38). God's Son took flesh and became man that he might overthrow the power of the Devil, and bring his works to nought (Heb. 2.14 f.; I John 3.8). The work that Christ had to do has culminated in his death on the cross and resurrection from the dead and was brought to completion in these last acts. It can be said of his whole life—from Herod's slaughter of the innocents and the temptation in the wilderness through all his teaching and healing miracles right to the very last, the last judgement—that his work is God's victory, the

---

[1] Here the problem no longer is what teachings 'must be believed' and what can be overlooked. Thinking of that sort is an infallible indication that the *kerygma* has been lost. The Gospel, therefore, has necessarily become a new law and a burden that is added to other burdens. Then it becomes a job of work to be 'religious'—instead of being a source of power.

[2] It is an entirely different matter that each term directs attention to a different aspect of the power of evil or, to use military terms, to a different division of the enemy's forces. Variety and unity are not in opposition to one another but really belong together.

release of men who were enslaved, the *catastrophe* and the judgement of
the power of Satan, all that is specially true of the death and resurrection. The powers which hold men in bondage were struck down in
Christ's death and resurrection (Col. 2.15 ff.; cf. Gal. 4.3). So men are
free through the work of Christ (Rom. 6.22; Gal. 5.1). God's acts do
not limit man's activity, but rather free it. That which is limited and in
the end beaten low, when finally the work of Jesus reaches its fulfilment, is the activity of the enemy of man, the slayer of man (John 8.44).
The two sides in the work of redemption, death and resurrection, come
to form a unity in the New Testament. This unity may be best illus-
trated by the shepherd, who at the cost of his life fights against the
wolf to save his flock (John 10.11 ff.), and who goes before his flock and
leads them to the place whither they could not go without him (John
10.4, 16; Matt. 26.31 f.; Heb. 13.20 f.; also Matt. 25.32 ff.).

But it is not just of the New Testament that the *kerygma* about Christ's
work is the centre. This is true of the *Bible*; it is kernel of the message
of all its collected books. That all in the Bible tends towards Christ's
death and resurrection is most readily perceived by fastening attention on
the contrasted pair, Adam and Christ. We may begin with Rom. 5.12-21,
where Adam and Christ are viewed as the points of departure for two
opposed dominions, a dominion of sin and death through Adam's fall
and a dominion of justification and life through Christ's resurrection.
Here Paul regards Adam's act as something that need not and ought not
to have happened, as 'sin', 'transgression' (v. 14), 'disobedience' (v. 19),
while Christ's act was, on the other hand, 'justification', 'obedience'
(v. 19; cf. Phil. 2.8, where Jesus' act is certainly contrasted with Adam's
as obedience with disobedience). Jesus' obedience brings about the collapse of the alien dominion of sin and death that came into existence
through Adam's defeat in temptation. It is a conviction common to the
whole New Testament that Jesus carried through his work in obedience
to God's will under continual attack and disturbance, that he was 'in
every respect *tempted* as we are' (Heb. 4.15). Thus a unity can be
detected in all the different events: the temptation in the wilderness,
the temptation by Peter (Mark 8.32 f.), the temptation to help himself
and come down from the cross (Matt. 27.40), are but expressions of the
continual assault by one and the same enemy (the same phrase occurs in
Matt. 4.3, 6; 27.40). Satan wants to lead Jesus away from the path of
obedience into the way Adam trod, the way where a man makes God's
image his own possession and uses it for his own advantage (cf. Gen.
3.1-5 with Phil. 2.5-8). Adam grasps at life and gets death; Jesus bows

in obedience under death and wins life, not to possess it, but to give it to us through the Word, as God gives and creates life through the Word (Gen. 1.1 ff. and John 1.1-18). Through the act of Jesus, the enemy's rule over men is destroyed. Now once more they can live as men, in innocence and purity, as men did before sin came.

Bound up with this is a general tendency in the New Testament to see the redemption in Christ as a renewal of the original creation. In this thought of the return of original innocence, there is nothing new over and above the thought of the victory over Satan, it is but a corollary of that. If behind all is the living God, the Father of life, then Satan's dominion implies an obstruction of the work of creation and Satan's defeat implies *eo ipso* a new and free development of that same creative work. The conception of a continued growth towards maturity and eternity is, again, no new addition to the major conception that Christ defeated Satan. Since the creative work springs forth freely and unhindered, greater development must also come about (John 1.50 f.; 5.20 f.; 14.12). Since Christ's victory over sin and death takes place in two stages, in all essentials in the death and in the resurrection on the third day, and then finally and fully in the *Parousia* and the last judgement, man is now free to fight against his own enemies in the conflict of spirit against flesh, but in eternity he will be free to triumph and to sing the songs of praise (Gal. 5.13, 17; Rom. 8.11 ff.; Rev. 19.6).

2. The Old and New Testaments are thus united

The eternal resurrection life is nothing different from the present life of man; the only difference is that our life now is a life of struggle against the enemies of human life, our life then will be a life without disturbance from unnatural elements, since the last enemy will have been defeated (I Cor. 15.26). And all that freedom, in its every moment, now as in the future, is a fruit of the victory of Christ which is already won in the cross and resurrection. That very creative power that was present in God's Word at the beginning, that power to call life into being, belongs to the Word when it becomes flesh in Christ and in him carries through its work of transformation.[1] The man who was created by God was blighted by Satan; Israel's struggle is a struggle for his rescue and release; Christ's death and resurrection is the victory over corruption and is man's restoration.

---

[1] Genesis 1 connects with John 1 and Rev. 19.13. The NT Word and OT 'wisdom' also merge into one another. Eph. 3.9-11 should be brought into the same chain of thought as John 1.1-14, Col. 1.15 ff. and other passages; cf. Prov. 8.12-36.

If we think exclusively in terms of the scheme of promise and fulfilment it may look as if the connexion of the Old and New Testaments is somewhat intellectual, consisting of certain sayings in the Old Testament pointing forward to the New Covenant. In that case we lose the deep and organic connexion brought about by the fact that God is engaged on the same activity throughout the whole Bible, an activity that looks to the future. Throughout the activity is the same, and yet Christ brings something new. Christ's death and resurrection stand at the heart and centre of Biblical preaching and, as a consequence, each part of the Bible has something of its own to say: it is *our* history, humanity's history, our way to life, a way which reaches its goal in eternity when we shall be fully incorporated in Christ's death and resurrection, but a way which leads through conflict. To regard any part of the Bible as antiquated would be to regard ourselves as having reached our goal and not as still on the way thither. On the other hand, to regard the Bible timelessly, as an authoritative source of revelation, all on one level and replete with truths, would be to regard Christ as not having come into the world, and ourselves without a Master and still expecting one.[1] The Lord has come, the victory has been won. To listen to the Bible is to be conducted along the way that leads to Christ's total rule over our existence and over that of all people, that leads, that is to say, to the last day and to heaven.

Such a perspective as this, in fact, is concealed in the oft-repeated New Testament expressions that speak of Jesus' cross and resurrection as something which took place 'according to the Scriptures', 'that the Scriptures might be fulfilled', etc. Very few instances are to be found in the Old Testament where Jesus' resurrection is explicitly anticipated. In general it is very difficult to understand the New Testament historically if it is not kept in mind that something has been going on in the Old Testament, a course of action, an activity, a movement, which does not end in the Old Testament, but passes over into the work of Jesus. When Jesus acts, dies and rises again this movement is completed, just as a child's actions can point forward and be completed by the full-

---

[1] An authoritative Bible whose main characteristic is that it is verbally inspired is a book without a Master and consequently a book with a doctrine instead of a message, its only task to relate what God has already done instead of having to bring men into the sphere of God's continuing activity. In that way a gulf yawns between the holy events of the Bible and the holy events awaited in the last times. Thereby the present is emptied of content. The present, on the contrary, must take its place as a worthy element within the history of redemption that the Bible reveals and that the *Parousia* completes, because the present is the time of the preaching of the Word and God is active in his Word.

grown man. The beginning of strife in itself looks forward; it is the prophecy of victory even if no single prophecy is made. Other Biblical concepts—as, for example, sacrifice—could be dealt with as we have dealt with the concept of conflict. Old Testament sacrifice is an action that cannot come to an end until Christ has offered himself and, therefore, there is an element of prophecy about sacrifice. The thought of the Epistle to the Hebrews must at times have run along such lines. The whole course of events which is thus brought to the light of day, in spite of its length, is for all that too short, since it includes neither prehistory nor what is yet to be, man's future history towards which we are on the way. When these links are added to the chain of thought, then we see the beginning of the Biblical chain of events in the Creator's Word of power which sustains the life of the whole world, and its end there in front of us—in him who has received the name of 'God's Word', who slays the beast and frees us out of the grasp of evil (Rev. 19.11-13). Then it is impossible to regard ourselves as detached from God's activity and for the same reason we listen to the preaching of the Word and confess Christ as Lord. To stand detached would be to have no Bible in which there was a unity. The Bible has its unity in Christ, and it is for faith that the unity exists. Since it is only as a message that the Bible is a unity, it is understandable that the very centre of the message speaks of something, brings news of something that happened, as we might say, at the end of the Bible—not by any means in the middle of the Bible, but, on the contrary, 'in the last times', 'in the fulness of time'. So the centre of gravity of the Bible is in the relatively small part that begins with St Matthew's Gospel. That is what a message is like. In a message about a battle the end tells of the victory.

The unity of the Bible, it must be said, depends on the fact that Christ is Lord. Christ is the living Lord who rises up between the two Covenants, the two 'Testaments', fulfilling the one and laying the foundation of the other. It was thus that the Ancient Church in early days regarded the Biblical documents, when it took in hand the theological task of uniting the old books of Israel with the new books of the Early Church and the apostles. This was a task whose difficulty we seldom realize, and consequently we do not appreciate the theological ability that enabled them to carry it through. We look on the idea of a unified Bible, divided into Old Testament and New Testament, as something to be taken for granted, a development that came about more or less of itself by reason of outward circumstances. Behind the theology of the second century, however, lies a toiling with Scriptural statements and a labour of thought

which, in its unphilosophical purity and in its concentration on the
Word, has only one counterpart in the history of the Church, that is,
in the Reformation of the sixteenth century.[1] It is surprising to observe
how Luther discovers the same kerygmatic character of the Bible, and
how he also sees that the Scriptures are united in witnessing to Christ,
by which witness faith lives and which witness faith receives. Consequently Luther with surprising energy set forth the cross and the resurrection as the centre of gravity of the preaching of Christ: all the main
concepts of Luther's theology draw their content from Christ's cross
and resurrection, and are only fully understandable in their relation to
that Christological foundation. This is specially striking in the case of
those central twin partners, law and Gospel, *Deus absconditus* and *Deus
revelatus*, whose inner dialectic makes them empty speculative play-
things when contact is not maintained at every point with what for
Luther is the starting point, the foundation and the end of theology:
Christ's actual death on the cross and his actual resurrection. Luther
does not fit in the witness of the New Testament about Christ into a
theological scheme arrived at in another way, but stands empty-handed
without any ordered conceptual apparatus before the Word about the
death and resurrection. Then he begins to search for terms and ideas
with which it may be possible to express the realities in question. Even
when he employs the old medieval expressions, they are constantly given
a new content. For this reason, from the points of view both of theology
and of the study of Luther, it is unimportant from what medieval source
his terminology was drawn. The Biblical *kerygma* about Christ controls and sets its stamp on Luther's theology, from its centre outwards
towards the details.

3. The death and the resurrection are inseparable

What we have said implies that the death and resurrection together
constitute the centre of gravity of the preaching of Christ and of the
Bible. It is important that both events should be kept together so that
the cross alone does not take the central place, and the resurrection thus

---

[1] Irenaeus' interpretation of the Bible, which pioneered the way in this matter,
made the history of redemption the scarlet thread that runs through all the
Scriptures, the Old Testament as well as the New, thus bringing out both the
unity and difference between them. But with Irenaeus the word 'testament' did
not mean a collection of writings, but a work of God in the history of redemption.
When later on the terms Old or New 'Testament' immediately gave rise to the
thought of books or written documents, poverty of thought was already on the
way.

be reduced to something that but strengthens the completed work of the cross—nor yet that the resurrection is isolated from the cross and itself comes to be the kernel of the message. In either case the Christian message is lost. When the cross alone dominates preaching, faith becomes faith in what has happened, what is complete—and is now to be personally applied in an act of faith which takes a step back in time. Then belief in eschatology, the last things, is added on to that as an appendix. When the resurrection alone dominates, then God's act comes docetically from on high without any connexion with human conflict and, consequently, faith mistakes its enemy, despair, and instead is forced to match itself in intellectual manner against what is no opponent, intellect. The former aberration is orthodox and pietistic, the latter is hypermodern and anti-liberal.

The true significance of the resurrection cannot be maintained, nor can it remain the Gospel, if it does not come into conflict with death and doubt. We receive into our heart the message of the resurrection in faith alone, that is to say, when we die because faith is the death of the self. Outside death there is no resurrection. To seek to attain theoretical certainty about the resurrection, and to approach the question as purely one of truth, is to seek to have the resurrection *without* having to die. Always it is where law speaks, where agony and death hold sway, that the Gospel of Christ's resurrection speaks. For Christ's cross and resurrection belong inseparably together, the way to resurrection goes through death.

The cross and death are, however, in like manner emptied of content, are sentimentalized, if they are separated from the resurrection, and made objects of pious contemplation. In that case we want the religious circle where peace is without the Master who is risen and alive and on his way to the conquest of the world, of humanity; we want to contemplate suffering instead of listening to the Creator and Conqueror, and being brought within the ambit of his mighty world-changing acts of power. For Early Christian faith the cross was not the end but a way to be trodden, a conflict to be waged, to the end. For the man who now listens to it, the Word of the cross strikes down as a destroying power, whose work it is to kill the flesh, to drive out Satan, to crucify sin, and that can only take place at that point where hope of heaven dwells, where the promise is alive—that is, in the heart that already tastes the first fruits of the resurrection.

Cross and resurrection are, therefore, opposites—but inseparable. This is a corner-stone of Luther's doctrine of the *communicatio idio-*

matum, the sharing of attributes. The divine cannot be separated from
the human, majesty cannot be isolated from humility, the work of God
in the resurrection cannot be separated from the agony of the cross.
Seen from below, that is, from the position of the man who now listens
to the Word, this means that he hears nothing from God unless he is in
process of dying; one can only trust when he is in despair—that is,
when the self-reliance that can do without God is broken in pieces.
Hope in the resurrection is denied and empty whenever man manages to
build up his life on his own, for God is near to him that is of a broken
heart and Christ found his life through death. The history of *man* that
is contained in Israel's struggles, defeat and death reaches its end in
Jesus' death and resurrection. Redemption cannot be had through lifting
the resurrection out of this chain of events and making it a naked object
of faith. Death, Christ's death and our own death, belong together to
redemption, and we are baptized that we may die. But *God's* history
with men lies as well in the life and death of the elect nation and the
elect Son. Through Christ's death, God brings his eternal decree to
fulfilment: Satan is conquered, creation is cleansed and brought to its
objective. At that moment, when all men are embraced by Christ's
conquest, the fulfilment of the world has come. To that end preaching
exists. Christ, who in himself comprises God's history with man and
man's history with God, extends his dominion through preaching.
Christ came, died and rose again so that the preaching of the Word
might take place now. Christ brings the whole Bible together as a
preached unity, whose deepest content is unknown until that moment
when there takes place that for which the Bible exists—the preaching of
the Bible. For the world of men, to which the Bible speaks, is a world
in thrall, controlled by powers unfriendly to man. For that reason, only
through death and resurrection could Christ carry out his work in the
world. For that reason, too, of all messages only the message of his
death and resurrection can reach down into the despair that holds sway
over the heart of man. All other messages touch but the surface of
man's life.

V

THE BIBLE AND PREACHING

1. The centrality of preaching in the history of the world

WE have already maintained that preaching, according to the view of
the Early Church, is itself an act of God, and belongs to the chain of
actions that God carries out from creation to the completion of all things.
The preaching of the Gospel once had a beginning, and one day it will
come to an end. It began when Christ came, and shall endure till he
comes again as the visible King. In Mark 13.4-23 the disciples ask what
the signs are for the coming of the last days, and Jesus replies by describing the last days. In that description not only do unchristian errors,
earthquake, war and apostasy find a place but preaching does as well.
Special mention is made of the witness 'before princes and kings' of
Christians who had been arrested and accused, and of the preaching of
the Gospel 'to all nations' (v. 10). In Acts it is Paul, arrested and accused,
who is called to witness, and who clearly treats his witness as of great
significance since it is made before the Great Council and King Agrippa
and, as he hopes, before Caesar in Rome (Acts 9.15; 23.11; 25.11 f.;
26.32). Preaching belongs to the time after Christ's resurrection. It
belongs to the birth pangs by which humanity is delivered and brought
to life. Indeed, it was for the sake of preaching, that is to say—in the
final analysis—for the sake of the redemption of humanity, that Christ's
resurrection took place (Acts 26.23). In Acts 1 the disciples ask, as in
Mark 13, about the time of the setting up of God's kingdom, and in
reply Jesus speaks of preaching, of witnessing 'to the end of the earth'
(Acts 1.6-8). It is thus that Christ exercises his power: he is himself
present where the nations of the world hear the Gospel and are baptized
(Matt. 28.18-20; cf. Mark 16.15-20). Paul's work from Jerusalem to
Illyricum is the spread of the Gospel and, as such, a work of Christ
(Rom. 15.19 f.; cf. Phil. 1.12 ff.). The argument in Rom. 9-11 belongs
to the same scheme of thought. It is for us to let all who are waiting
hear of Christ's conquest, and like Deutero-Isaiah's bearer of good
news, carry the glad tidings of freedom to the conquered and the bruised

(Rom. 10.14-21; cf. Isa. 52.7). So, preaching must continue until the 'full number of the Gentiles come in' (Rom. 11.25). Then shall the end come (Matt. 24.14). It is, therefore, a token of the end that preaching is taking place at all. It belongs to the events of the last times, that God's Word rides out into the world of men (Rev. 19.11-16).[1]

Bound up with this is the fact that the fulfilment of the Old Testament prophecies in a certain sense is different from the Israelitish hopes from which prophecy sprang. For Israel all life was on one plane, which was at the same time earthly and spiritual, political and religious in one. For this reason it was most difficult, almost impossible, for a true Jew to believe that Jesus of Nazareth was the Messiah. The dividing up of the victory into these two moments, cross and resurrection, took away what was visible from the fulfilment and faced the disciple with a hard demand, the demand that he should believe and yet not see (John 20.29; II Cor. 5.7; I Peter 1.8). The cross was what all could see: 'the people stood by, watching' (Luke 23.35). The Risen One is revealed 'not to all the people, but to us who were chosen by God as witnesses . . . ; and he commanded us to preach to the people' (Acts 10.40-42)—that is to say, to occupy with the spoken word the period between Easter and the *Parousia* when Christ is invisible, to carry the Gospel to the people of all nations. The spread of the Gospel is a double one, geographical and historical, out towards the people and onwards towards the *Parousia*, 'to the end of the earth' and 'to the close of the age' (Acts. 1.8; Matt. 28.20). The war of the Lord is finished and the great blow is struck. Never again can Satan tempt Christ, as in the desert. Jesus is now *Lord*, Conqueror. But a war is not finished, a conflict does not cease with the striking of the decisive blow. The enemy remains with the scattered remnants of his army, and in pockets here and there a strong resistance may continue. That is the position of the Christian: his Master, Christ, has in his death and resurrection beaten the enemy, but in his own heart the tempter lives on, there the conflict rages between flesh and spirit (Gal. 5.17). The last judgement means Satan's destruction and the resurrection of the dead—that is, death's final expulsion from God's world (Rev. 20.14), the fall of the last enemy, because death is the last enemy (I Cor. 15.26). Then man will no longer need to 'believe without seeing',

---

[1] That Mark 16.20, Matt. 28.20, Acts 28.31 and Rom. 16.25 f. each end their description with preaching is really much the same thing as the *Maranatha* of Rev. 22.20 and of I Cor. 16.22. The doubleness of indicative and imperative—that is, of present experience and of expectation, event and hope—this doubleness in the Aramaic expression is also in preaching, and is, one might say, its real nature, because preaching combines Christ's resurrection and the *Parousia*.

for then Christ will be the visible King: 'we shall *see* him as he is' (I John 3.2), '*see* God' (Matt. 5.8); then, as it is repeatedly expressed in the New Testament, all shall be 'revealed.' The division into two moments is past, resurrection is visible, the body is there and all the world is there—all is once more on a spirit-body basis, as Israel hoped for all the time. Then for the first time Old Testament prophecy is fulfilled without remainder, fulfilled before the eyes of all—'every eye will see him' (Rev. 1.7). Until then it stands that God's kingdom 'is not coming with signs to be observed' (Luke 17.20) Prophecy is fulfilled in Jesus' coming in humility, in such a way as is described in Luke 4.21, 'Today this Scripture has been fulfilled in your hearing'. Faith's time is not a time for seeing, but the time of the Word, the time of preaching, the time of listening. The right interpretation of the phrase 'not see but believe' might be said to be 'not see but hear'.

Luther emphasized this with unusual clarity as the demand of the faith. 'The Word and faith belong together.' That the Scripture is fulfilled 'in your hearing' means for Luther that the Scripture is fulfilled in such a way that it still needs to be *proclaimed* that it is fulfilled; it must be announced not just once for all but incessantly, because only in the Word can the fulfilment be maintained, only in hearing is certainty to be found. When it is preached, preaching is not something beyond that which is given in the New Testament, but preaching is the New Covenant, that is to say, the fulfilment, fulfilment 'in your hearing'. The New Covenant is the Gospel and the Gospel is the glad news.

The spiritual realm has, then, the character of a 'kingdom of hearing' —a fact which makes understandable the absence of any thought of associations or institutions in Luther's conception of the Church. Men remain at their worldly occupations and tasks and do not need to leave them—heaven *is heard* everywhere on earth; hands work and hearts listen to the Word. In temptation we desire to see and know and understand; we cannot hold fast to what the Word says; we cannot retain the truth that is offered in the Word, and we refuse to venture unless we have a more secure footing than we have in the Word. Here is the root of all temptation. The forgiveness of sins is something promised me by the Word, but what I see is my sin. Faith in the forgiveness of sins is only possible as sheer reliance on the Word, and to cast oneself on the Word is faith. No more secure place can man find until the resurrection of the dead when Satan is overthrown. Before then he is allowed, in response to his demand to 'see' and 'know', only to see and know of his death, and just these are the premonitory signs for faith that the cross is being reared up and that, consequently, the resurrection is drawing nearer. For now, in this interim period, before the world's regeneration, Christ's cross and resurrection must spread abroad in the life of man so that all may die and rise again as the body follows after the head in birth. When men have passed through death and resurrection, they emerge into the eternal world where Christ rules for all to see. We are living in the shadows where nothing is seen. 'But even if you do not see you shall see by hearing.' 'Stick your eyes in your ears.'[1] 'He who will not take hold with his ears but wants to look with his eyes is lost.'[2] Now is the time of preaching, travail time, before the world is born anew. One thing only matters: to hear what Christ says.[3]

For this reason Luther lays great stress on the fact that the Gospel is a spoken word, not primarily a book, but a Word that is heralded abroad. The Gospel is 'a good message'.[4] 'It is really not what is found in books and what is spelled out with letters but rather an oral preaching, a living Word, a voice which sounds into all the world, and is openly heralded forth, so that it may be heard everywhere.'[5] That Gospels had to be written was itself a weakness, 'a great breach and a quenching of the Spirit'.[6] When that took place it was not intended that written material should replace the earlier spoken word but, on the contrary, that the spoken word should be able to continue thanks to their accounts: 'The Gospel is, and cannot be other than, the account or the story of Christ.'[7]

In order that the Gospel might be preached the Gospel was written down. For this reason the outward course of events is not fully described by the evangelists, for in what they say the apostles intend to preach

[1] *WA* 49, 360.28 f. (Sermons, 1544; Stolz MS). At one and the same time temptation doubts Christ's resurrection and the forgiveness of sins. Sin and death belong together. So forgiveness of sins is 'life and blessedness'.

[2] *WA* 37, 202.14-22 (Sermons, 1533) in Rörer MS.

[3] Luther fits the relations between the water and the Word in baptism into this scheme of thought. The water is *seen*, the Word *heard*. When baptism takes place faith must rely on the Word, and so baptism (death and resurrection) is actualized in the course of Christian life. See *WA* 37, 202.22-30: 'He set us in baptism, and, so far as it is visible, baptism is water. He has set us in preaching which is just the breath of a man. For the eye, water is water, but I must not follow my eyes but must listen to what he says. . . . It seems so small, yet it was also small that he who allowed himself to be crucified should thus take away sin and death and hell. Yes, we must believe it, we must hold on to it with our ears.'

[4] *WA* 10(III), 68.1-7 (Sermons, 1522).

[5] *WA* 12, 259.5-13 (Exposition of I Peter; Cruciger MS).

[6] *WA* 10(I.1), 626.19-627.3 (Kirchenpostille, 1522).

[7] *WA* 10(I.1), 9, 6-20. Cf. *WA* 50, 629.17-20: 'We are speaking of the outward word preached by men, preached by you and me by word of mouth. For Christ has but left behind him an outward sign, by which his Church and his holy Christian people may be known in the world.'

about Christ. To approach the fact of the cross and the resurrection with the idea that the evangelists have provided us with a document about past events, and that the main question is about the exactness, the adequacy and the detail of the document, implies an almost complete lack of understanding of what took place. At least, it is taken for granted that the events in question have no relevance for us. The evangelist who wrote down the 'document' presupposed the very opposite, that no future reader of his words could read them without receiving from them life or death, and the evangelist hoped that he would receive life (cf. John 20.30 f.). As he wrote, the plan and every detail without exception was controlled by this presupposition. Consequently a particular passage tells of an outward act of Jesus, for the whole life of Jesus was outward acts, but linked therewith is a message, for Jesus was the Redeemer of the world—that is to say, the Redeemer of every reader, of every hearer, until the end of the world. To preach is 'to bring what has already happened into history and to proclaim it before the whole world' until the 'deed' comes to be 'the use of the deed' (or the Word), until 'reconciliation' comes to be 'a message of reconciliation' (see II Cor. 5.19).[1]

2. The centrality of preaching in the Gospels

We may say, then, that the outward deed is accompanied by a Word by which it passes into preaching; that which has happened proclaims a message—that is to say, it works in the hearers, in the readers. But it ought to be noted that 'the Word' which thus accompanies the act is not added by Luther, nor by the preacher of today, but by the Bible itself. Indeed, we turn everything upside down if we talk about 'addition' at all. On the contrary, it was that he might preach that the evangelist wrote down the historical accounts. As Martin Dibelius said, 'In the beginning was the *kerygma*'. When the evangelist thought of the Word as the beginning, he did so because he conceived Christ's birth, life and work as culminating in preaching and as destined from the beginning

[1] In his exegesis of I Tim. 2.6 along with Rom. 16.26 and Eph. 3.5, Luther says: 'Note this passage and others like it. Redemption itself is distinguished from the preaching of redemption. If a hundred thousand Christs had been crucified and no one had said anything about it, what use would that have been? Just betrayal to the cross. But when I come to this we must draw this deed into history and divulge it to the whole world. . . . To the deed must be added the use of the deed, that it may be proclaimed by the Word, held by faith and that he who believes may be saved. Therefore let it be agreed: to the work of redemption belongs the preaching of the Word which does no more than inculcate the work of redemption' (*WA* 26, 40.9-17; Rörer's MS).

E

to be the Word that goes out to all nations (Acts 26.23). That in turn
rests on the fact that Christ from the beginning is the Word (John 1.14),
God's Word which creates the world and all the imprisoned, waiting
people in it. It is out to the people that the creative Word wishes to go,
and when the enemy of man is slain in Christ's resurrection the Word
goes forth once more with the power of the Spirit. The different thoughts
are happily combined by Paul when he says: 'All this is from God, who
through Christ reconciled us to himself, and gave us the ministry of
reconciliation; that is, God was in Christ, reconciling the world to himself, not counting their trespasses against them, and entrusting to us the
message of reconciliation. So we are ambassadors for Christ, God making
his appeal through us. We beseech you on behalf of Christ, be reconciled
to God' (II Cor. 5.18-20). About this passage R. Bultmann says that it
shows how the act of redemption 'makes itself contemporary in the
preaching of the Word'. 'By means of the cross God has set forth the
means of redemption, the Word of redemption. To my mind, preaching
itself belongs to the history of redemption.'[1] Luther's attitude to the
New Testament is, in fact, very like that of form criticism—both often
make a certain saying the focus and meaning of a passage. Both like to
take 'the Word' as the preacher's text, around which the contents of a
passage cluster and which is directed as a *kerygma* towards the hearers
or readers whom the writer has in mind.

Such exegesis holds that an activity is manifest in the Gospel stories.
The Gospels do not remain away back in the past, neutral and biographical, for us to go to them and make them the object of our activity,
our historical investigations. Of course, that attitude can be adopted,
but, in that case, it has to be admitted that the Gospels are poor documents and that what is written of them by those who approach them
thus is, for the most part, sheer hypotheses, conservative or radical, as
the case may be, but still hypotheses. To do justice to the unique nature
of the Gospels we must rather listen to the *message* that they bring to us,
and whose content we can determine historically without resorting to
the making of hypotheses. *Then* the Gospels are seen to be very good
documents, for in that case we are asking about what was important for
those who wrote them down and, accordingly, the material provides the
answer we are seeking. When we ask our question in this way the activity
in the material is immediately apparent—the will to proclaim, which
sets its stamp on every story about Christ, particularly in the striking
culmination in a *saying* of Chrst with which the account of something

[1] In *Jesus Christus* (1936) p. 89.

he did so often ends.[1] Christ heals and forgives, acts and speaks. The sick, the possessed, those in need of help and burdened with guilt, who in all the Gospels surround Jesus, belong by inner necessity to the message of the Gospels. These people—with whom every hearer or reader of the Gospels can identify himself, and in whose company he can reckon himself to belong, however much he may be a criminal before impending judgement, without the possibility of making any amends (Luke 23.43)—are an irremovable part of the Gospels, unless the *kerygma* is to go by the board.[2] Otherwise the acts of Christ become miracles on a stage, intended to be looked at and admired. In fact, however, they are a message about God's presence and forgiveness, a message which is intended for all who have been born in the demoniac condition of the human race and have the opportunity of hearing the Word about Christ and his acts until the end of time. Men everywhere are in the same condition of slavery under which the men about Jesus suffered, and Jesus comes just as much to us as to the men who are described in the Gospels. To us he comes in the Word, in the Gospel; that is what the New Testament implies in every case. God loved the *world* and gave Christ for it, so that all who believe in him should not perish but have everlasting life (John 3.16). The evangelist wrote Jesus' signs in his book that those who heard of them or read of them might believe and have life (John 20.30 f.). God's action in Christ develops into the *kerygma* for the world.

When Luther thinks of preaching he traces out certain features which remind us of wholly modern and radical exegetical principles. He especially notices the relation between action and word in the Gospels. 'Where we have narratives about events accompanied by sayings, we take the

[1] Such a passage is itself a sermon, for everyone who reads or hears the passage with the presupposition that Jesus is his Master hears Jesus speaking to him in the Word. It was as a word to be spoken in a gathering of people that the passage was first written down. If this way of looking at the different passages be extended to take in all the material that is found in the Gospels, we have partly an event, Christ's death, cross and resurrection, and partly a 'word' in which that event culminates—and the Word is the apostolic preaching with which we are confronted in the Acts and the Epistles, the proclamation of the living Christ. A collection of writings like the New Testament is in its entirety a sermon. In fact the great and all-embracing New Testament message of Christ's cross and resurrection is set forth in every single story in the Gospels.

[2] This is another feature of the structure of the Gospels which Luther, with keen eye, observed and emphasized. A feature like this is not there because the evangelists made up their minds to put it there, but because it has a right to be there, since it is based on the fact that Christ was like that. The proclamation was born out of something that really happened, but what happened was a message even when it happened. It was first understood as a detestable message, and written down by the evangelists as a good message.

sayings to be the main thing. Here is a safe rule: to interpret the Gospels properly pay attention to the sayings, especially the sayings of Christ.'[1] The Gospels describe the outward course of events. That is our foundation; if the events did not take place, the sayings that interpret them lose their anchorage and importance. The event, however, is not the point at which we stop, since in that case Jesus would be in the past. Through the Word which interprets it, the outward course of events comes to have power and relevance for me as I now hear the story. In the preaching of the Gospel, which is contained in the Word, that which once happened comes to be alive in me as I listen to the Word in faith in the living Christ: 'and there the passion of Christ and his resurrection come into force'.[2] The *kerygma* found in all the separate stories is that which is basic to the whole New Testament, the *kerygma* about Christ's death and resurrection; or better, Christ's death and resurrection is the stream that flows deep down in every individual passage, the stream under any particular event described in the Gospels, for example, the stories of the son of the widow of Nain and what Jesus did for him, the healing of the lame man and so on. He who leads from death and depravity to life and light has himself passed through suffering and darkness to conquest and resurrection and he leads everyone along the same road now. In that instant when he receives the Word the listener finds himself on the way. The conflict against sin goes on; the new life of man is likewise going on, and, taken together, these are the death and resurrection of Christ, for Christ comes in the Word.

It is not the case that one has to read chapter after chapter in the Gospels and wait until he has got as far as Christ's death before he can find the message. All that Jesus did from the day he first set out is a unity; every single passage has something to say about the one great redemptive act in which he was everywhere engaged, and the unity of the proclamation is still there, whatever limited part of the redemptive history we may deal with in a sermon.[3] Everywhere it is the proclamation of 'Jesus of Nazareth . . . who went about doing good and healing all that were oppressed by the devil. . . . They put him to death by hanging him on a tree; but God raised him up on the third day' (Acts 10.38.40).

[1] *WA* 34(I), 318.12-14 (Sermons, 1531; Rörer MS).
[2] See *WA* 34(I), 318.15-319, 4.
[3] Since the chapters of the Gospels were composed out of what were originally isolated fragments, all of which were bearers of a message, the best way to understand the Bible is often just to read the isolated fragments in the Prayer Book. There they stand as passages for sermons, isolated passages, passages for the congregation, the Church. These three traits are more truly and originally characteristic of the New Testament than is generally realized.

To associate preaching only with the death and resurrection, and to take no notice of the actual contacts between Jesus and needy men in the Gospels, would involve an obvious risk for preaching, for then the preacher would cease to be a messenger and become instead a purveyor of information. In an age like that of Luther, when the theological compass had gone astray, but when the characters of the Gospels were looked upon as relatively well-known contemporary figures, it may have been a wise plan to concentrate in preaching on the basic themes of the Pauline and Johannine writings, and to allow these precedence over passages from the Gospels. But in our day, which suffers the errors of Docetism, and which has the 'basic conception' thoroughly in mind but is strangely powerless when it comes to relating the actual life of every day to this correct basic conception, it is, *mirabile dictu*, necessary once more to go back to the world of the Synoptic Gospels, if we are not to lose the full-orbed faith of the Early Christian and Lutheran Gospel.[1] The Synoptics stand, in this respect, on the side of the Old Testament, and safeguard the setting of the work of Christ in common, outward history. They hold us fast in our true position and they insist that reconciliation is not a superficial addition to what is human, but, on the contrary, the redemption and the health of the human. They continually bring us back to the truth that Christ comes to us in the earthly need in which we stand, and not in the religious realm which we have made up for ourselves and in which Christ never is. In spite of their swarms of signs and wonders, they awaken us to Christ's *humanity*, and thereby to the Gospel and to grace. It is as God that Christ can help us, but divinity would be no help to us, if it were not here where we are, 'in the likeness of sinful flesh' (Rom. 8.3; cf. II Cor. 5.21).

3. The Bible itself overflows into preaching

We have seen earlier that the Biblical documents, as a whole, make known God's acts, and to that extent are sermons. We have seen, further, that the chain of the events that the Bible describes attains its decisive stage in Christ's death and resurrection. For this reason the Biblical *kerygma* has its centre of gravity in the proclamation of the cross and

[1] The Reformation certainly restored the Pauline and Johannine *kerygma*, but not as a speciality within the Bible, but as an uncommonly clear and well thought-out expression of the message which the Bible as a whole bears. If we consider Luther as a restorer of the Pauline conception in contrast to another in the New Testament, e.g. the Synoptic, we shall certainly interpret Luther, and possibly Paul too, in a Docetic manner. The Paul who is opposed to the Synoptics has no right to the name: his real name is Marcion.

Easter. The whole Bible is concentrated in this message about Christ. The Bible itself overflows into preaching, and is itself active when the preaching of Christ to men takes place. 'Preaching and God's Word', the order of words used in Luther's exposition of the Third Commandment, is not the sign of a mechanical combination of disparate elements, but of an organic relationship—for our preaching today has its centre of gravity in Christ's death and resurrection, just as the Bible has. If we wish to say in a word what must happen to a man to transfer him from the realm of sin to that of righteousness, we may say that he must be ingrafted into Christ's death and resurrection, his sinful flesh must be crucified and a new man arise. For this reason he is baptized; for this reason he receives the Lord's Supper; for this reason the Word is sent to him, both the chastening law and the regenerating Gospel. Here, then, is the third major entity, the redemption of man, which has the very same centre of gravity as the Bible has and as preaching has too. When the preacher goes to the Bible, he goes to the place where the message that meets man's central need sounds forth. Indeed, he goes to the creative Word out of which man's creative life flows—God's Word, which is Christ become flesh. The Word and men are intended for each other. This creative Word speaks to us out of every Biblical passage, and since it is creative we must listen to it without demanding such a comprehension of it as will free us from the need to listen afterwards to particular passages. Every such wish of putting ourselves above the Word instead of under it, of mastering the Word instead of allowing it to master us, implies a failure to see that God creates by his Word and that we are being created; we behave as if we were perfect, fully created. In fact we are on the road towards the resurrection of the dead. We stand in the course of God's activity only when we listen, listen to the preaching of the Word, just as we progress only when we journey a particular part of the way. The way in general can be thought about but not journeyed; 'the Word in general' can be thought about, but not heard.

Faith is listening to the Word, hearing God's call, sharing in God's activity. Thereby man emerges as a part of God's mighty action that began when God by his Word uttered the command and the world stood forth (Gen. 1) and will end when the dead shall hear the voice of the Son of God and live (John 5.25-30), when they shall hear his 'command' and rise up (I Thess. 4.16). It is not strange that the word of the preacher is with power and gives life, for preaching is a link in a chain of creative words: preaching possesses, as a continuation of the Bible, of God's Word, the same might which once created the world, and shall one day create the world anew. The Word's unifying work binds together creation and completion. For this reason the Bible is a unity from Genesis to Revelation, a unity that cannot be preserved otherwise than by the preaching of the Word today—that is to say, than by the setting of men in the series of events that binds together the prehistory of creation and the future of hope. The all-embracing history of mankind which the Apocalypse envisages is not yet complete; world-mission implies its approach, but not yet its appearing. In preaching, it might be said, we strain towards the unity of the Bible. Christ's words in the New Testament point backwards to the Israel of God in such a way that they penetrate behind Israel's call to the creation of the world and the history and destiny of the whole human race. Christ is the Redeemer of the world, the Saviour of all men from death. But he is that as we now hear and preach the Word so that the resurrection of the dead may come. If we are to speak of a 'theology of preaching', it must, by inner necessity, be a theology of the whole Bible in that meaning, not just a theology of the New Testament but a theology of both Testaments, a Biblical theology of both Testaments. Because it is one and the same enemy with whom God is in conflict from the Fall of man until the last judgement, and because we are in thraldom to that very enemy, and only because of that, it means something to preach the Bible today, to preach Christ for us. Let this connexion be disrupted in the slightest, and logically all preaching should be discontinued. Refusal to travel the false road involves travelling the road we have indicated. Retain preaching; face the problem of what it really is; and *from that point of view* read the Scriptures, for only then are the Scriptures read with their own presuppositions—consequently only then can they have their full meaning.

The unity that thus belongs to the Bible involves, moreover, a quite definite view of ourselves. This is a simple consequence of the character of the Bible as a message.[1] We cannot believe just what we wish about ourselves as men when we hear the *kerygma* of God's actions. With the intention of making clear the singular nature of Biblical preaching, we shall now pass on to the actual situation of the man who listens—the situation with which preaching has to come to grips and which it must presuppose if it is to be genuine preaching at all.

[1] An *exposition* does not necessitate any presupposition about the reader's or the hearer's existential situation, but it belongs to the very nature of a *message* that it must always presuppose something about the receiver. A message of liberation is sent to a prisoner.

VI

CONQUERED MAN

1. The creation of man by the Word

WE shall now discuss the man who hears the Bible, hears preaching; for preaching would be falsely described were it not given a setting in a particular, consciously defined and analysed anthropological context. It is not to be thought that by keeping silence about man a correct theological view of him is half-unconsciously attained. Silence, on the contrary, is the surest way to an unexamined and uncritical acceptance of the heathen view of man, which is not compatible with the Gospel but which belongs to the general cultural atmosphere of our day.

Just as important, however, is the fact that when we set out to analyse the man to whom preaching is addressed, we deal first with man in his conquered state, and second with God and the Devil. That is theological anthropology: it does not develop into a discussion about man as he is in himself, but ends in a treatment of the two powers who control man's situation, *every* man's situation, God and Satan. Even before the minister begins to preach, the conflict between God and Satan determines the listener's situation, *every* listener's situation. In both the Ancient Church and Luther, this fact is clear and indisputable. Life is not open to man without the work of the Creator. Confronted with life we are confronted with something which God is in the process of making, and since God creates by his Word, that means that God speaks to us from our actual human life, from the event, from what is going on around us on all sides. The words 'God said', which are followed again and again on the first page of the Bible by the words 'and it was so', uphold all being and give life and existence to all—as Luther says. As long as a created being is in existence, for so long endures that being's Word; the creative Word behind all that is outward maintains existence, and repeatedly makes contact with us in the meeting of men and events.[1] As usual,

---

[1] Cf. Luther on Genesis 1: 'When you hear this saying *and God spake*, beware that you do not think that it is a passing saying such as we men speak; know that it is an eternal saying, which is spoken from eternity and continues to be spoken. As little as God's being ceases, so little ceases that speech without

when it is a matter of the Word Luther stoutly maintains that the Word cannot be seen in creation, cannot be touched or handled, but can be 'heard'.[1] One New Testament passage that, for Luther, gives support to this conception of the relation between the creative Word and the present condition of the creation is II Peter 3.5-7, about the heaven and earth being created by the power of God's Word and 'by the same Word . . . stored up for fire, being kept until the day of judgement'. There the present existence of the world is envisaged as dependent on God's Word. God has not just been the Creator, he *continues* to be so. And since the creative Word took flesh in Jesus Christ he is, in his Word, the Upholder of the work of creation: 'upholding the universe by his word of power' (Heb. 1.3). In him men are created anew (II Cor. 5.17; Gal. 6.15); they are raised up through him from death and live again, are born anew.

There exists not only a life-giving Power but also a power that destroys, leads astray and corrupts. God's recreating activity is his answer to a hostile destructive activity. Immediately following on creation in the beginning came sin, 'and death through sin' (Gen. 2.17; 3.1 f.; John 8.44; Rom. 5.12). God's continued activity is carried on in the face of opposition and disturbances; it is at one and the same time conflict and creation, and when the final and transformed new creation emerges in the resurrection, it will emerge as a victory over the last enemy (I Cor. 15.26). Creation and sin are the two most important factors which regulate human life. Even in the Old Testament the creative work of the Lord is regarded as a conflict against death, chaos and hatred. That is still more the case in the New Testament where the Spirit and the new man stand in opposition to the old man of flesh and where sin and Satan are portrayed as real enemies against which every Christian has a hard battle to wage. The events of the last days are conceived in the same categories of conflict: life's victory is itself the

---

which the creature would not enjoy his existence in time. But it continues to speak and goes on without interruption, for no creature can maintain his own existence. Therefore, so long as the creature exists, so long will the Word also exist: so long as the earth bears, or is able to bear, so long that speech will continue without intermission. As Moses shows us God in all his creatures and through them leads us to God, let us understand him, so that we may think when we see the creature: *see, there is God!* That means that all creatures in their life and work without intermission are acted upon, and maintained by, the Word' (*WA* 24, 37.21-38.10).

[1] 'Believe,' said Moses, 'it has been spoken. Thou dost hear, thou dost not see, nor touch. This word is in the creatures as long as God speaks. When he doesn't speak, that is, when he withdraws the power of the Word, they have no power' (*WA* 24, 38.6-8).

bringing to nought of the Antichrist and the Serpent. The destructive powers continue to make their attacks all the time that God is engaged on his creative work. Such attacks are not expected to end before the end of the old order itself.

Accordingly, we are always coming across the idea that God creates by the Word that goes out of his mouth or by his Spirit, the breath of his mouth. God's creation by the Word and God's 'breathing in' of the breath of life (Gen. 2.7) are, basically, one and the same. Man's life is from God's Word or from God's Spirit: man lives from that which cometh out of the mouth of God (Deut. 8.3). When God in Christ speaks his Word to men, and when God in Christ pours out his Spirit, these are, basically, one and not two things, an objective speech and a subjective experience: the Spirit is the Word's own Spirit, the wind of the Word. When the Spirit comes, the Word is heard. The miracle of the Day of Pentecost is the miracle of preaching, that all the world's inhabitants understand the Word when it is spoken (Acts 1.8; 2.1-42). The pouring out of the Spirit in John's Gospel also implies a sending forth into the world (John 20.19-23). This account corresponds with that of the creation of man in Gen. 2.7, the 'breathing in' of the breath of life: '. . . he breathed on them, and said to them, "Receive the Holy Spirit".' God creates anew by giving his Spirit, creates life and renews the face of the earth (Ps. 104.30). It is the Creator of the world who raises Jesus from the dead and so accomplishes his plan in spite of the noise and opposition of the fiends (note the connexion in Acts 4.24-28); the same Creator now gives his Spirit, so that the Word freely has its way in public preaching and the sick are freed from the unhealthy condition which is alien to creation (Acts 4.29-31). The creative Word 'calls into existence the things that do not exist' (Rom. 4.17), and so establishes in the world that which is new, which up to then could not exist; the creative Word gives life to the dead and shall one day call the whole race of men to come forth out of their graves (John 5.28 f.). It is significant that when Luther wants to set forth the power of the Word in the Lord's Supper, he turns back to the same account in Genesis: in the Lord's Supper the same power is met with that brought forth life and all things and that can still fashion all things anew. The judgement of God implies that the earth is 'without form and void' just as before the creation (Gen. 1.2; cf. Jer. 4.23), but forgiveness is life and blessedness. He who relies on the Lord—'the fountain of living water' (Jer. 17.13)—continues to receive life and health from the hand of the Creator. 'He is like a tree planted by water, that sends out its roots by the stream'

(Jer. 17.8). Sin is the breaking of the bond that unites us with the fountain of life, God; that is, sin is death.

2. The image of God restored by the picture of Christ

Man has a special place in creation in so far as he was created 'in the image of God' (Gen. 1.26 f.). 'When God created man, he made him in the likeness of God' (Gen. 5.1). Seth, who was Adam's son, was, in his turn, like Adam, 'after his image' (5.3). The description of man as created in the image of God only appears sporadically in the Old Testament. That is bound up with the fact that the creation of the whole human race was of lesser interest, so long as Israel existed, than the creation of a special people; in that period, the deliverance from Egypt, and the events related to that, occupied the same place as the prehistorical creation came to occupy after Israel had fallen and Christ had risen from the dead. Israel's purity was a deliverance from the besmirching that the idolatry of the other peoples implied and a return to the first days of their election, but the purity of humanity is a deliverance from the universal uncleanness due to the sin that ravages the heart of everyman, and a return to the beginning of creation.

For this reason the terms 'image' and 'likeness' begin to appear once more in the New Testament Epistles just as they did in Old Testament prehistory, but now 'image' and 'likeness' are, typically enough, something to be attained, something that lies ahead—the goal is approached by growing together with Christ, which takes place in the Church, in the body of Christ. But full likeness is only attained in the resurrection of the dead, when sin and death, the enemies of man, are defeated. Christ is the image of God (Col. 1.15); cf. Heb. 1.3. To become like Christ is to become man as the Creator intended he should be (Gen. 1.26 f.). Those who are called are intended to be the images of God's Son, likenesses of him (Rom. 8.29). The new man is created in the likeness of God (Eph. 4.24). The growing likeness to Christ leads man out of the realm of the powers that destroy him and into the true life of man, which is fully attained in the resurrection of the dead. Until then struggle and growth go on: we are changed into his image as we rise from glory to glory (II Cor. 3.18). Through death and resurrection the road leads to 'likeness', by 'becoming like him in his death' (Phil. 3.10), by the 'cross'; as Luther says, it leads to eternal life in which man's body attains to likeness with Christ's resurrection body (Phil. 3.21). Then we shall see him, not just hear his Word as now, in the time of faith, and with seeing shall follow 'likeness' (I John 3.2). Until then the conflict to drive out Satan must rage, for only then will it be crowned with total victory.

That such conceptions of 'image' held a central place in the theology of the Ancient Church, e.g. in Irenaeus, where they served to knit together Christology and anthropology, is well known. It is less well known that Luther accorded the same conceptions great significance and—and this is the important point here—that for Luther's view of preaching they are absolutely basic.

'He who trusts in God,' says Luther, 'returns to that from which Adam fell.'[1] But God is eternally Creator who always renews. It is, accordingly, unallowable to call the first creation a perfect state, for in that case a deistic and passive picture of God would result: creation would possess a perfection which it could, in certain cases, lose and, in certain cases, regain—all quite static categories. 'Understand it, then, in this way: when God begins and carries through his works they are complete, but when God has still work to do and is engaged on it then it is not complete. Now it is plain to be seen that he is continually working and creating.'[2] Ongoing work like this, the most revolutionary since sin came to power in the world, is taking place in the shaping and refashioning of men into the image of Christ, a chiselling-out process which will end in death and resurrection.[3] After the Fall, indeed, Adam was a conquered man, a slave of Satan and death. But for that fate he was not made; thraldom under the enemies of man is opposed to God's plan in creation which is realized instead when Christ, God's image, conquers sin and death and afterwards fashions humanity into likeness with himself, in his body, by means of the preaching of the Word.[4]

The day for preaching, according to the viewpoints of both Irenaeus and Luther, is the time between the ascension and the *Parousia*. During that time there takes place the incorporation into Christ, an event which attains its goal in the resurrection of the dead. The central point of

---

[1] *WA* 24, 18.28 f.

[2] *WA* 24, 20.21-29. In this way Luther escapes the rigid alternatives of restoration or evolution where no continuous creation is envisaged, no growth under struggle.

[3] 'We must bear his image and be made like to him. It belongs to this image also that he was born and suffered, and all that belongs to him, his resurrection, life, grace and virtue is to this end that the same image should be in us. Of this type are now all heavenly men, that is, those who believe. Thus, you see what "image" and "likeness" mean' (*WA* 24, 50.29-34). The passage is an exposition of Gen. 1.26 f., which is compared with I Cor. 15.48 f. Cf. Irenaeus *Adv. haer.*, IV.61.2 [Harvey; Massuet and Migne, IV.37.7].

[4] Cf. *WA* 24, 49.23-50.29; *Adv. haer.*, V.8.1 *et passim*.

preaching is Christ's death and resurrection, which are continually being presented anew to the congregation and are to come right down into the earthly life of every Christian and take shape in suffering and crucifixion for the well-being of one's neighbour, in new birth and hope for the day of Christ. That preaching has the character of epic, narrative and painting was often deeply pondered by Luther. That it sets forth the course of events in which Christ is the main person, describes his death and resurrection, provides a picture of Christ, is, according to Luther, bound up with the fact that man is created 'in the image of God'. He must become the image of God if he is to be man, that is to say, if he is to be redeemed from the violence of the Devil, and Christ is the 'image' who has redemption. Christ is the living Word who, by becoming man and living his life, by dying and rising again, speaks to us and tells us what the heart of God is like.[1] When the picture of Christ is delineated for us in preaching, faith receives a picture of God through the Word, and this picture, received by faith, is 'God's image' for which man was created. When God sees faith—that is, Christ in man—then God must say, 'There is my image, so created I Adam; as my image is in that heart, so am I in majesty.'[2] Luther later refers to II Cor. 3.18, the saying about how 'we all, with unveiled face, beholding the glory of the Lord, are being changed into his likeness from one degree of glory to another'. His plan achieves that change on the last day. Until then, however, that process of transformation, that image-making, must go on without any break, and it goes on when Christ is preached and we listen to preaching in faith.[3]

For this reason the Bible is a book that relates what God did, a book that describes events and does not deal in conceptions, a book which describes and depicts, not one that puzzles things out and is lacking in pictures.[4] Even from the beginning God gave his Word in pictures, 'set forth in pictures', and clearest of all pictures is 'God's image' himself,

[1] 'He pictures himself in us through the Gospel just as he sees us fashioned by Christ who is the living Word. . . . My Word is there; as my visage and image and as you see my face, so is my Word. As you hear me here on earth in the Word thus in majesty is my image shaped, conceived and has its being' (WA 37, 452.4-8 (Sermons, 1534; Rörer MS)).

[2] The passage continues: 'When we thus make God's image our own, and day by day become more like him, II Cor. 3 begins. Here he shapes himself as he is; we ought to grasp it and press it to our hearts more and more, so that we may know his feelings towards us' (WA 37, 453.1-6). This passage is an exposition of Matt. 8.13, where faith is said to be exactly that on which God takes action. This was a very important Scriptural statement for Luther. Cf. Irenaeus, Adv. haer., V.36.   [3] WA 37, 459.26-461.18.

[4] 'Thus from the beginning God set forth his Word in pictures' (WA 27, 386.14 f. (Rörer MS)). Luther gives many examples.

Christ, the living, incarnate, human Word, into whose life we are incorporated when he is proclaimed and we believe. Especially when preaching from passages in the Gospels, Luther in the very first words often begins thus: 'This passage from the Gospels depicts . . . describes . . . paints . . . gives us a picture', etc. In this way Christ and his deeds occupy the central place from the first, and hold it till the end. Since Christ is the Living One, his actions as they are described in the Gospels show how he *now* acts with *us*. The men in the Gospels were not afflicted with different troubles from ours, but with the same—and he who conquered their enemies by his acts conquers ours too. The victory over Satan is Christ's death and resurrection which took place that redemption might be ours through the Word and baptism (Rom. 6.1-11). Our union with Christ's death and new life (Rom. 6.5) is the forming of the 'image' of Christ in us, the return to the purity of creation which will come about when the enemy of man has been slain and sin driven out— that is to say, in the resurrection of the dead.

The conception of 'conformity' in Luther centres wholly on these two events, Christ's death and resurrection, which two become in us the chastisement of the old man by the law and the birth of the new man through the Gospel, both of them equally the work of the *Word*. The centre of gravity in preaching is Christ's cross and resurrection, which in the coming of the Word make claim to be given shape in the life of the listener. If that takes place they achieve man's redemption, and result in the downfall of man's enemy, sin. This downfall is accompanied by disturbances and trouble for man himself, but it is a downfall all the same. If sin were not crushed, then it is man that would be lost. One of them must be destroyed—both cannot remain. And Christ comes, the Word is preached, that Satan may yield and man may be redeemed (Heb. 2.14 f.; cf. I John 3.8). There will be opportunity later to develop our treatment of this conception of 'image' from another point of view; what we wanted to do at this point was to link up preaching with God's *creative* work, as Luther sees it. God makes man to be man through a succession of acts—a series of mighty words. Were God to break off his work, then human growth would come to an end and death would reign. The Fall brought about the corruption of human nature. 'Man before preaching', man apart from the creative Word, before he is spoken to, is *conquered* man.

What is given to man in Christ is not, then, a supernatural addition to human life, but his own free growth towards true life. What the New Testament has to say about 'growth' is linked up, as part of a system with the doctrine of the two ages. What Christ achieved becomes the possession of his Church, his body, in that every single Christian is 'holding fast to the Head from whom the whole body . . . grows' (Col. 2.19). Christ has triumphed, and the Christian shares in Christ's triumph but, all the same, must fight on until the great day of the end comes. Then the triumph will be complete and at the same time 'growth' will reach its maturity. With the fulness of Christ all will have reached their goal. That day, now unseen, is set as the goal for the eye of the faithful, who just now are distressed and taste of death and the cross (cf. II Cor. 4.16-18); thereby 'the inward man' is renewed; he grows and increases in power (Eph. 3.16). Maturity of growth is 'redemption', the final triumph and freedom (I Peter 2.2).

Since for Early Christian faith the last day is closely linked with the onward march of the Word in the world of men, the increase of the Church by the preaching of the Gospel is accomplished, in a way that we find it hard to understand, by the growth of Christians to 'mature manhood', 'the fulness of Christ' (Eph. 4.13).[1] Mission, the 'growth' of the individual and the coming again of Jesus—these three are for us at different points on the road. But from the Early Church's point of view there must have been a very close connexion between them.[2] The Gospel makes its way to the end of the world, and all Christians grow in the struggle against temptation. Both these events come together in Christ's triumph over the world, which completes the triumphal progress of the Gospel among the nations and which in itself implies a conquest over the sin of every individual, the full possession of the body by the Spirit, the resurrection of the dead and the annihilation of Satan (cf. Col. 1.6).

---

[1] It is interesting to notice how Luther combines the conceptions of 'image' and 'growth' with that of 'conflict' with Satan. See *WA* 37, 459.38-460.35: 'Thereby we are shown that it is no easy matter nor of our own power to believe this or to understand these pictures, but it is God's gift and his doing alone. He bears our weakness and lack of understanding, thus assisting us forward. Otherwise we only begin to believe and abide by the Word, as he himself says by the Prophet Isaiah: "As a mother bears her child and nurses it so will I also bear thee." For it is not quickly that a child is born into the world from the womb of its mother, but grows slowly, eyes, ears, and all the members after each other until a whole, perfect, living human being is there. We too are very unformed objects whom God must accompany with his Word and Spirit that we may grow in faith from day to day until we are perfect and until, as Paul says, Christ achieves his image in us. We must always continue to look at that image, so that we may fully take it in and become like it. If the Devil often makes a scratch or a speck in it, then we must keep on cleaning and polishing it until it is fully clean again. Then man will be newborn and not just that, but perfect also, as St Paul again says, "to the measure of the stature of the fulness of Christ".'

[2] The increase of the Church implies that the 'Word of God increased'. There must be some connexion between 'the increase of faith' in II Cor. 10.15 and the spread of the Gospel in the following verse.

When that takes place, man will be free. Until then a tyrant, a barrier, restrains him. Then at last the 'image' will be clear and pure, 'God's image', in which he was created.

3. Preaching's conflict with sin, death and guilt

All this means that Christ must come, and preaching must be carried on, if man is to be man. The creative Word is the same all the way from prehistory's 'Let it be!' till the mighty Word of the resurrection. Just now, in this middle period, preaching is the mode of existence that the creative Word assumes. Without God man would be abandoned to destruction; as a prisoner in the hands of God's enemy he could only die. But imprisonment is undeniably the position in which he finds himself until Christ's—that is to say, until the Word's—advent. If God does not speak, the world of man disappears. We have just now drawn certain lines from the creation in the beginning, through Christ's assumption of humanity to the eternal fulfilment—and everywhere we have seen 'growth', creative activity, interwoven with the conflict against the Devil: man will be fully created and loosed from the hold of the destroyer on the last day. We must now cut short all these considerations, and confine ourselves to the fact that to the work we have described preaching belongs. If preaching is eliminated from this chain of events not only is there a vacant space where preaching once was, but in all its evil destructiveness satanic activity ravages unopposed and unfought in the field where man should normally 'grow' through taking to himself 'everything that proceeds out of the mouth of the Lord' (Deut. 8.3; cf. Ps. 28.1; Matt. 4.4). In the defeat of Adam the enemy of man won the field and man has no power in himself to overthrow this diabolical activity. The man to whom preaching is addressed is the man who is *conquered*. We shall examine his servitude briefly under three headings —sin, death and guilt.

Sin means being an enemy of God, being drawn into the opposition to God which is the mark of the fallen creation. Sin's nature consists, at its deepest, in unbelief—that is, in refusal to accept the message of God's love, in hardness of heart and blindness before Christ. As a result of that man feels an inescapable need, in all conceivable situations, to 'look out for himself'—first of all in the raw, egotistical greed for possessions, then in the finer, religious way of being as pious as possible, of accumulating Christian virtues, to which the greatest importance is attached: 'All this have *I*, in greatest humility, won for myself'. It is generally impossible for him who is in thrall to see through his own self-righteousness; there is but one way on earth in which such a tower of self-righteousness can be brought down—and that way is through the death of the body of him who is enslaved, which brings to an end the egocentric building and razes the illusion to the ground. All that God has done to free man, all that Christ has said, done and suffered, God's Word, baptism, and the Lord's Supper, all without exception can be twisted into their opposites and used in his 'religious activity' by the perverted man, that is, by Satan. No Biblical writer is so on the alert for this sort of human enslavement as Paul. No one enquires with such pertinacity as he about the true *righteousness*. Luther asks the same basic question as Paul, and both arrive at the same radical answer: righteousness is *Christ*, who died for our sins. Both see the present Christian life as Christ's struggle in us against the enemy, and regard the resurrection of the dead as Satan's final fall and annihilation. One of the great misfortunes of our modern Christianity is that our preaching at the present time does not come to grips with real sins, but generally with imaginary ones—so that often even men who otherwise have a good sense of judgement feel an unrealistic aversion to the very term 'sin'.

Sin brings *death*. This occurs because sin is separation from God who is the Creator, that is to say, the fount of life. To be in rebellion against God is to be at enmity with the only one who has life in himself. All life is of God's creation: all life—since it is life—is contact with God. Sin breaks the threads by which vitality is supported, and finally death becomes lord. According to the Christian faith death has no place in a world free from sin. In our fallen world, however, death, sickness and want of health appear almost normal: while, on the other hand, Christ's resurrection—which is the advent of purity in abnormal surroundings—appears unbelievable. Among the New Testament writings it is the Johannine group which are dominated by the question of *life*. In all the New Testament writings, however, it is faith in the resurrection which is the conviction dominating all others. The Johannine question about 'life' to a very high degree controls the thought of Irenaeus. Just as Paul and Luther stress the fact that righteousness is Christ, so John and Irenaeus hold fast to the fact that life is Christ. But according to the faith of the Ancient Church and of the Reformation, Christ gives life to men as they share in his cross and resurrection— that is to say, in an action of *destruction* which leads to life. Death and sin are both enemies of God, but God uses death, the one enemy, as a tool and helper to slay sin, the other enemy—that is, to slay Satan, whose death is part of God's plan of redemption for man (Rev. 20.10, 14).

F

The death of sin is experienced by man as something that shatters his own ego, as the destruction of his old man; but the sinful self is not entirely suppressed until the body has died. God's use of death, nevertheless, does not mean that the enemy becomes a friend. Death also shall be conquered, but only at the last. 'The last enemy to be destroyed is death' (I Cor. 15.26). The final triumph over the enemy of man implies also the fall of death, that is to say, the rescue of man. That is the resurrection of the dead: with that the last stronghold of the power that destroys human life has been taken. The maturity and full freshness of man's life can only then be experienced. A major difficulty for preaching today is the fact that modern man in theory regards his situation as that of a humanity in which nothing is lacking: he is the seat of judgement before which Christianity must prove its claims. That is the superficial *theory*, but deep down is the realization that he is not free but cut off and far away from the sources of life. Our preaching, however, does not succeed in making a rent in the theory, and uncovering the depths beneath.

Sin also brings *guilt*. Certainly sin is a power from which no man can escape and which exercises tyrannical violence over us. Guilt does *not* imply that man spots a weak point in sin's dominion, sees the full possibility of being other than he is, of being free from sin, and so acknowledging that possibility, admits that he is guilty and not just held in thrall. Rather does guilt imply that before God he becomes aware that all humanity, indeed the whole cosmos, is in rebellion against God and that *he shares in it too*, even consents to it, and into the activities against God he himself enters just like the rest. All therefore may equally excuse themselves because of sin's character of violence and fate. In a word, sin implies that man understands that *he himself* is Adam, as the story in Gen. 3 tells him. Adam, the man, described in the story of the Fall, is I myself. Here, as elsewhere, the Bible is 'the story of Everyman', but I myself am also Everyman in the Gospel, to whom Jesus says 'your sins are forgiven you'—and it was to many that he spoke thus. These men are there in our Gospels that Christ may speak the word of forgiveness to us. Both in the New Testament and in Luther's thought the forgiveness of sins is of central significance; the word of forgiveness is the weapon which is first employed against the power of Satan, a word with which the enemy is hunted out of our *conscience*. Now that the conscience is free the continuing control of a foreign power over the body is a torment that can be endured and that will totally cease in the resurrection life. Wherever sin dwells, there law

It's a promise not a realization

reigns. God's own creative will becomes law where man in his fallen condition sets himself up against the Creator. Forgiveness is the casting out of sin and guilt from the conscience, and along with them the law is cast out as well. So far as the body and the world are concerned, however, law and secular authority continue to rule, awaiting the coming of the last day when Satan shall be overthrown and Christ visibly becomes King. In heaven there is no sin, no death, no guilt, no law. On the other hand, Christ, as man, was put under the law; his suffering on the cross was a struggle against God's judgement in the law, a bearing of God's wrath. But his resurrection shattered not only the power of sin and death but also that of the law and guilt and opened the kingdom of heaven in which all these powers are set aside, since there God's enemies are no more.

Just as it can be said of our preaching today that it does not deal with real sin, nor expose the agony caused by death, but with an odd 'good will' glosses over the thraldom of man, so it can also be said that the real consciousness of sin in the depths of the soul, on the one side, and the proclamation of the Church, on the other, do not meet each other today. It is a paradoxical situation that the forgiveness of sins is being declared continually in all our cities and villages and that, at the same time, year after year in the very places where that is the case scores of people are to be found who are tormented by unforgiven sin and cannot find a way out of their torment. Oftener than one imagines, these guilt-burdened people listen to the words of our preaching and absolution without the thought of God's forgiveness of their sins crossing their minds for a moment. Something must surely be lacking in preaching when people experience this inability to hear. Proclamation itself must, in this case, be of such a nature that the hearers do not link up the realities in question with the life of every day—not, that is to say, with the ordinary life of the world but rather with that so called 'religious' life which is really nothing at all but a pure fiction, the Emperor's new clothes. Needed here, as in the story, is a real child who can cry aloud that a 'religious' relationship cut off from all earthly relationships is nothing at all. So that we might not succeed in worming our way into such a realm, which in any case we could not reach, Christ became *man* and forgave whoredom, theft, embezzlement, fraud, etc.—not only forgave them, indeed, but took them on himself, lived amongst sinners and died as a thief.

The difficulty with which we are here confronted, that of effecting a meeting between the Word and real sin, death and guilt, is unavoidable so long as we do not see man's life in general as a work on which *God* is engaged, and the destruction of each man's life—no matter how profane, biological or economic a destruction it may appear—as a work on which *Satan* is engaged. It is a hopeless task to achieve an attitude of faith towards existence just when the Word reaches man, if up to that moment each earthly event is regarded as unrelated to God. Even 'before preaching'—to use a term we have used already—God's work and the enemy's work were being carried on in the life of every man. Preaching is not a new beginning, but a new phase in a conflict that has been going on for a long time, a conflict between creation and sin, between God and the Devil. We shall, therefore, now turn to the general conception of life based on the category of conflict, which constitutes the background for faith in the living Word.

Church is not Jonah going to Nineveh. It is Nineveh after Jonah's visit

VII

CREATION AND REDEMPTION

1. Redemption: a critique of Pietism

IF we wish to describe briefly the leading convictions which set their stamp on the religious thought of the last two centuries, we may say that during them the life of man has been regarded as something we have in ourselves, which God neither gives nor creates. On the other hand, we need God in order to be able to make something *out of* our lives. Life is raw material which religion, ethics, culture, etc., take in hand. Raw material has come into existence through a series of natural causes, and on these a 'religious' aspect cannot be imposed. God comes on the scene somewhere about the middle of human life when the question of 'religion' arises.

By an extension of this same point of view to the history of the human race, the conclusion is reached that about the year 1 B.C. God took a hand in dealing with the raw material that humanity offered. As long as optimism and evolutionism prevailed it was easily possible to regard Christianity as superior to all other forces engaged on the task of shaping the material—a sort of cultural summit—as the nineteenth century did. When, however, heathenism takes a firm enough hold, that claim becomes unendurable to so-called 'secularized' people who refuse to undergo such radical remodelling, and desire instead to have more of the raw material—that is to say, of human life—left unmodelled.[1]

In face of this danger ecclesiastics are abandoning the nineteenth-century cultural synthesis: now, with polemical intent, redemption and

---

[1] In the real situation in which we find ourselves, though the secularists do not appreciate this, sin and death play their part. The desire for 'freedom' implies therefore the desire to let loose the enemies of man—and this is just what is taking place in the moral desolation of the present time. The greatest difficulty in the present situation is caused by the fact that those who protest against the forces which destroy human life nearly always protest as well against the human life which God has created, and do not wish it to have its freedom. It is impossible to straighten out this tangle, in which neither side is in the right, without challenging, and waging war on, the ethical outlook that has followed in the train of Pietism and is responsible for one of the main defects in the religiosity of the present time.

the Church are being set in opposition to the secularist attempt to remodel the material—that is to say, against the shaping of human life. In comparison with the clearly thought-out matter-and-form ideology of the Scholastics, this way of viewing the problem may appear to be obscure, but basically it is clear, and therefore convincing to him who has once got it into his head.[1] No one can think in these categories theologically without longing for Rome. Churchmanship conditioned by such an atmosphere of thought points to Rome—even if it recreates the pristine purity of Lutheran orthodoxy one day, resurrects some cultic usage of heathen Sweden of long ago the next and, just to be on the safe side, turns to actual social problems the third.

The Ancient Church did not think of Christ as an 'improver' of man's life, but as its *Restorer and Redeemer*. The same conviction was equally strong in Luther, who fought relentlessly against theories, foreign to the Bible, which grew up in the Middle Ages.[2] The first point that must be kept in mind by anyone who would understand the theology of Irenaeus or Luther is that *man's life*, as man's life, is a work of *God*, that it has its meaning as the creation of God *before* we begin to make something specially holy out of it.[3] Though we ourselves have invented many ways of organizing the life of man we have not, on the contrary, invented the life of man itself, but God the Creator has. From that it follows that man's life is better than our ways of organizing it: God's work is better than ours. It is a totally different matter that the life of every man is evil and twisted; that rather strengthens the affirmation that it was originally created good. Because of sin, man's life can never be raw

---

[1] This way of putting the problem is clear so long as the Church's work is regarded as essentially a consecration of that which is profane, and no opportunity is allowed of correcting the unbiblical philosophical conception which lies at the source of this conviction.

[2] A counterpart of Luther's polemic against the spirituality of the Scholastics and the Fanatics (*Schwärmer*) is offered by the struggle of the Ancient Church against Gnosticism. In both cases, Biblical conceptions were the cause of the opposition.

[3] See Irenaeus, *Adv. haer.*, V.3.3 [2-3]. For Luther, see *WA* 10(I.1), 199.27-200.8: 'For it is not to be denied that the natural life, which even the unbelieving have, exists through him, as Paul says in Acts 17: "In him we live, and move, and have our being". Yes, the natural life is part of the eternal life, a beginning of it, but it ends in death, because it does not know nor honour him from whom it comes. He therefore cuts it off, so that it must die eternally. Again, those who believe and know him in whom they live die no more, but the natural life is continued in the eternal, so that it does not taste death.' Then John 8.52 and 11.25 f. are quoted. Here Luther sets forth the relation between the life here and life in the resurrection exactly as Irenaeus does: these two forms of life are not two different things but are fully identical, nothing being added in the resurrection. That which is new in the resurrection is that sin and death, the enemies of man, which we fight against here are conquered there.

material which is to be moulded, but is rather in thrall from which it must be freed. It was to rescue prisoners that Jesus came into the world: the evangelists make that clear in one story after another. Indeed the picture of Jesus as the driver out of demons and the healer has not only religio-historical significance, but is also highly theological in essence.[1]

The very fact that Jesus came into a world where suffering and thraldom were present, and *there* went about as a rescuer of men from the bonds which bound them, is of the utmost importance. Nothing new is argued out of a supposedly new and theoretical revelation. No new 'religion' is started. No attempt is made to propagate or spread a newly discovered system of thought or to refurbish an old one. Instead Christ goes around with his disciples in the places where there is need —in such a way that he thereby meets his doom. When that happens, in the victories that the Redeemer wins at the cost of his own life, the kingdom of God has come. Those who wrote the Gospels had a clear insight into the significance of this: they continually give us a picture of the Master who conquers in the depths but is never a 'success', never 'achieves' anything, never raises himself out of his anonymity. Today the same insight must regulate the proclamation of the Word of Christ —that is to say, the certainty of victory and a scepticism about so-called 'results'. To desire it otherwise is to desire that the proclamation of the Word should cease being a conflict against Satan and become instead the spreading of an ideology, that it should be a 'movement', as it is called, a spreading of ideas—in other words it is to desire that seeing should take place now instead of at the last day.

Every miracle of healing that Jesus does is—it may be said—a phase of the great miracle, the resurrection of Christ. Since the resurrection constitutes the conquest that the whole New Testament proclaims, we have that crowd of sick men in the Gospels who find healing through Christ's Word. To tell of such events is to preach the resurrection of Christ with the special kerygmatic address which such preaching of the resurrection should have, if it is to be of the Early Church; that is, to preach the resurrection of Christ as something that God did with us, with men. From of old death reigned because sin reigned from of old. Now Christ comes and is tempted in all points as we are, as Adam, but does not fall. Conquest of temptation was the beginning of Christ's

[1] Since 'save' and 'Saviour' have acquired a certain significance from the revivals of the last century it is advisable to employ in their place the terms 'redeem' and 'Redeemer'. Otherwise, there is a real danger that their original meaning will disappear from the homiletical usage of today.

resurrection. Satan holds the human race under both sin and death; if anyone succeeds in bursting the chain of sin he will certainly come at last to shatter that of death as well, even if on the road thither—and that goes by way of the cross—he is fearfully wounded. All Christ's work— his temptations, his labours with the sick, his preaching of the forgive- ness of sins, his death and resurrection—is one single conquest over a foreign power which held men subject when he came to earth. And now that conquest abides in Christ's Word. We who today hear the Word find ourselves under the same dominion of sin and death, and we have the Conqueror with us because we have the Word with us. The Word is, as we have seen before, the link between the resurrection of Christ which happened once and our own which lies in the future. That con- quest achieved on the field of battle will one day be visible to us. Until then it is the conquest that is preached, for our ears to hear. Our situ- ation 'before preaching' is then the same as the position of men when Jesus came into the world. In the evil within us the same enemy of men is at work as in the evil in them. In the subjection of our bodies to death the same unnatural condition shows itself as in their illnesses. Existence, as man's existence, is charged to the full with conflict between God and Satan.

With men 'before preaching' God too is present. Life, just because it is life, is an ongoing work of God. We cannot, in fact, understand what it means to be totally abandoned by God—therefore, as Luther pointed out, we cannot understand Christ's conflict on the cross. There would be no word of any release, any reconciliation, any redemption, any salvation, were life not under subjection to death, in a blasted and evil state. Christ does not come to Satan's own world when he comes in the Incarnation, but he comes to *his* own, to the men of the Creator who have been led astray into enmity with God. All humanity sees the rain- bow in the sky, and the bow is the sign of the covenant between God and *the world*, 'every living creature of all flesh that is upon the earth' (Gen. 9.8-17). The God who chose Israel and gave them circumcision has not totally abandoned the other nations to death but has concluded a covenant with them too—a covenant of grace, whose kernel is that destruction, extermination, shall *not* have full scope, that is to say that the 'Flood' shall not come again (Gen. 9.11, 15). Judgement is stayed, heaven and earth are spared (II Peter 3.3-7). To live as man at all is the result of receiving something every day; it is a fruit of the Creator's act of grace. We can all say, 'It is of the Lord's mercies that we are not consumed, because his compassions fail not' (Lam. 3.22, AV). Did the earth not have sun and rain life would be over; that the sun now shines and the rain now falls is due to the positive action of God (Matt. 5.45). When the question is asked why life should be given in Christ when it existed before his coming, that question makes it plain that what thinking in terms of *conflict* means has not been understood. Why should Christ be tempted on the cross when he has already been tempted in the wilderness? How can Satan be cast down at the *Parousia* when he has already been cast down at the resurrection on the third day? In a battle the *final* victory is in danger in every single phase of the struggle: he who is to be finally victorious must be victorious stage by stage, he who is to be defeated at the end is beaten stage by stage. Life at creation is the same life that Christ redeems—but when Christ comes it is a *threatened* life, a life doomed to death. Through his victory it can 'rise' and 'stand upon its feet', as it is often expressed in accounts of healing miracles—rise up to victorious battle until it 'stands up' for ever out of the graves and triumphs with the Lord.

2. Creation: a critique of Barthianism

He who at creation was intended to live with the Lord and not to die is man. He is created in the image of God, created in Christ. When he is rescued from death and sin what was intended in his creation takes place, for the Devil is no independent and evil principle who is God's counterpart eternally. Were that the case his fall at the last day would bring about something entirely different from what obtained at creation: of the two original principles one alone would remain, God. But God alone has created all, even the beings who afterwards fall and become evil. Life, just because it is life, comes from God. The enemy cannot create, cannot even exist in himself, can only kill, only damage what has been created. When the enemy has been overcome, creation is pure and fresh and God's kingdom has come. But the process through which the creation is cleansed is long.

Already in Israel's liberation from Egypt and its changing history from then till the coming of Christ the purifying process was going on, without the poison being fully eliminated. Against the background of the ruin of humanity as a whole, Israel was called, so that in this people the sin of the world should be redeemed, and the Word of redemption should go forth to all humanity, for the repair of whose ruin Israel was called as a representative. Just as Israel was freed from the enemy through the Exodus from Egypt, but only gradually attained its king-

dom in the reign of David, so humanity was freed from the enemy
through the resurrection of Christ but only gradually, after journeying
through the desert, struggling the while, does it attain to an abiding
dwelling in the kingdom of God through the resurrection of the dead.
Sin, which was never annihilated in the days of ancient Israel, but continued to live on below the surface, was conquered by Christ, but in
such a way that the conquest *comes* from him to us, comes through the
Word, until he himself shall come visibly.

In Israel's struggle against her enemies, the vestibule of Christ's
conquest, we hear, therefore, of ourselves, of our struggle against our
enemies now in the interim period of faith and of the Word which is the
vestibule of Christ's final conquest, that which shall be visible. Christ
fulfils the Passover, Israel's feast of thanksgiving for the Exodus—for
behind Pharaoh another hides, a stronger enemy, whom only the incarnate God, and not Moses, could overcome. The same God comes
to us through the Word; he comes when Satan's hold is strongest and
most unyielding, comes to the *sinner*, to him most of all.[1]

When the Gospels tell of the healing of the sick what they are really
talking about is redemption: where death gives ground life is being
victorious. The Creator's world is depraved, and depravity is seen first
of all—to use modern language—as biological degeneracy, not so mark-
edly as social degeneracy; bodily disturbances are more apparent than
disturbances in the social framework. The Ancient Church liked to
think along these lines when formulating its ideas on redemption, making the contrast between life and death its basic theme. Luther, on the
other hand, with far-reaching consequences, followed out another Early
Christian line of thought, which is to be found both in the Gospels and
in Paul: sin and death represent depravity, while forgiveness represents
healing.[2] This definite concentration on sin involved a penetrating investigation on Luther's part of the problem of *society*—or as one might
say, of the spiritual content in social depravity. Here, in his teaching on

[1] Jesus' love of sinners is easily sentimentalized if the aspect of conflict is
passed over. When Jesus seeks the sinner, he seeks him whom the *enemy* torments: the forgiveness of sins is the destruction of the enemy and the restoration
of man.

[2] The conviction, found everywhere in the New Testament, that sin is the
primary degeneracy, bringing death in its train, is shared without any shadow
of a doubt by the theology of both the Ancient Church and Luther. For this
reason forgiveness is for Irenaeus the primary factor in healing, just as it is for
Luther. But the accent is on life in the Ancient Church and on forgiveness in
Luther. If anyone feels like criticizing this as 'one-sidedness', taking the Bible
as his starting point, his criticism must be directed against *both* Irenaeus and
Luther. In our own situation we cannot mechanically reproduce either the one
or the other.

vocation and on secular authority, Luther works out his basic conception of existence that makes real and living for his time the conception of life which characterizes the Gospels.[1]

The view of life that easily slips in with modern theology, according to which the world is bare and empty of any relation to God when the Incarnation comes as a bolt from the blue, or when Christians go out into it with their Christianity, is, therefore, basically contrary to the Bible and to the Reformation, and makes all preaching impossible.[2] On the contrary, we are all born into a world where God and the Devil are both active; our own existence with its daily experience of light and darkness tastes God's goodness and the destroyer's evil. When we hear preaching we hear the call of him who created us. In our 'yes' to Christ our pristine purity is released from its prison; the repressive power of the enemy that holds sway over our lives is broken in pieces by him who comes from without and who is stronger than we are. Under his dominion man receives life anew as a gift of which he cannot be deprived whatever happens. In the service of his Redeemer and Lord he is commissioned to serve, in his own place in the world and until his death, those about him, his neighbours, and thus 'exercise' his office.

In our day it is extremely important that over against the influential Barthian theology, which is to be found even where no mention of Barth's name is made, we should keep alive this fundamental belief in creation and distinguish constantly between creation and sin without

---

[1] The fact that everyone comes under secular authority is in itself a sign of the dominion of sin. Authority is based on force and exercises violence when what is good cannot be done with willing heart. Thereby God keeps under his *law* the whole world that he has created and creates but which has fallen and is in revolt. From one point of view, man finds himself, thanks to God's law expressed in secular authority, *in the old covenant*, not in the empty, profane void, but under discipline—men are subdued and waiting as when Christ came into the world. All institutions and official positions drive men to good works towards their neighbours: no one in society can avoid serving others. In any official position the God of law is at work. He is not far away but near at hand and keeps on with his creative work employing all men as his tools and instruments; so the work of the world gets done. But the man himself, the person in the official position, is, indeed, a prisoner under the power of sin, and so under compulsion in all situations to look after himself and thereby to do his neighbour down. Perhaps he can 'use' his official position aright, and stand in the life-giving service of God—but he can also 'misuse' it, and stand in the death-bringing service of the Devil, so that both he and those about him pine away. In use and abuse the conflict between God and the Devil surges backwards and forwards over the whole area of social life—in home and family, in local affairs and politics, in civilian life and in military, in the ecclesiastical field and in education.

[2] Barth with his dogma of the Incarnation and Christian Socialists with their 'world betterment' are both of them in agreement with the atheists that the world has no connexion with God—before he 'comes down' or before their own 'attack' respectively.

allowing ourselves to be frightened of the usual invective against 'natural theology', 'liberalism', etc. If today the theological stream is not diverted at this point, it is not just a peripheral detail of the Christian faith that will suffer; it is the Christian *kerygma* itself, at its very centre, which will be suppressed. The centre of gravity of the preaching of the Early Church was in Christ's death and resurrection, not in the Incarnation in itself, not in the virgin birth as the meeting place of 'God' and 'man'. All is brought into relation to the main message of the death and resurrection.[1] God and man are not two poles that stand over against one another. It is possible to retain that unbiblical viewpoint while expatiating on the Incarnation—indeed, it thrives in company with the concept of a bare incarnation—but God, by the power of Christ, lifts men out of the kingdom of darkness, strikes man's enemy down, and gives life to man. If the cross and the resurrection are to retain their New Testament position at the centre of the message, then a revision of the opposition between transcendence and immanence must be brought about. The Lutheran dualism of law and Gospel in the Word performs just that very revising, anti-speculative function. God's work meets us *sub contraria specie*, hidden under the work of death. It must be so, since we are in thrall to sin; when our sin, which insists on ruling in our being, is killed, we receive life but it seems as though it were death. The lifegiving function of the Gospel is indissolubly bound up with the condemnatory and punitive function of the law; the cross is fast bound with the resurrection. If this intrinsic duality of law and Gospel is abandoned and replaced, as in Barth, by a single 'Word' above the law and the Gospel, then there follows also a new metaphysical cleavage, so that within the single Word we discover a higher, transcendent sphere, the Word of God (*Gottes Wort*) and a lower sphere, the word of man (*Menschenswort*). Thereby the Platonic doctrine of two worlds becomes supreme in theology. What is specifically theological and Christian is introduced later in the thesis that 'God' and 'man' meet and are brought together in the Incarnation. But in that case the mere meeting between God and man becomes the centre of the New Testament, while struggle and victory in the death and the resurrection have lost their place as the centre of the *kerygma*. This is the chief accusation that must be brought against Karl Barth's theology.

When, as happens in the Barthian theology, God and man are set in

[1] For Barth an empty incarnation is the main thing; much else is afterwards added to that but what is thus added has *no essential* significance. Neither in the New Testament nor in Luther has the virgin birth a central place, but for Barth, on the contrary, that is just what it has.

opposition to one another and, in addition, the distance between them is stressed, the result to be expected is that unbelief is regarded as the only really natural thing. So there arises a strange affinity with the widespread heathen cultural atmosphere of today, within which also unbelief is alone really 'natural'. In its survey of life as a whole such a theology feels itself at one with almost all movements of every age, provided they are irreligious. What makes the theologian different from the others is that in addition to this view of life which is without faith and which he shares with the others he imagines a 'paradox', and posits that x equals God—a paradox which is beyond the human realm and to which faith stands in relation. We move first of all on a purely naturalistic human plane where it is meaningless to talk about God, and then afterwards we discover faith, the great exception, the irregularity, 'an exceptional bulge in an otherwise straight line of human events'. Thus from the very beginning a point of view is adopted that forbids faith any relation to human life in all its fulness and denies that what is given in faith signifies the deliverance of man from his unnatural condition, his restoration to the estate in which he was created. For Luther, unbelief is *demonic*. It is not 'human' to doubt and 'paradoxical' to believe; on the contrary, where doubt arises, it is diabolical powers that strive for mastery in human life. So, for Luther doubt is not of the intellect but is *despair* about life and redemption. Where faith arises, Christ comes and drives Satan out of the conscience, so that man can breathe and live, free and unrestrained as a child, and in this state of true humanity he can fulfil God's will in the ordinary and earthly life of every day.

Scepticism about the message is, accordingly, not just the human and irreligious plane over which, thanks to an outpouring of the Spirit, faith can hover freely. Where scepticism is found, that is a sign that the God of this world has *blinded* the understanding so that 'the light of the gospel of the glory of Christ, who is the likeness of God' (II Cor. 4.4) cannot be seen. Someone is thus active in opposition to the Creator wherever unbelief is found—that is to say, where death is found. Just as we saw before that the existence of human life is the expression of a lifegiving activity of the Creator, so we now see that that unbelief, unresponsiveness to God's Word, is the expression of a destructive and blinding activity of Satan. In neither case is man free and his own master. In both something happens to him: he is the battle-ground between two who wish to have him for themselves. But these two are not comparable: God is man's rightful Lord, Satan a false lord, a usurper, a thief, a robber. This distinction between God and the Devil, their contrasted claim on man, is not something which should be added to the contrast between life and death to complete that contrast, for Satan's subordination to God and his helplessness before God are implied in that very contrast itself. When it is said that God is life, it is implied that man becomes man by receiving from God; and when Satan is said to be death, it is implied that man loses his humanity when under Satan's dominion, for Satan is a murderer (John 8.44). The question of the legitimacy of God's claim, and of Satan's, on man is a question that provides its own answer, as is always the case when true sovereignty emerges: the dispute is not settled in favour of the rightful claimant, instead it is clear that the rightful claimant never disputes with the underling but allows him to be just who he is, and thus proceeds with his work using the subordinate usurper as his tool without taking away his evil. So shall it be at the last day when the faithful of the Lord shall attain to fulness of vision and shall see that the death, discipline and evil under which they suffered on earth, and in which Satan always works, but brought them nearer to life and destroyed the hold that sin, their enemy, had on their inmost being. The enemy executes that which God has determined shall be (Acts 4.27).

3. The task of the preacher is to do battle

Man's position 'before preaching' is, accordingly, determined by the undecided and stern struggle between God and the Devil. To speak of the last day, of the final victory and the full redemption, is to speak of something that is being accomplished by the Word and mediated by the preaching that is now going on throughout the world, which is the link between Christ's resurrection and our own. Redemption is not just something of which we hear in the Word. It is something which is even now happening to us, when we encounter the Word; the Word is the creative Word which brings its work to birth in us. Through the creative Word which comes to us in preaching we are redeemed—that is, we become men; for Satan, the murderer, is forced to let go his hold on us. But 'man before preaching' is the defeated man, who has not been fully freed, who is still held in the jaws of death. Since the task of the Word is to give battle, and as such, is carried through in the teeth of continual opposition and with perturbation of mind, Christ has instituted—and here we are on the threshold of the next chapter—a special *ministry* of the Word, has undertaken a direct *sending* by which messengers are sent right into the enemy-occupied world of men, sent 'as sheep in the midst of wolves' (Matt. 10.16).[1] It belongs to the nature of the office of preaching that it has its place in the battle between God and the Devil, and that it *must* have its place there—must continually, with conscious intent, take its place there. Both in the New Testament and in Luther do we detect this characteristic of the office of the ministry. A contrary wind, a noise of battle—such is the preacher's native element. Musty quiet, contentment on left and right, are indeed signs that touch with the Word must have been lost.[2]

As Christ came into human life and did not add a wholly different life to that which had existed before on earth, but instead redeemed the very life, endangered and doomed to die, with which he was confronted, so with the coming of the Gospel a spiritual authority enters the world of men, which on account of its sin is wholly shut up by God's law under secular authority. The earth is full of 'offices', and yet the spiritual office must be added to them. The Church is a standing witness that life is eternal: she opens the door to heaven where the life of man is to be redeemed by Christ. It is not a wholly other life she offers to us in the Word, but the only redemption for the life of man which is what she has been charged to preach, life's release from the two enemies—first from sin through forgiveness and next from death through the resurrection, so that the life which is freed thereby becomes everlasting. For this reason in the third article of the Creed, in closest unity with confession of belief in the Church, faith utters these words: ' . . . the forgiveness of sins, the resurrection of the body and the life everlasting.'

---

[1] That the disciples are sent as sheep in the midst of wolves implies that in themselves they are helpless and unable to protect themselves against the violence to which they may be exposed for the sake of the Gospel. Christ strove with enemies but he did not make a stand against the crucifixion. Referring to this, Luther emphasizes that the spiritual realm must be without external might and have but one weapon, the Word. On the other hand, there is no eagerness for martyrdom in Matt. 10.16. The rest of the verse runs: 'so be wise as serpents and innocent as doves'. Luther's opposition to a 'self-chosen cross' is well known. He who seeks martyrdom is just as self-centred as he who flees it. What matters is that the messenger should proclaim the Word and in faith afterwards take what comes to him without counting on success or fearing opposition.

[2] Cf. Luther in the Larger Commentary on Galatians: 'Bernard also saw this. According to him the Church is in best state when from all sides she is being attacked by Satan's violence and devilry and in worst state when peace reigns on all sides. Striking, if somewhat incorrect, is his quotation of that verse in Hezekiah's song of thanksgiving, "My peace is my bitterest bitterness" (Isa. 38.17, Vulgate), put in the mouth of the Church in times of peace and security. Paul (Gal. 5.11) sees it as a sure sign that it is not the Gospel that is being proclaimed if it is proclaimed without upsetting the peace' (*WA* 40(II), 53.36-54.12).

VIII

THE MINISTRY OF RECONCILIATION

1. The commission of the ministry

WE now turn our attention to the preaching of the present time. Preaching means that Christ comes now. He who hears the Gospel hears Christ speaking and meets with him. To be heard in the world Christ himself has sent out messengers, and instituted the ministry of preaching. The ministry of reconciliation is a ministry of the Word, and Christ is in the Word; he comes in the Word.[1] At this point, however, we are confronted with a difficulty for our thought. Preaching is to paint a picture of Christ, the crucified and risen—is to tell of him, set forth God's action in him. To this extent the preacher speaks about Christ. It is difficult to see clearly how such speech can come to be Christ's own words to his hearers.

A link that binds the two modes of speech together is offered by the accounts in the Gospels which often describe something Jesus did and then bring the story to a climax in a word Jesus spoke—a word for us, which allows us to hear the Lord's own voice and transforms the action of which we have been told into one that has to do with *us*. how?

But there is yet something more important—the unique unity in which, according to the Biblical viewpoint, the messenger and he whose messenger he is are bound together. When the messenger speaks, he who sent him speaks. The messengers whom Jephthah sends to the King of the Ammonites are Jephthah himself and, therefore, they speak, though many, in the singular, 'What hast thou to do with *me*?' (Judges 11.12 f.). The messenger there in the place whither he has been sent can speak of his master who has sent him and his words are not the sender's own words but rather words about him, but in the same moment that the

---

[1] Cf. Luther on John 20.19: 'His coming is nothing other than what he preaches through all the world. For he who is a Christian and preaches him, does not himself do the work, but Christ; when we hear the Gospel, we hear Christ himself. His is the voice that speaks, and his the word that is spoken. So when Christ comes to us, no one sees him or touches him, but he is perceived by the heart alone and stands "in the midst"—that is, in our heart' (*WA* 20, 364.38-365.5; Rörer MS).

master's *message* is passed on the character of the words is altered: they now are those of another person than they were before, for the voice of the sender is heard when he who is sent speaks. In this way Jesus Christ is the one who has been sent, God's gift to the world. Accordingly, sometimes Christ speaks about God as though God were wholly other than himself; sometimes, again, Christ speaks and acts in God's stead, and then he is God, the Word.[1] Suddenly, without any connecting link, the Gospels pass from one of these types of Jesus' speech to the other: it is a sign that the idea of 'sending' and 'message' dominates the New Testament thought. Now, in his turn, Christ sends his apostles: 'As the Father has sent me, even so I send you' (John 20.21). For this reason it is natural that those who are sent forth on the one hand speak *about* Christ and tell of his doings, and, on the other, speak Christ's own word so that he comes to men through what is said by the preachers he has sent. But it is this latter, Christ's presence in the Word, that is the content of the message and that makes preaching preaching.

Sending is an action of Christ by which he stands forth as Lord over the world, making claim to all nations. It is after the resurrection that Christ sends forth his messengers into all the world until the end of time. At the same time he makes promise of, and bestows, his Spirit, which is a sort of first fruits until that time when the world shall be born anew and the dead rise again. These messengers have the same task in preaching as Christ himself had: 'to proclaim release to the captives' (Luke 4.18)—something that he did because the Spirit was upon him (cf. Isa. 61.1). Through his ascension Christ receives the same power as God, and since God by his power can be everywhere and is not locked up in heaven, Christ's ascension implies that Christ is everywhere on earth where his messengers proclaim his Word.[2] The foundation of preaching is the ascension of Christ and Pentecost, the outpouring of his Spirit which sprang from it. Out in the world are the prisoners who need release. How are they to take to themselves a message they have not heard? 'And how are they to hear without a *preacher*? And how can men preach unless they are *sent*?' (Rom. 10.14 f.). Thus Early Christian faith sometimes begins by establishing the necessity for redemption and the need of the world of men, and then afterwards pictures Christ's

[1] Jesus shows the way and he is the way; he gives the bread of life and he is the bread of life; he teaches truth and he is the truth—difference passes into identity. Especially in St John's Gospel, where the conception of sending is unusually clear, we often stumble on double conceptions of this type.
[2] The run of events in Mark 16.19 f. is striking: the ascension, the preaching of the eleven, the presence of the Ascended One in the preached Word; it is the same basic conception as in Acts.

G

death and resurrection and their inevitable outcome in two events—the
sending forth of messengers of good tidings and the preaching of the
messengers throughout the world. By sending forth preachers the Redeemer comes to men who are in need. That it should reach them
belongs to the work of redemption; otherwise it would not be full
redemption. Sending and preaching, therefore, both belong to Christ's
redemptive work. Christ's work of redemption takes place when men
preach about it. For this reason Paul too can begin with Christ's work
and from that pass on to sending and preaching, and thus come to those
in need of redemption, unreconciled men. In II Cor. 5.17-20, Paul speaks
of the same thing as in Rom. 10.14 ff., although here the order is
reversed: reconciliation, the ministry and word of reconciliation and,
last of all, the message that the messengers carry into the world of men.
'We are ambassadors for Christ, God making his appeal through us'
(II Cor. 5.20). God's action in Christ passes over into the preacher's
message about Christ which is to go to the ends of the earth.

The ministry is, then, a necessary constituent part of the message.
Anyone who considers that the ministry can be eliminated has not
thought through the conception of Christ's *sending* of the apostles, a
conception that belongs to the very core of the New Testament. 'Sending' implies that Christ speaks in preaching—that is to say, preaching
cannot be carried on on the basis of the preacher's personal inner experiences, but depends on a commission, received from a sender, which
even determines *what* is to be preached. Freedom for Christ's preachers
of any particular age to preach almost anything—for example, what the
educated would like to hear—cannot be allowed. The outward dress of
the message, its formal shape, language, imagery, can change from time
to time, but the content and core undergoes no change, from Christ's
resurrection to the last day; the offence that the message causes is
basically the same in every age. The abiding element, which is unaffected
by changing times and types of preachers, is Christ himself, who is in
the Word because he has sent it forth, speaks through all the preachers
of all the ages, uses them as his own tongue and lips and through them
dons the clothes of every generation. The ministry is, accordingly, something that the Word—that is to say, Christ—uses to advance through
the nations to the ends of the earth and through the generations to the
end of time, the *Parousia*.[1]

[1] Continuity between the holders of office in different ages is, accordingly,
due to the fact that the living Christ works all the time. Christ's word, spoken
and heard today, binding together Christ's resurrection and Christ's *Parousia*
is the link in the chain of events and contains all the continuity that is necessary.

What is primary is the Word, which is destined to endure as long as humanity endures; the means by which it presses forward is the messengers who hold the office of preaching the Word. With the coming of the Word, the Church arises in all nations. We are not to think first of an outgoing Church and then of its message, the Word. The Word is no other than the creative Word, which took flesh in Christ and now goes out to his world. First of all is the Word, before it is only chaos. The Word creates, the Word sustains (John 1.3; James 1.18; I Peter 1.23-25).[1]

2. The authority of the ministry

Discussion of such questions proceeds on the presupposition that the Word is *clear*. The Bible has its climax in a message which is perfectly plain, but which raises a headwind when it is sent forth into the world just because it is so plain. Humanity is unreconciled, bound, opposed to God, in need of redemption—therefore the Lord *sends* his messengers, therefore the preacher must rely on his commission, his sending—in other words, on his ministry. To the Word the ministry belongs. A totally different view of the ministry emerges when the Bible is regarded as obscure, as the locked box that no ordinary man can open. In that case there is an idealization of a human function, the function of the interpreter, because the ministry is regarded as primary: to the ministry the Word belongs, the ministry holds sway over the Word. 'Understanding the Scriptures' is regarded as something unbelievably difficult so that *something else* may be held as holy: the box must be locked so that the opener, the possessor of the key, may be held in honour and esteem. Those who stand for this ideology are to be recognized by the fact that in discussion of the Bible's message they only waken to life

The need of an ecclesiastical succession implies doubt about the living Christ: the theological basis for such a succession is that Christ *was once* alive and established a ministry which later was passed on by means of a visible ecclesiastical causal chain—a belief which is essentially akin to belief in a verbally, inspired book handed down to us.

[1] Put together the concept of creation and the missionary command, as the Early Christians did, so that the Gospel is thus given direct and immediate relation to the world, the heathen world, and it becomes easier to understand how firm and strong are the foundations of the World Church without apostolic succession. But nowadays the Gospel is regarded as bound up with 'the churches' and thus these churches are regarded as missionary bodies. The modern tendency away from special missionary societies towards the Church's own missionary work cannot itself make us think along Biblical lines, for the Word remains strangely imprisoned in pious human organizations. The old missionary society has become sufficiently 'churchy', but at the same time the churches have become missionary societies. Eighteenth-century speech is a sticky dough from which our generation has not succeeded in extricating itself.

and take an interest when it is apparent that two or more interpretations
of the meaning of the Bible are possible. 'See', they say to themselves,
'someone must decide who is in the right; someone is *the authority*, the
only question is who it is.' They never regard *the Bible* as the judge,
and the lack of agreement as itself a witness to that fact, but always
regard the authorized interpreter as the judge, and their highest ambition
is to avoid the unauthorized interpreters, to avoid listening to more than
one authority.[1] They fail to understand that thereby they cut themselves
off from the possibility of listening to the Bible and set up a human
entity as lord over the Scriptures and as their own lord—lock up the
Word and lock up themselves. Some adherents of the ideology of the
locked box look up to the ecclesiastical teaching ministry as the holder
of the keys, others regard the one who is truly converted, truly born
again, the pneumatic, with the same devotion. With respect to the
principle involved there is no difference in this regard between the
High Church and Pietism, between the institutional church and the
'gathered' church. The theology of apostolic succession and the theology
of the regenerate have been minted in very different atmospheres, but
in both cases the Word is placed under a guardian.

We have, however, seen earlier that the message of the Bible is clear.
The clarity of a matter does not mean that all are united about it, nor
that anyone bows in his heart before the claim it makes. Men are often
in disagreement about the clearest matters and they often hear something whose correctness is apparent without acting in conformity thereto.
Preaching has vast tasks in every generation in spite of the Bible's clarity,
for preaching is not first of all a work of enlightenment of an intellectual
nature, but is God's action against a demonic *realm* in which man is,
and which actively upsets even the interpretation of the Bible and sets
the spirit of division loose in the Church, to split asunder the Body of
Christ and once more crucify and slay him. So the clear Word has a
ministry, which is the ministry of the Word, the ministry of preaching.
The reason for the ministry is not that the Word is unclear so that one
needs to go to the ministry instead of direct to the Word to listen to it
—in that case there would be much reason to talk about 'the word of

[1] The question of authority is for the ideology we are considering the only
really serious question; diversity of interpretation is accordingly a very burning
issue. If the Word is, on the contrary, conversation with man's heart and
conscience, it will quickly be seen that the Word speaks even when the interpreters are in disagreement. Indeed, sometimes the relevation of the Word
becomes fully evident only when interpreters disagree, and it is seen that they
disagree about the meaning of the Word—and therefore bow before the Word
in the midst of their strife, so that no man, but only the Word, is holy. Then it is
understood that the Word holds Christ as Lord over all.

the Ministry', rather than 'the ministry of the Word'. The ministry derives its authority from the message. It is wholly wrongheaded to derive the authority of the Word from the ministry. Allow that reversal, and the Church becomes superior to the Word and Christ is locked up in the Church instead of being its Lord. Often nowadays in Sweden, the Church is thus regarded as superior to the Word in spite of the fact that there is no support for that in the Bible, or in the Reformation, or in the constitution of the Swedish Church. It must, indeed, be questioned if the fact that quite by chance in the sixteenth century the Swedish Church preserved the apostolic succession has not been a positive source of damage to the spiritual development of our Church in the last decade and led it along false paths which bring us to inner uncertainty and division.[1] There are in Europe Church bodies whose constitutions allow succession to have an essential place. But a Church such as the Swedish cannot suddenly incorporate into itself a mode of thought that drives the Reformation message from its central position without setting up thereby an inner crisis. A choice must be made. If the choice is based on the Bible there is no shadow of doubt what the result will be.

That it is a matter of 'either-or', and that there can be no wobbling about between both, is specially evident when both theses are formulated negatively. Luther, for his part, could see the Church of Christ even in the Rome of the Pope, because the *Word* was there. Where the Gospel is heard and where the sacraments are administered according to Christ's institution, there Christ comes through the mist of false theology which is hung over the Word, baptism, and the Lord's Supper: the faith of the heart can hear the Gospel in all such bodies and can lay hold on the promises of the Word. There is, of course, need to eliminate false usages from such a body, and to make the message of the Scriptures clear to all by straightforward preaching.[2] But a Lutheran theologian can never regard another Church in such a way as to believe that it lacks something that it must be for us Lutherans to provide. It is the Word that has primacy over the Church and those Church members in the other body do, indeed, to hear the Word; they only need understand something

[1] It happens that the confusion is most evident in the conception of the sacraments and in worship, but it cannot be restricted to that; theological principles, by inner necessity, seek to cover everything. *One* position at any rate is hopeless —eclecticism. Certain conceptions are simply impossible to combine. That is the case with the conception of succession and that of the Word as the basis of the Church. The one totally excludes the other.

[2] It ought to be noted that Luther never left the Church of Rome. Within the Church he preached what he believed he found in the Scriptures—and was driven out.

that is already theirs. This freedom in our relation with others is a gift of the Word.[1] No one is so free and so bound as he who is rooted in the Word. The situation changes entirely when Church or ministry is set above the Word. Then the source of life of the Church is no longer in something that comes to the Church and creates the Church but is *in* itself, once and for all deposited *in* the Church by Christ. If then any body has, on the way between Christ and the present day, lost succession, it cannot derive the true and genuine life of the Church from the Word, nor from baptism, nor from the Lord's Supper; what is lost is lost until the right ministry is brought from some other undamaged Church.[2]

We do not intend, at this point, to enter on a discussion with European churches that think along these lines. Carrying on such a debate would be a task in itself. What we intend to emphasize is something different: that this conception of the ministry is incompatible with the central message of the Lutheran Reformation, incompatible with our confessions, and devoid of support in the Bible.[3] To adopt such an ideology about the ministry now would be to abandon the line followed by the Swedish Church for 400 years. The confused eclecticism that prevails on occasions in Sweden about such questions is due entirely to the fact that the two positions have not been thought through, nor their incompatibility seen.

It is an entirely different matter that the Word cannot be conceived apart from the Church. In the conception of the Word the conception

[1] The Swedish Church, therefore, finds it no problem how far she is to recognize the Church of England. She does that freely and willingly on the basis of her own presuppositions and without for a moment looking at the matter from the Anglican standpoint—that is, without attaching any significance to her own possession of succession. Were she to regard the possession of succession as essential to her own existence as a church, she would have to regard the Churches of Denmark and Norway as defective. If such a doctrine finds its way into Northern Lutheranism, the Reformation message will have been quite washed away. Sweden's Church, in entire freedom, is in full communion with both the Lutheran and Anglican Churches. She would not enjoy more freedom, but less, were she to adopt a point of view about her past that is foreign to her, since she would thereby introduce a clear contradiction into her own house. We may very well feel pleased with the Swedish succession, as something significant from an ecumenical point of view, and yet hold a conception of the nature of the Church wholly true to the Bible and the Reformation without any compromise with the Anglican conception.

[2] As soon as this negative sentence has been formulated the possibility of formulating without any qualification the positive sentence that the Word and the sacraments constitute the Church is destroyed.

[3] Even to Irenaeus the concept of the ministry here being discussed was unknown. There are elements in Irenaeus' theology not to be met with in the Reformation, but taken as a whole there is no element which *conflicts* with the Reformation.

of the Church is also included. It does not follow from this that the Word has its basis in the Church just as the Church has its basis in the Word, so that some sort of dialectical relation should exist between the conception of the Word and the conception of the Church. A father or mother cannot be thought of without thinking of a child but the relation between the two sides is simple, undialectical, and irreversible—the child derives his life from the parents, never the other way round.[1]

The Church, then, draws its life from the Word, never the other way round. Any other view results in an empty conception of the Word—a 'Word' which somehow arises in the course of history, so that a 'Church' can exist before it. But the Word in the Church is the creative Word, from which man and the world take their beginning. The Word took fleshly form in the man Jesus, arose with life from the dead, and now is heard in the preaching to which I listen, thanks to the action of him who is risen in sending it forth. Christ is in the Word, and sustains the Church—that is to say, he creates us men anew through his creative Word. The order in the relation between the Word and the ministry, as between the Word and the Church, is irreversible. If the Word is here, then an unbroken relation with Christ exists too; nothing is lacking. If, doubting the power of his Word, we begin to look around for an unbroken historical connexion with the apostles, we cannot come closer to the Christ who *has* risen from the dead, shall one day come again, and today speaks his *Word* to us—that Word which is the source of life from creation's morn till the last day. Instead we put more distance between him and us. Christ comes in the Word. The ministry is the instrument the Word uses as its highway to advance and be heard. The power of the ministry is the power of the Word, and not of consecration. The present Lord is he who is at work in the ministry as soon as the Word sounds forth. It is not the case that the Christ of the past cut a channel through the ages and that his power is lessened if any break in historical continuity takes place. The message gives authority to the ministry; consecration, on the contrary, gives no authority to the message. Consecration is but the choice of someone for a *task*—not the setting of him in a channel of power.

[1] Cf. Luther: 'The Church is engendered through the Word. Therefore, you must say that the Church is less than the Word. Why, then, do you say that the Church is superior to the Word? It is the same as saying that the child is superior to the mother. But, on the contrary, it is the mother who bears and nourishes the child. So here. Christianity is a child, pure and simple, a mere babe apart from the Word. She is judged and guided by the Word; therefore she cannot judge the Word of God; if she does so, she is a harlot, not a mother' (*WA* 17(I), 99.26-31; Roth MS).

3. The priest and the congregation

The whole conception of the Church becomes somewhat warped when in Lutheran circles the term 'ministry' is taken to refer exclusively to the ministry of the *clergy*. In Anglican circles, such isolation of the ecclesiastical office suits passably well, for there the Church is built on the continuity of consecration in the episcopate, which confers authority on the other holders of ecclesiastical office. Ordination of a Lutheran priest implies that in a Church where all are essentially priests, a household of God, he receives the special *task* of preaching the Word and dispensing the sacraments.[1] The particular office which the priest holds is for Lutheranism but a special case of a general sharing out of vocations. The ministry of the priest is no *more* a ministry than is that of the mother or the doctor; it is simply that he has a *different* ministry from theirs, a totally different. The preacher's ministry alone represents the spiritual authority and the heavenly kingdom; all other ministries exercise secular authority and uphold, in one form or another, life on earth. The priest has his own special task, a special commission, which in essentials is identical with the sending forth of the Gospel after Christ's resurrection; the other ministries have another meaning, each its own special nature. The word 'ministry' is a word without content until it is known *what* ministry is in mind. Indeed, the practice of going around talking about 'the ministry' as something definite is an objectionable usage for a Lutheran priesthood, and implies in itself a false cleavage between the congregation and the priest, however modestly it may be done. If an older concept of the priesthood is to be brought to life again, that can only come about by a renaissance of a total conception in which the conception of priesthood is but one facet. Preaching must be addressed to *all* in the pew as those who have tasks, vocations and ministries from God in the places where their lot is cast on earth, whether as parents or teachers, factory workers or farmers. Among them is their priest who has *his* ministry, which is a gift of Christ for the well-being of the congregation. Otherwise the world is profane and without tasks of God's giving, destined to make contact with God through the priesthood and its actions. Such a view of the Church and the priesthood is but a hindrance to the Word.

As soon as the priesthood is given its right setting, however, along with other ministries, it becomes fully understandable how the congregation can take an active part in the selection of its priest. The

[1] See I Peter 2.9, Rev. 1.6 and 5.10.

congregation does not thereby institute the office of the priesthood from below, for it rests on Christ's commission. So little does the congregation institute it that, on the contrary, the congregation is brought to birth by the coming of the messenger with the Word. In similar fashion we daily receive our bodily life from God by the carrying out of duties of their ministries by the fathers, mothers, servants, etc., whom God placed on earth long before we were born. New people are always taking on these tasks, and it is normal that their fellow-men should introduce them to them. Even in the concept of ministry a certain tendency exists nowadays towards Docetism: as soon as it is said that everything is not determined from above, as soon as human activity is allowed to play its part in anything, a dread of Liberalism easily seizes hold of people. When the human element is so pushed aside, there may be good reason to fear that the content of the Bible will itself be pushed aside. We have seen earlier that Israel *is* humanity, that its election makes it the representative of all humanity and that God in his actions with Israel has all nations in mind. This implies that Jesus' twelve apostles must be regarded from two different points of view. They are *sent* by Jesus; that is the one side. But at the same time they *are* all Israel, and therefore they are humanity as well. When Jesus sees them, he sees humanity; that is the other side. They are not sent out docetically from on high, as divine and therefore supernatural into the midst of humanity, but when they go out, and the Church is gathered together, the new, fresh, redeemed humanity springs forth. To set the ministry over against the congregation is Doceticism; it is to set God over against man, and deny the Incarnation. The ministry of the priesthood is a ministry of the congregation: the congregation acts and is present when the priest is called to his task. But the task, which is the Gospel, comes from Christ because he has sent him.

Christ, too, is true God and true man. Since he sends, we are not elevated above humanity, but are right down within it. If Christ stood above, he would not be the Redeemer. But now he is a man like us. He is called the Son of Man—the highest divine name of honour and yet the name of a man, a name that betokens hidden, needy majesty and that bears witness to the everyday simplicity in the coming of his kingdom. In the Word he comes; for human eyes he is but poor. His poverty is related to his kingdom, which is the realm for service, footwashings, suffering and love. He could not have assumed the bearing of a conqueror without falling into just that thraldom which is Adam's—that is to say, he could not have lifted himself up out of the place of a servant without thereby losing his conquest, the conquest of the Redeemer. In his kingdom no other rule can be in force than that the servant is first of all (Mark 10.42-45).[1] Intentionally narrowing the application, we might say that the ministry of the priest stands *under* the congregation, just as Christ was deeper down than his Church has ever been. And Christ sends and commissions with the words, 'A disciple is not above his teacher' (Matt. 10.24), 'nor is he who is sent greater than he who sent him' (John 13.16; cf. 15.20). He who has a ministry suffers for the church (Col. 1.24).

No picture is more vivid in this respect than the typical New Testament picture of the *shepherd*. The word 'shepherd' in the New Testament is a term which relates to the ministry and at the same time, like almost all Early Christian terms relating to the ministry, is a description of Christ. The shepherd seeks his sheep and gives his life for them (John 10.11-16). When Peter is ordained as a shepherd (John 21.15-19), he is ordained to die. It is the same kingdom of service and suffering that Jesus possesses, for from of old 'shepherd' was a name for the *king*; it is a kingly work to care for the weak and unprotected (Micah 5.2-6; cf. Matt. 2.6; II Sam. 5.2; Ezek. 34.23 and 37.24; Ps. 78.70-72). They who are shepherds in the congregation and have a share in Christ's sufferings for his flock are not to set themselves up as 'overlords' (I Peter 5.1-4), but as servants (I Cor. 3.5), helpers of one another's joy (II Cor. 1.24). In this way they stand in the forefront, for the servant in this case is the first—they go before the rest as the shepherd should go, forward from suffering to glory.

The life of the congregation is, indeed, lived in expectation that the world will be reborn, in expectation of the Great Shepherd, of the victor's crown. The ministry is not everlasting, any more than preaching or conflict is. There is a time between Easter and the *Parousia* when Satan, though conquered, tries to keep his empire intact; that is the time for the ministry. In the fight between God and Satan stands the ministry —and that applies to every ministry, that of the priest and all others, for all are in the conflict, are toiling and waiting.[2] While the conflict lasts the ministry is indispensable, for in conflict commands and tasks are indispensable; where Satan still is active divine *authority* must be active too. Even in talking of the Good Shepherd, the Chief Shepherd,

---

[1] All Jesus' temptations are but a single temptation, from the desert till his death—the temptation not to serve, but to desire to exercise authority.

[2] Cf. Luther in 1531: 'In that life we shall have neither wife nor child. There all different positions (*die Empter*) will be at an end. There all will be alike' (*WA* 34(II), 27.3-5; Rörer MS).

and those whom he sends forth to be shepherds of his flock, there is an echo of battle. Christ is the Saviour of his flock in that he takes action against Satan, against the wolf, the destroyer of the flock, and by his own conflict and death overcomes him (cf. John 10.11 f.). And when he sends forth his messenger he sends him into the midst of need and danger, into the midst of wolves.[1] Shepherds of God's congregation find themselves in conflict because they are shepherds, for wolves never spare the flock (Acts 20.28 f.; cf. I Sam. 17.34-36; Amos 3.12). But when the Chief Shepherd shall appear, when Christ shall come and the enemy be annihilated, the watchful service of the shepherds will end, for then the Lord himself will lead his flock to the fountains of living waters: 'the lamb . . . will be their shepherd' (Rev. 7.17). The shepherd-ministry of the Church is a ministry of conflict, which can be laid down in the city that needs no temple (Rev. 21.22).

The ministry of preaching has, accordingly, its place in the history of redemption. Once it began, and one day it will end. When the day comes for sight, then the Word will no longer need to be preached to those in thraldom, because there will be none such when the enemy is no more. Until then it is a case of waiting, listening, trusting, without seeing. Having thus considered the ministry of redemption from a temporal point of view, we have also reached a vantage point from which to attack the problem of the Word and faith.

[1] 'As sheep', Matt. 10.16 runs, not 'as shepherds'. Here it is the picture of Christ as a lamb which is presented.

IX

THE WORD AND FAITH

1. Christ and I are present in the Word

ONE day Christ shall be a visible King. But now Christ is in the Word; now he is preached by the messengers whom he has sent; now he lives in the cloud in the heart, which faith is. The time for the Word is the time that precedes the last day. The time for faith is the same time, the time before sight shall come. The Word and faith belong together.

We have seen earlier that the Bible is a witness to God's actions, that it speaks of a long series of deeds which the God of the Word did with his people. In the last pages of the Bible we are not told of the last acts of God, but instead the expectation prevails of new acts to come, completing the whole. Even at this very hour the same expectation prevails in Christ's Church. In other words, God's series of acts is still going on and is not yet completed. The living Word, which is God at work, has its home in the present. Preaching is not just talk about a Christ of the past, but is a mouth through which the Christ of the present offers us life today. In the Word we become partakers of that which took place and of that which shall take place—that is, of Christ's death and resurrection and of our own death and resurrection. The latter are nothing else than an extension of the power of the former to *us*; that which shall take place is a fruit of that which has taken place already. Christ will have fully risen when his Body has risen and his Body is the Church—that is, we are his Body. The fulfilment of God's promise began when Christ came and what is now happening in the Church through Word and sacrament takes its place within the fulfilment which thus began and which is marching towards completion. The New Testament, the New Covenant, draws our present time into the event that burst forth in the latter part of the Bible, and that will come to its conclusion when God becomes 'all in all' (I Cor. 15.28).[1]

---

[1] Irenaeus, *Adv. haer.*, IV.56.1 [34.2]: 'For in his coming he himself fulfilled all things, and still in his Church fulfils the new covenant foretold by the law even to the consummation.'

This unity of what has already taken place, what is still in the future, and the present, is fully understandable only when it is kept clearly in mind that man is suffering an unnatural oppression, which is alien to him and inimical to his life, and that Christ carries out his great work in opposition to this same alien oppression. If I make clear to myself what this means it will become apparent that what has already taken place (Christ's resurrection) was, even when it took place, something that happened to me who am now alive, for he who conquered my destroyer did something to me, even if he did it before I was born. In the same way, Satan's final fall, and death's destruction in the last days, are events happening to me, since they who fall and are dethroned are the same as the enemies under whom I now languish. The accounts in the Gospels of Christ's death and resurrection sound wholly 'objective' and far distant when they are read out, and the word of prophecy about the last days displays an immense cosmic drama before our eyes—we have difficulty in fitting ourselves into these large paintings, for there is no place for 'subjective' elements. Modern man feels a need to paint himself into the picture of God's work, but the mighty objectivity of the Bible does not allow of that in any way. Consequently, he likes to turn Christianity into a 'movement' among other temporal movements, in which he can be enrolled and in which his contribution is noticeable. Basic to this whole attitude is the presupposition that man is not a slave and that no Satanic might exists. If the reality of thraldom, of the enemy, is realized, then no search is made for a subjective creephole which leaves a place for 'man', as it is usually expressed—for now I know that I, as all men, am present since the enemy is present. It is *our* destroyer's defeat that is being spoken of when the Gospels in their brief way describe Christ's death and resurrection; it is *our* death and *our* sin—powers of which we are daily all too conscious—that are spoken of when the events of the last day are being described. There is no need to insert ourselves into the picture. To stand in the present and look back to Christ's work is to stand and look back on our own lives, see our own health streaming from its source; to look forward to Satan's fall is to look forward to the goal towards which our whole conflict and pilgrimage presses forward.[1] Where the Word speaks to us today Christ is *there*. All he did once is *there*. All he shall do is *there*, gathered together, pressed small in the Word, and now it offers itself to our hearts.

[1] 'Believing' can therefore never be just some extra to living. To succeed in living is to believe. If faith is lacking, human existence is lacking also; that is choked which ought to have the chance to grow.

There is a point involved in what we have just said that we shall have to think through in this present section—namely, that the series of God's actions, the chain of divine events of which the Bible speaks, creates us. For man is not created all at once, so that he should thereby be fully created and that then a new process might set in, a process that would only do something 'with' him, would be a complement to his human existence, a specially religious existence on top of the ordinary self-evident existence. Man's coming into existence is a series of events, and when we get to know what is basic in that series it is seen to be bound up with the series of God's events that the Bible makes known to us. God creates through the Word from beginning to end. Faith, which lays itself open to God's action in the Word, means the coming to birth of what is human. To be man is to be the object of God's actions, to be created. Man lives because God speaks. The creative Word is the same through all the long series of God's actions, the very same Word of God from the 'Let there be . . . ' of Genesis till the Word of power that shall sound forth in the graves (John 5.28 f.). All the time Christ is the Word. But the Word becomes flesh, sends out apostles and sustains the World Church—when the Son of Man is born, dies, and rises again, struggling against Satan and conquering him. Now, between Pentecost and the Consummation of all things, *preaching* is the means by which the eternal Word functions. The preaching that is now going on is an organic part of the series of actions that God carries out from the beginning of time till the great judgement day for the world. Since man's coming into existence as man, his redemption from the hold of the life-destroying powers of evil, is a result simply of this divine action, it is not permissible in analysing preaching to set 'objective' and 'subjective' over against each other.[1] We shall deal fully and critically with this erroneous conception. If preaching is eliminated from the series of God's actions then something is eliminated by which man receives life, is brought to the end designed by his Creator, and a satanic world-destroying power comes sweeping in over the field of humanity just as an enemy gains access to a town when a gate is left open. The presence

---

[1] The basis for the distinction between 'subjective' and 'objective' is that man possesses his own human life and now 'meets' God as another party in a religious situation, whereby redemption comes about ('redemption' being regarded as something different from life itself). No account is taken of a third party, a power that holds man in thrall (sin being regarded as a quality that a man can 'have' without his humanity being thereby encroached upon). Thus redemption and sin are regarded as something which different parts 'have', where they stand over against one another; there exists, in fact, a sort of 'faculty theology', which shows certain similarities to 'faculty psychology'.

of the Word is man's life and the absence of the Word is man's destruction. When the implications of this double thesis are considered, and their correctness realized, the distinction between 'objective' and 'subjective' is cast aside as inadmissible in this connexion.

2. God and man are active in the Word

The main problem in the matter of the Word and faith is the problem of the part that God plays and the part that man plays. We feel an instinctive dislike, for the most part justifiably, for both solutions in which different lines of thought usually end. If we take God as active in the Word, and man as active in faith which seizes on the Word, then activity is shared co-operatively between God and man and grace is given too subordinate a place. To escape that, it is said that faith is God's work in man. Thus all activity becomes God's. The Word and faith are both God's actions with men. Thereby synergism is avoided, and grace is pure. But as a penalty, the meaningfulness of the call to faith, of the call to fight the good fight of faith, is lost. 'God is all and man is naught' as the catchword runs.[1] It can scarcely be said that any other possibility than these two is available. Theoretically, it might be considered that all activity is man's and that God is wholly passive, but that would imply such an obvious contradiction of all that the Bible proclaims that no one puts forward such a solution. Anyhow, under no circumstances could that be a solution to the problem of the Word and faith. For when we make use of the expression 'the Word' we regard God as active, as speaking. The two possibilities we have discussed offer the only conceivable solutions—and we dislike both.

Speaking generally, we may say that if in such a situation *no* good solution to a problem is possible, if *all* answers to a question are incorrect, then there is something in the question itself, in the way of posing the question, that is wrong.[2] It can be said *a priori* that according

---

[1] It is striking that such a catchword should have been coined in an anti-liberal epoch, as a reaction to the nineteenth-century deification of man. But in this case, the rejected outlook of the age is in reality retained, only it is turned topsy-turvy. It may well be that nineteenth-century theology had a false outlook. In that case, it is not of the least help to react against it; it is better to forget about such a violent reaction against it and instead sit down calmly and work out unpolemically a new outlook.

[2] The basic mistake in the particular approach to the problem we have discussed may well be that in the case of God and man, a disjunction is being made between activity and passivity. Thereby a definite truth is denied, namely man's crookedness, his sin, for that implies activity, *evil* activity on man's part (and a wrathful activity on God's part). The thought of passivity looks innocent, but implies a whole theology, and a false one at that.

to the Biblical view there must be unity between the Word and faith with full unbounded activity on the part of both God and man. It must be we ourselves who, in our approach to the problem, bring our own presuppositions with us, which, being foreign to the subject, hinder us from seeing.

Another instance, common in these times, of two activities which stand in a certain relation to each other might be taken. Let us imagine that the people of a certain place are living under an oppressive occupying power, which robs the occupied country of its freedom and means of life, and that a deliverer one day lands on its coasts to take up the fight against the oppressor. There we have a situation which is not at all different to that which the Ancient Church envisaged when thinking about redemption and salvation. But all the same we have not yet come to what correspond to the parts played by God and man. God in Christ is the deliverer, but it is man who is delivered. Only when we turn our attention to the situation of the oppressed people are we face to face with that which corresponds to men in redemption. Here we must raise the question if there is any need to postulate a relation of *exclusiveness* between the activity of the deliverer and the delivered. The deliverer is no less active because the delivered do something themselves. The possibilities of action, previously restricted, are not decreased because of the activity of the deliverer; instead they increase. Deliverer and delivered can often directly *increase* each other's activity. It must be admitted, of course, that the illustration we have chosen does not fully mirror the situation in redemption. The sinner is not occupied by sin against his will, but with his consent. Satan wishes to have our concurrence, just as God also does. That implies that the contrast between activity and passivity cannot be applied to the question that concerns us here. Man is often regarded as a passive, neutral, horizontal entity, on whom the divine power strikes down 'straight from on high' at an angle of ninety degrees; and in accordance with this, intellectual explanations of how God can be active without being active are worked out. But the course of thought in Rom. 6.12-14 is different: 'Formerly you made your members available for sin as instruments of wickedness. Now make them available to God as instruments of righteousness.' An evil activity against a good activity, a conflict—*that* is the basic conception of the New Testament. Not for a moment is there mention made of passivity, nor yet of vertical lines, nor of man as 'nothing', as 'zero', etc. What is first of all clear is that man, however he may turn, is active. So the question how man shall acquire this activity beforehand may be dis-

missed as an incorrect question. The question is transformed to one of
conflict between God and Satan. Man's activity is brought into play on
both sides in this mighty cosmic duel.

The problem of the Word and faith is insoluble if it is thought that
there is first of all a natural, human position where faith plays as yet no
part, and then faith is looked on as something different from this. For
here man is regarded as man without faith and without God, and therefore man is independent before God: from the very beginning the
concept of grace is shattered, an injury which is not repaired by afterwards loading all the activity on God and making man entirely empty.
We must begin aright, that is with the fact that there are only two
possibilities: that we can believe or not believe, but that in either case
we are active, for there is no way of being passive.[1] Of these two possibilities, unbelief is not something natural, purely human, but is demonic,
is possession; and faith is, accordingly, *not* a raising of man to the
supernatural, to a specifically religious sphere, but in faith is simply
life, freedom from the 'murderer of man', a return to his origin, to
fellowship with the source of life, the Creator.

With that we have almost reached our decisive point of view. The
picture of the liberator who makes a landing and drives out an oppressor,
thereby adding his might to that of those whom he frees, can be useful
in that it saves us from the false picture of God and man as two poles
between which activity and passivity are to be shared, but the illustration
of conflict is wholly unsuited to the task of setting forth in a positive way
the relation of God and man.[2] The three parties, the oppressed, the
oppressor and the deliverer, are in fact three comparable entities. None
of them has created the other two. But God is the Creator. Man lives
solely by being created by God, and when God creates, life springs
forth in freedom as if it had a source in itself. No relation between two
human beings can in any way show a comparable relation to that between the Creator and his creation, for every action on the part of the
created being implies, in that it is an action of a created being, a gift of
life on the part of the Creator. As long as the created being is pure,
uncorrupted by the power inimical to the creation, its free growth is
nothing but a creative activity of God (cf. I Cor. 3.5-9; 15.37 f.). But
even when Satanic power has fallen and has begun its rebellious work,

---

[1] This is also the reason why it is inconceivable that the Word should be
without influence on man. If it does not deliver it hardens.

[2] Another implication of this is that the illustration does not fully show the
relation between God and the Devil. God's supremacy cannot be expressed in
a picture like this.

H

God still remains Creator, the Giver of life, and even Satanic power, while engaged on destruction, is forced to serve God's power, to drive God's children nearer to him, to slap God's children in the face that they may not exalt themselves (II Cor. 12.7), but rather in weakness share Christ's power, that is, be created, grow and live (II Cor. 12.9 f.). If this view of the relation between God and man is kept clear, then man's struggle, his striving, and his work may be spoken of in the strongest terms, and at the same time God may be described as working 'in you both to will and to work' (Phil. 2.12 f.). The concepts of creation and conflict go well together, and can with advantage be woven into one another. Man is created and the actions of the created being are those of the Creator. Man is enslaved to Satan but delivered by God, and the activity of the delivered becomes one with the activity of the Deliverer. Neither line of thought makes it necessary to contrapose God's act to man's, but in both cases it is natural to see God at work in man's life, at work in his freedom and in no way limiting that freedom.[1]

3. Faith in the Word is true human life

Up to now we have often spoken of man in relation to God without specially talking about faith, which was really our theme. It is bound up with this that we have spoken of God's dealings with man without specially talking about the Word, which was also really our theme. The Word and faith—that is God and man. God acts, God creates through the Word: man derives his life from the Word; without the Word he would not exist; to believe is to receive life, that is to say, to live. The course of reasoning we have been following has brought us appreciably nearer to an understanding of the problem that is inherent in the relation between the Word and faith.

Earlier we made reference to the importance of the concept 'God's image' for Luther and the Ancient Church. The Word contains the image of Christ, depicts him in his death and resurrection. Faith receives the Word, and in that way receives Christ, who impresses his image on man through faith and pervades him in the struggle against the sin that he finds within him. The inner struggle in man's heart, the death of the old man and the resurrection of the new, is Christ's own death and resurrection in the man who listens now. There must be a reminder that faith is the way along which Christ travels in his journey to the

---

[1] In Barth there is a tendency for God's freedom and man's to limit each other, a necessary consequence of regarding man and God as opposites.

Parousia—that is to say, till he comes to be seen of man. Men are formed in the image of Christ when in faith they receive the Word, and Christ is 'God's image'—in other words, that for which the whole race of man was created. To become like Christ is to attain the true life of creation, to be redeemed from the enemies of creation, to be saved. When God sees our faith he sees Christ, and therefore God must say, 'That is an image that is like me, just as I created Adam in my own image.' The whole conflict right up to the last day is about the purity of creation, and therefore about Satan's downfall, and therefore about man's redemption. An event is going on in the world of men, and when that event has reached its completion man will be man, creation will be complete. Just now we have not reached that point, but we are on the way, continuing the conflict, listening to the Word without sight. That is—seen from below, seen by us, seen from the human standpoint—the same long event, the same chain of actions that we caught sight of in our analysis of the Bible, a chain of actions which began with the creation, is not finished at the end of the Bible but is still going on today—going on just in this way that *preaching* is going on. The present phase in man's coming into existence is listening to the Word in faith. The present phase in God's redemptive history is preaching, the Word. Man is created in faith and grows in the Word. 'The Word' and 'faith' imply God's action and man's free life in one.

With that, we have reached the point where the temporal aspect of the Word and faith must come in. We have just now looked at the matter from the point of view of creation's faith and from a totally different point of view, that of conflict. God creates through the Word and from the Word man draws his life: faith is man's free unhindered life. God does battle and frees man by the Word. In that way man obtains his redemption from the enemy. Faith is—to repeat—man's free, unhindered life. Man's conflict and exertions, his most determined efforts, his unrest, prayers, and longing, all belong to the same faith, which is, indeed, as Luther said, 'the most powerful of all actions'. To live thus, in conflict and growth, is to be man—that is, to receive the riches that the Creator bestows. But the category of time needs to be taken into account. It is in a definite phase of God's history with us that Christ works through the spoken Word. If in the expression 'the Word and faith' an upper sphere, the Word, is first thought of and then a lower, human sphere, faith, timelessness prevails from the first, and one thing is certain: within the framework of timelessness the Bible can never be comprehended, for it is totally shut out, and philosophy dominates.

When that expression, 'the Word', is heard, the first thought must be of Christ and his sending forth of the Word, his command to his messengers to go out with the message—and, accordingly, of Christ as visible King on the last day when the time for preaching is over, when faith's day is past and seeing has begun. Between these events, that is, today, the Word goes forth in its forward march towards the days to come, inceasingly making for, and striving after, what still lies ahead, the resurrection, and rebirth of the world. When, further, that expression, 'faith', is heard, the first thought must be of 'pressing towards the goal' (Phil. 3.9-14), 'the assurance of things hoped for' (Heb. 11.1), the certainty of the resurrection on the other side of the cross and death. Faith is the event preceding sight, just as the Word is the event preceding the *Parousia*, the wholly future, the visible. The Word and faith belong to the same period of time as the ministry of redemption. Preaching belongs to the Biblical chain of events, that is, to man's creation, which attains its final destination when man attains to the resurrection of the dead.

Now we have got to confront the temporal view with the two aspects we have mentioned—the concept of creation and the concept of conflict. It is not possible to resolve a problem of this nature in any other way than by moving about from one standpoint to another; after having grasped one point then it is possible to return to that vantage point from which one started. It is advisable to begin by thinking in temporal terms and then going on to the idea of *conflict*. Thereby it becomes abundantly clear that this aspect of conflict is bound up with the temporal aspect. Faith's time is the time when conflict with sin is going on. Sight's time will come, when Satan shall be overthrown and when all earth's sin shall be judged at the last judgement. On man's side the cosmic revolution in the last stage of human history consists in passing over from the conflict of the spirit against the flesh to the Spirit's conquest of the flesh, the Spirit's possession of the body (Rom. 8.11, I Cor. 15.44 f.). Faith's conflict is a conflict to attain to the resurrection of the dead (Phil. 3.9-11). But the power against which the conflict is carried on—'the flesh', sin, Satan—is a power which, according to the belief of the Early Church, destroys man. This power, fought by the Spirit, does not belong to the true creation, but involves the destruction of man, that is, 'death'. To be rid of that 'death' is Life; it is to be redeemed, to be back in the freshness of creation. The conflict goes on, in hope that reaches out to the future; *faith* lives on the *Word* and in the struggle seizes on 'things not seen' (Heb. 11.1). All this means that the grip of the enemy on the man whom God has created is slackening; man is receiving life, he is being created anew.

We have passed, then, from thinking in terms of time, by way of the idea of conflict, to the thought of creation. On the way, moreover, faith in creation has received a clearer content than it had at first. Creation did not take place just at the beginning of time, but God's creative work goes on all the way until the resurrection. Creation is not restricted to a sphere that is undisturbed; rather, God's creative work goes on in the midst of continual disturbance, in the midst of conflict and in the midst of evil in the hearts of men, all the way till Satan's downfall. The Word is a decisive act of war, an onslaught on the demonic power in the world of men, an onslaught against our old man himself, who must be slain if the new one is to be able to arise in spite of hindrances. Faith is man when he breaks free from the control of what is alien to him—that is to say, is the free, unoppressed man, God's own creative work. Unbelief is the Satanic act of war, an onslaught against the work of release, a diabolical attempt to hold man within the prison camp, to maintain the cleavage between him and his source of life, his Creator, and that is deadly to man. To stretch out towards the Word and from it to obtain life—that is faith. If we look to the Word, look to God, look away from our own ego, then true undamaged human life will emerge; man's life springs out of the fountain of the Word. If we let our attention wander from the Word, then we shall not fall away from faith into passivity, into what is purely human—instead, unbelief will come in, which is the enemy's destruction of what is human; for the man who is cut off from God is immediately Satanic and his human life, being eaten away, dies. The Spirit is life and the Spirit is in the Word, not side by side with the Word. Since the Spirit is in the Word, therefore he is in the heart that believes the Word, hangs on the Word. When man turns to the Word he turns to true life—that is, to what is usually called 'the subjective'. When man turns away from the Word (as the supposedly 'objective') to the 'subjective', the human element that is sought for, he turns, to put it exactly, *from* human life. Though this is the situation, the words 'subjective' and 'objective' ought to be avoided in the analysis of the relation between the Word and faith.

Faith is our death and resurrection; it is to let go our selfish will, and let the Word have freedom to accomplish its destroying and lifegiving work, which is none other than Christ's death and resurrection as they reach us and assume rule over us, for the preaching of the Word in our ears is the coming of Christ's death and resurrection over our threshold, as Christ advances in his vast journey, as the crucified and risen One, through the history of men, by means of the Word, towards his appearing, the *Parousia*.[1] By coming thus through death and resurrection among men, God in Christ becomes the Creator and Conqueror and his work in the world, through which he advances, is the restoration of human life.

[1] The connexion between Christ's death and resurrection is the connexion between the humanity and divinity of Christ, a connexion and a unity which is retained even now when Christ comes to us in the Word and faith. To separate faith from the Word would be to separate the humanity of Christ from his divinity. Christ as man is in our humanity; he does not just come to us when faith is strong and stand without when faith is struggling, for Christ's humanity is a tempted humanity, our own faltering and doubting humanity, which does not hold the Word in its grip but gropes for it, stretches out towards it, listens as one listens to a cry from someone unseen. That was Jesus' position in Gethsemane and on the cross, and it is our position in faith in the Word.

X

DEATH AND RESURRECTION

1. Preaching must answer: did Christ rise?

WE have now to deal with the most fundamental problem of preaching
—the problem of its truth and justification. We have earlier gone into
the questions of the unity of the Bible and the total content of its
message, of the position of man as he listens to preaching, and of the
actual preaching that is now being carried on by the ministry of the
Church in the congregations that exist at the present time. But we have
never really raised the question whether we can truly and justifiably
preach the content of the Scriptures today. We have not faced the
problem that arises when someone makes the objection: 'Very well,
that is the content of the Bible's message, but I suggest that there is
neither justification nor reason for preaching this historically given
message. There is no occasion to proclaim the conviction, springing
from faith, of a certain group of men in Early Christian days.' The
theologian may perhaps point out that he is only making a scientific
analysis of documents, but the preacher cannot do that. From a scientific
point of view the Bible and the Koran are possibly not essentially
different documents. At any rate the theologian does not need to keep
the difference between them clearly in mind in justifying his choice of
the Bible as his subject matter. But the preacher *preaches* the Bible.
It is meaningless to run away from the fundamental question of the
reason why it is possible and imperative to preach.[1] We propose to raise
that question here.

---

[1] It is impossible to preach if the Scriptures are only regarded as a historical
quarry without valid claim to be heard. To carry on theological science is not in
the same way impossible. Preaching is the act by which the Bible makes its
message heard today; it is essentially just the activity of the Bible itself, mediated
through a man of the present time who preaches. But a voice, a message, goes
forth also from other historical documents. Christian preaching is a service
rendered to a certain message. No one who actively undertakes such service can
avoid the question if he does so justifiably or not. Reference to ordination, in
this case, is not enough. It is the justification for there being priests at all that
is called in question. Nothing except the truth of the message is sufficient basis.
If, so far as its essence is concerned, the message could not be proclaimed

As a summing up of the double thesis which will be more fully supported in what follows it may be said immediately: (1) that the only valid ground for preaching is the factual nature of Christ's death and resurrection, and (2) that if this factual nature is treated as a purely scientific question then Christ's death and resurrection are no longer central to the question. These two sentences may be formulated thus. (1) *Not faith but only the fact in which faith believes is a valid ground.* (2) *The fact in which faith believes is no longer the same fact if faith is absent.*[1] In what follows we shall move freely from one of these sentences to the other.

It is advisable to start with a somewhat remote example from another sphere of life. A Professor of Law explains and provides a commentary on a law. His mode of procedure is the same whether it is a law of his own land or of a foreign land. But a judge in a court judges according to the law of the land. The law of his own land is valid in that land, and the action of the judge is an expression of the authority of the law. It is not the case that the Professor of Law is acting objectively and the judge subjectively. Both have entirely objectively fixed tasks and both can display a personal subjectivity in carrying out their duties that is injurious to the matter in hand. The exposition of, and commentary on, a Biblical passage given by a Professor of Exegesis is no more objective than that of the preacher; both exegete and priest are charged with wholly factual tasks, because they are both dealing with passages of the Bible—though, undeniably, *different* tasks, just as the legal scientist and the judge have *different* tasks *vis à vis* the laws.[2] The preacher assumes

among shipwrecked people on an isolated island where there is no bishop and where nobody has been ordained, it cannot be proclaimed at all.

[1] It should be noted that sentence (2) does not wipe out sentence (1). The basis is a fact. All humanity, however, is included in Christ's death and resurrection, and therefore the commission to preach is included too; to redemption belongs the word of redemption and the ministry of redemption (II Cor. 5.18-20). If this latter is cut away so that only the first fact is left (Golgotha and Easter) then the first fact is altered. An effort is often made to narrow down the problem so as to reach the point where it may be decided whether belief is reasonable or not, but in narrowing down the problem the question is already answered in the negative. Decision has already been made against faith when that point is reached. In the contrary case, that is, when the question of faith is answered in the affirmative, when one bows before the message, there one rests on Christ's actual death and resurrection. If faith is regarded as in essence quite untouched by the question of fact, then it is not Biblical faith that is in mind, but, for example, a mystical experience, or an attempt after auto-suggestion. Biblical faith is faith in a divine authority over men exercised through historical events.

[2] In an unexpectedly large number of cases related tasks of work, each occupied with the same material, are carried on alongside each other. There is no reason for differentiating between them with the help of the *clichés* 'subjective' and 'objective'. As for the difference between the exegete and the preacher, it is

that the Word of the Bible *decides*, just as the judge assumes that the law decides. So far does the parallel extend between the judge and the preacher. For this reason the preacher must necessarily keep it clearly in mind that the Word of the Bible *is applicable to us*. But the parallel goes no further. The message of the Bible applies to us in a totally different sense from a law. It must, all the same, be possible to say why the Bible's claim to be preached is justified. If we cannot say that, then we are lost in a jungle of writings derived from the history of religions, just as a judge is in a jungle of laws derived from the history of law—without the right to preach, without the right to pronounce judgement.

If we speak mostly about the resurrection alone, and not about the death and resurrection, that is to be explained exclusively by the fact that no person capable of judgement denies that Jesus died. The death and resurrection essentially belong together and ought not to be separated from each other, but for the present it is none the less useful to isolate Christ's resurrection. Were we to accept it as a hypothesis that Christ *is* risen, with all that is implied in that belief—exaltation, right to judge, his ability to give life, his power for all time to forgive sins—then we should have in that very fact sufficient ground for preaching to every generation and to all peoples on the face of the earth. In Christ's resurrection, then, the source of life for all who are called men would be provided: to discuss the justification for preaching would be to discuss the justification for truth and life. The presupposition, now and then unspoken, behind every attack on Christianity is the conviction, in many places taken for granted, that Christ never rose from the dead. That is the inmost kernel of the whole question of Christianity's 'to be or not to be'.[1] If Christ is risen then undeniably majesty belongs to the Word today. If Christ is not risen, then the Christian message lacks meaning for every serious man, and the propagators of Christianity may devote themselves to the task of describing, for those who are not given to thinking seriously, the regrettable ethical consequences of the disappearance of religious faith, in the dim hope that someone will manage

to be admitted that the temptation to subjectivism is greater in the case of the latter than for most men, since he comes under the influence of an (objectively incorrect) theory of preaching according to which the preacher should reproduce his own personal experiences and nothing else.

[1] The question about faith in a personal God, which in debates about religion is often regarded as the central question, is, on the contrary, a relatively peripheral one as long as nothing is said about what God is regarded as being and doing. An affirmative answer can be made by widely different religions on the face of the earth, several of which are definitely hostile to the Christian message. The Christian creed is, by its very nature, confession of Christ as Lord, the Risen One.

to believe sincerely without being convinced about the truth of the
matter.

Very few professional theologians spend their time nowadays on such
work of an apologetical nature. Nearly all of them, however, avoid the
question about what *happened*, the question about the facts. They
restrict themselves to the question of the meaning of 'the documents',
'the texts'—what this or that author intended in his use of certain words
or 'statements'.[1] If it is correct to speak of a certain Docetism, a shrink-
ing from what is human, as the main danger of present-day anti-liberal
theology, then this refusal to let go the documents and face the question
of fact may be one of the sources of this Docetism. There is no coming
right down into the human sphere, into what has taken place, but a
stand is taken on a 'view' which is to be found in written sources. The
Word is not flesh, not human life, but a 'view of faith': the divine
hesitates and holds back from daring to become historical and allowing
itself to be handled by the unbelieving. Theology did good work in
recent decades, reassuring men in the time of crisis and in the general
chaos after the first world war. But the preacher must work away from
home; his Word must descend to the world, into the human life of a
parish, into the earthly communities where books and 'views' make a
very airy impression. The Word of the preacher is, in essence, a Word
about something that has *taken place*.[2] That is involved in the very word
'preaching', what a herald announces, and every preacher knows, when
the moment for preaching has come, the weight of the question of fact.

[1] In certain ways exegetes and systematic theologians are united in their
fundamental approach. The positive value in this position shows up against the
background of the habits of theologians of an earlier age who did not regard
interpretation as a task at all. The risk that is run is that the question of truth
can be treated as a matter of indifference. Truth in that case simply amounts to
the question whether the sources contain faith's conviction. This is a Professor's
question about truth; it is not a preacher's. If a preacher adopts such exegetical
methods on the one hand, and a subjectivist theory of preaching on the other,
he dare not preach. The liberal theory of preaching raised, indeed, the question
of truth, but in this form: is what is said in the pulpit genuinely felt and experienced as true by the preacher personally? But preaching must rest on
certainty. The message declares *what has taken place*. That is why the message
is there in the passage of Scripture; and that is why the priest can personally
stand for it, and be honest and sincere when he speaks.

[2] Cf. Luther's exposition of the Gospel for Christmas Day on Christmas Day
1529. 'Today you have heard that I have simply attempted to explain the story,
because it was in order that this story should be told that the festival was
instituted. If it were to happen that this story were itself forgotten then there
would be no foundation for that. . . .' Once Luther wanted to preach about
things sublime, but now he knows that he must just keep on telling about what
happened when he preaches: 'these stories cannot be preached enough in the
simplest possible way. Formerly I wanted to go further but I was a fool. . . . '
(*WA* 29, 657.2-9; Rörer MS).

To fly from the question is impossible, for that would be to fly from preaching itself to lecturing, to lecturing about religion, to theological discourse.

The question of fact that we are now raising means, speaking generally, for him whose life-work preaching is, the question of the factuality of the resurrection of Christ. To be confronted now and then with legendary details in the passage for the day only causes trifling difficulty when one is certain that Christ is risen. Now and then historical criticism can with advantage be indulged in in the pulpit. It gives more life to the kernel of the text than an accumulation of orthodox commonplaces can provide.[1] But when that is done, it must be in the service of the main message: he who feels it necessary to pass on to the congregation all his doubts about the historicity of the details has, it may be conjectured, an egocentric attitude to the work of preaching.

As a general truth, we may say that we today who have not lived through the downfall of the dogma of verbal inspiration, but who from childhood regarded it as outmoded, have a better opportunity of reaching the centre of the Scriptures than supporters of verbal inspiration had. But if, when we have reached the heart of the message—Christ's death and resurrection—we are in doubt about the full reality of the event with which we are here concerned then, indeed, all is lost. It is profitless to start to collect the fragments of the New Testament that remain. The resurrection is indispensable if preaching is to be carried on at all. To say this, to argue from the fictional nature of the resurrection to the impossibility of preaching, is but to quote the New Testament. When Paul visualized the possibility that Christ had not risen it might have been expected that the first consequence he would have drawn from that would not just have been the hopelessness of preaching, but, for example, the hopelessness of faith. But Paul says: 'If Christ has not been raised, then our *preaching* is in vain and your *faith* is in vain' (I Cor. 15.14). That is the order. In the Biblical chain of actions that we have often come across, preaching is an act of God in the present, the link between Christ's resurrection and the resurrection of all the dead in the future.[2] Had Christ not risen, there would have

[1] Christ's death and resurrection as the firm and inerasible centre keep the proportions clear here as elsewhere. The complete humanity of Christ's sufferings sets its stamp also on the humanity of the passage. The divine would not be here, but always a bit away from us, if it were not here in this way, in these uncertain passages. The Risen One apart from that cross would not be the Risen One but someone else, an unincarnate one who had not 'emptied himself taking the form of a servant'.

[2] See what follows: 'Then those also who have fallen asleep in Christ have perished' (I Cor. 15.18).

been no risen Lord to send these preachers forth, no Spirit would have been given, and no life bestowed in the Word. But in that case preaching could give no reason for its existence, for preaching's indispensable foundation is the risen Christ.

2. The nature of preaching's answer

The question of Christ's resurrection cannot, however, be treated as a matter of purely scientific truth. Paul says not only that preaching is vain if Christ is dead, but adds: 'and you are still in your *sins*' (I Cor. 15.17). According to the same basic conception of preaching that we have often outlined, the Word of the preacher is an attack on the prison in which man is held. If the living Christ does not dwell in the Word, then preaching has no power to open the doors, but is degraded to an attempt at religious suggestion: in reality man remains imprisoned as before. The factuality that is here involved implies also the factuality of our imprisonment and, as a consequence, we are outside the area where it is only a matter of asking about what has 'happened' as a matter of history. When we are speaking about imprisonment we are appealing to the hearer's own self-condemnation: it can be conceived that man believes he is free and in that case there is little that preaching can do. To those who believe themselves free the Gospel has scarcely anything to say—except that they are *not free*. One sign and token, among others, of imprisonment is death, which threatens every man, colours every phase of his existence and makes ineffectiveness something with which he is well acquainted.[1] To have accustomed oneself to slavery is not to be free. Even to share this slavery with other beings is not to be free. The life that is offered to man in the Word is the 'standpoint' from which alone realization of the whole extent of our slavery is possible. If life is not viewed from the Word, then it is possible to close the door of his prison cell and call that relative freedom. If, on the other hand, im-

---

[1] The essence of unbelief may be said to consist in the thought that it is absurd that there could be something wrong, something irrational, in that which characterizes not only me, but also my fellow-men. Restricting himself to comparison with 'the others', man loses the ability to take account of God and the Devil and he is inclined to find gods and devils only among 'the others'. The former he finds generally in the other sex—sexual religion is a typical post-Christian product in Europe today—the latter in the political field where devils are localized in certain lands and become wonderful, post-Christian devil-idols. The Christian man knows that he has God and the Devil in his own heart, and views 'the others' as a body to which he too belongs, from which neither divine idols nor their counterparts on the opposite side can be picked out. He knows he belongs to the body of mankind, which is enslaved and in need of release just as he himself is.

prisonment is seen as something that is the fate of the whole human race, then the intellectual difficulties in the accounts of Jesus' resurrection drop away. For in that case it is seen that the *whole* argument against his resurrection arises out of the historical situation where slavery is the order of the day. Christ is free from sin and, therefore, he is free from death. It is not supernature that stands forth in Christ's resurrection but man, free unbound man.[1] But the possibility of seeing the matter thus is dependent on a self-condemnation, which in itself is faith, faith in Christ.[2] There is an element of decision involved in this mode of thought. The question has ceased to be just a question of truth in a scientific sense.

Against this it may be justly objected that such a course of thought leads to the dissolution of the factuality of the resurrection, for then faith decides if Jesus rose from the dead or not. But in that case, it has been overlooked, it may be said, that Jesus' resurrection was an outward event according to the Gospels, that the grave was empty and the stone rolled away (Matt. 28.2 ff., Mark 16.4 ff., Luke 24.2 ff., John 20.1 ff.). It was the custom in theology once to say nothing about that. But since then it has come to be seen that the Gospel story is still more difficult to understand historically if the empty tomb is cut out, if it is accepted as if it were not accepted, accepted, that is, as 'a sign' of the resurrection without essential significance being accorded to it. As we shall soon see, it belongs to the essence of the resurrection that it should be the resurrection of the whole man. A resurrection that was not the resurrection of the body, a resurrection not within the limits to God's powers set by creation, is no resurrection, no divine act, but the immortality of the soul in disguise.[3] But if it is the case that Jesus in the

---

[1] For this reason the resurrection of Christ is, in itself, redemption for men. In the Ancient Church the joy of Easter was anchored in a very strong conviction that all men are enslaved. Death was not natural, but an enemy slain by Christ. See the present author's *Man and the Incarnation*.

[2] The deep inner naturalness of the resurrection of Christ is connected with the deep inner unnaturalness of our own situation. But to regard our own situation as unnatural is, in itself, faith, for it is the recognition that God is right when he says in his Word that we have departed from him.

[3] That we speak at this point about 'the body' is, it is true, partly a result of polemics. If we were content to use the language of the Bible there would be no reason to use other terms that 'the resurrection', 'the resurrection of the dead', 'the resurrection from the dead'. But when language that is foreign to the Bible breaks up the unity of man and recognizes a spiritual, as distinct from a bodily resurrection, one is driven, in order to keep true to the Bible, to regard it as highly necessary to accentuate the body, as was the case even in the second century against Gnosticism. Thereby, it is undeniable, a certain crudity is imported. In the same way, if the parallel is permitted, a crudity is imported into sexual love in romantic circles.

ordinary sense rose from the grave, that is an event that belongs to the world of ordinary experience and cannot be isolated as just 'a view of faith'. If it is quite simply true that Jesus rose, true in that way, then it must be possible to argue that those who say that Jesus did not rise not only put themselves outside Christian faith, but also are mistaken about an event that took place. It is in this direct form that the question about the fact of the resurrection is often posed for theology. Those who ask the question do not mean that it is up to theology to prove the factuality of Christ's resurrection. Proof is not native to it; not even for those of that day did the accounts try to provide proof. But those who, from without, raise the question of truth for theology are exclusively concerned to ask if believers believe that the account of the resurrection is true in the ordinary sense.

It is easy to see that he who asks the question is talking about the resurrection without mentioning God. The background of such questions is the belief that reality is what is given in space and time. The encounter with Christian faith is turned into the question of what reality is: the problem is whether Christian faith has contact with another reality than that which is given in space and time, a transcendent reality, or if Christian faith is only a subjective attitude. The question of Christ's resurrection is important *because* the resurrection represents an event belonging to the reality that is subject to time and space, though originating in what is possibly a different reality, divine reality. This general viewpoint, somewhat varied, is, as a rule, the presupposition of those who ask the question. We are not going to enter into a discussion with the questioner at this point. Rather, it is our task to examine the method by which theology answers the question on behalf of faith. There are three possibilities: it may be answered that the accounts of the resurrection given by Christian faith are true, or that they are not true in the usual sense or, following the example set by us theologians when we are hard pressed, the question may be declined as foreign to the view of faith.

If one replies that the resurrection is not true in the usual sense, then one is shown to have the same general view as the questioner. Without any further discussion the matter is clear. If the reply merely says that the question is badly put, that again shows the same general point of view as the questioner. For that implies that the alternative, true or false, cannot be applied to the story of the resurrection, since that is a religious matter.[1] If the question be asked what conditions must be ful-

[1] In our exposition the resurrection of Christ is important for this reason, that

filled before a judgement on an external event can be placed in the category, true or false, the reply must be that the account in question must lack religious meaning, must be a plain account of something factual. As soon as an event provides a basis for an article of faith the alternative of true or false is out of place. The *basis* of faith, on this view can never be an external event; the basis must be free of contact with an event externally perceived.[1]

It is quite apparent that in this way there is agreement on the concept of being, according to which the gulf between immanence (what is given in space and time) and transcendence (what is embraced in faith) is self-evident, only the agreement is not carried to its logical conclusion. The stories in the Gospels deal exclusively with external events, but in no case do they intend to be merely accounts of something that happened. *All*, every sentence, is proclamation, is faith. Accordingly, not a line is to be found in these accounts to which the alternative, true or false, can fittingly be applied. That Christ was born, said something, and died upon the cross would then be articles of faith and not suscep-tible to the alternative, true or false. It is possible that some hold that point of view. We have, however, started with the hypothesis that the person in question isolates the resurrection and finds its history dubious in contrast to the other events of which the Gospels tell and which the New Testament as a whole regards as central. The wholesale sceptical attitude we have no reason to discuss. The total result of our course of thought till this point is that if we are confronted with the question of the truth of the story of the resurrection there are only two possibilities:

a historical investigation of the content of the *kerygma* leads us to Christ's death and resurrection as the basis and centre of gravity for preaching. If, then, it is quite obvious that the Gospels are shot through with legendary elements, the question to what extent the resurrection on the third day is of that nature is important. That God, on the contrary, is not just a transcendent reality and that different kinds of reality cannot be postulated at all, if the Christian Gospel is not to be Platonized, is regarded here as something fully settled.

[1] Faith rests, according to the New Testament and the Reformation, only on the Word. That word cannot well be the Word of Christ's resurrection if it is meaningless to ask if a resurrection took place. It is rather the Word of God's love, of forgiveness, of justification (for in the case of these words it is unjustifi-able to raise the question of factuality as we raised it in the case of the resur-rection). After having thus arrived at what is characteristically Christian from such a Word, consideration is given to the Incarnation, the resurrection, the sacraments and so on, and at all these points a manifestation of the same basic motif is discovered. This mode of procedure, however, does not correspond with the construction of the *kerygma* of the Primitive Church, for there *events* are themselves the basis on which all 'conceptions', faith and hope rest. He who is to preach today, to carry the same *kerygma* to the men of our time, cannot ask about what was *thought* in the early days of the Church but must ask about what *happened*.

either give up the Christian faith, or admit that the story of the resurrection is true, true in the usual sense.

It does not follow from this, however, that the story of the resurrection was written down just as a report about discoveries that had been
made. It is not theology, which, in order to avoid the claim of the story
to be true, makes it into proclamation and lifts it above the plain of
factuality. From the very first it was the evangelist who recorded it as
kerygma, a *true* message, but still a *message*, intended to lift its hearers
and its readers out of the imprisonment in which they were locked up,
a message about the conquest over an enemy, intended to be carried in
haste by heralds over the earth till all his enemies should be destroyed.
They who deal with the factuality exclusively, weighing the alternatives,
historic fact or subjective conception, are perhaps trying thereby to
reach the point where they can decide whether they ought to believe
or not, but those who thus search are not searching without having
their own presuppositions. It is of the very nature of scientific truth
that the seeker shall be an observer and not a slave. The question
whether we are slaves or not is not left an open one but answered
negatively at the very beginning of the investigation. The moment a
man admits the condemnation passed on him by his own conscience and
recognizes that he is not fulfilling the task and meaning of his life, that
he is imprisoned in his own inmost will, that moment he seeks as a slave
seeks. His search is not without presuppositions, for he who sees himself as a prisoner believes already in God and the Devil.[1] There is no
neutrality here: one passes from unbelief straight to faith without the
chance to be in between. And when one who is held in thrall is the
seeker it is quite clear that Christ's resurrection cannot be isolated from
his death. The *kerygma* is not a *kerygma* about Christ's resurrection:
the *kerygma* is a *kerygma* about Christ's death and resurrection, both in
one, bound together, indivisible. We only divided them here because
intellectual doubt accepts Christ's death as factual, but proceeds in the

---

[1] When we are without presuppositions we are always looking at something
different from ourselves. For that reason science can be without presuppositions.
When it is the factuality of the resurrection with which we are concerned there
is an attitude to life involved in the question, and to that extent an element of
religion, of counter-belief, which argues that in searching for truth a question of
faith can be answered in the negative. As we shall see in the conclusion of this
section, where we return to this problem, even this seeking for truth is marked
by what might be called an anonymous slavery, the closed mind of the intellectual
conscience in which man is shut up without an organ with which to perceive
'guilt', without ability to understand the meaning of 'condemnation' and without
need of 'forgiveness'. To a man like that Christ's resurrection must be preached
as the *truth*.

opposite way with his resurrection. From the point of view of the Biblical message there is no reason to separate the two: on the contrary they are bound together indissolubly. At this point it is profitable to discuss briefly what is involved in their unity. In that way we shall understand better *why* giving up Christ's bodily resurrection means giving up Christian faith.

3. The significance of Christ's resurrection for our faith

Death and resurrection belong together, since redemption is Christ's struggle and victory. It is as our redemption that Christ's conflict and victory concern us, and bring about *in* us our death and resurrection. Faith in Christ's resurrection is faith in the action of the resurrection upon us, and this faith is itself our resurrection day by day.[1] But there can only be resurrection from the dead. He who does not die does not rise again. The opposition against which faith strains is despair under condemnation. In the face of an agnostic attitude of mind faith in the resurrection cannot establish itself, for such an attitude would be in conflict with the concept of faith in the resurrection. The Gospel of the resurrection speaks to the heart where law and judgement speak, where death and anguish dwell; in other hearts it is silent. Approaching the story of the resurrection with only the question of factuality in mind means trying to approach the fact of the resurrection apart from the fact of death—without needing to be condemned, without needing to die. It is to be unable to approach the fact of the resurrection at all. For both Christ's death and his resurrection took place for the sake of our death and resurrection. That is why it belongs to their essence that they not only took place once upon a time, but must necessarily be *preached* now and until they have taken place in the race of men at the last day.[2] To isolate the question of factuality makes it impossible to retain Christ's death and resurrection in the central position. A wish is embedded in the question, a wish not to be condemned; and it diverts the questioner from the real issue. The way to the real issue lies through his own death.

[1] Resurrection day by day is, of course, in like manner inseparable from death day by day. The life of the Christian lies concealed under his death; he tastes death when things go against his ego.

[2] Cf. Luther: 'Therefore as well as the resurrection of Christ we must hold to our own. For they belong together; there must be a complete resurrection. It follows, then, that if we are not to rise again Christ did not rise, and *vice versa*. Therefore, if you do not believe in your own resurrection you cannot believe in Christ's resurrection. For the head cannot be without members' (*WA* 49, 396. 1-397.1; Stolz MS).

The Word must begin by speaking against ourselves if it is ever to reveal its content. To believe is, as Luther said, to believe in our own resurrection. If our own resurrection is eliminated from the issue with which we are dealing then there is eliminated something that belongs to that issue. The fact that faith believes is no longer the same fact if faith is absent.

The different versions in the New Testament of the appearance of the risen Lord to his disciples are a direct help in understanding the matter, just because they are unlike and varied. Even more significant is the fact that faith in Jesus' resurrection was even in New Testament times linked with discipleship, with the older discipleship or—for example, in the case of Paul—with later discipleship, that is, with fellowship in Christ in suffering and in the Spirit (cf. Acts 10.40 f.). Christ's resurrection takes place and has effect in that it conditions us and has an effect upon us who are Christ's body, his Church. Just as his death cannot be disjoined from his resurrection without his resurrection being *eo ipso* given up, so his Church cannot be disjoined from his resurrection without his resurrection being *eo ipso* given up. It was Christ's body which rose from the grave, but we, his body, are the Church. Between Christ's death and resurrection there exists the same unbreakable bond of union as between Christ's humanity and divinity. He is God in that he divests himself and redeems us; he acquires majesty by suffering on our battlefield. Our humanity is his humanity; we are already in him in his redemption, because we are being tried, tempted, and put to death. Like a group of men, occupied with the limited tasks of their time, so the Church is the humanity of Christ and, as such, is united with his divinity with just as little chance of living on and enduring as he had—dying as he did and, therefore, rising again, sure of an eternal future as he is. The resurrection is no miracle of transubstantiation in which what is human and temporal disappears, for that which will die is not temporality, not what is human—that, on the contrary, is what is to be redeemed. Therefore sin must die, the Devil be driven out and annihilated, in *battle*, which implies suffering and conflict for man.[1] No single episode in the conflict, for example the resurrection, can be isolated from the rest. Death and resurrection belong together.

But—to return to the question of factuality—if the resurrection,

---

[1] In the Church both death and resurrection are taking place; for this reason, in the Church what is divine is not separable from what is human, but where the divine power is at work in the Church there the Church is altogether human, a fellowship at a meal of bread and wine. Transubstantiation's Church is a Church which is divine because it is not human.

through which Christ lives, is to have a limit imposed on it within the created world, what would that imply? If it is not going to be possible to say that it *happened*, and that it happened as an outward event, then an attempt would have to be made to visualize man's life without his body. To abandon the body to a neutral existence will not do. Jesus has lived and died; the factuality of death we regard as accepted. If the factuality of the resurrection is called in question, then Jesus' body is regarded as held by death and, at the same time also—from the same point of view—Jesus as redeemer. A moment's reflection on the significance of that should be enough to show us how theologically questionable is that position.[1]

Concealed behind this there lurks the major opposition of spirit and matter, which is not in line with Biblical thought. Faith in creation is rejected as soon as it is held that the resurrection of Jesus does not apply to his body and yet that it is still meaningful to talk of the resurrection as distinct from the immortality of the soul. This is a variant of the conception of religion as a special sphere above the human. Life on earth is raw material, the result of a series of natural causes, about which faith has nothing to say. God comes on the scene when the religious question arises. And the Christian documents give a special answer to those religious questions, an answer supported by a unified and organic view of all points, among them being the question of the resurrection. When Christianity is so conceived time is, in essence, forgotten: Christian faith has its content in the form of an organic unity of thought supported by a master motif. The element of hope and waiting for a

[1] It ought to be noted that the Gospels clearly presuppose Christ's bodily resurrection. He who raises objections to that sets limits somehow on the resurrection. He who starts off with belief in an unlimited resurrection does not, on the contrary, make deductions from a position that he has adopted beforehand, but his point of departure is the story as it has been handed down. In the former case a position taken up beforehand necessitates a certain theological structure in what follows. In the latter case, on the contrary, the message of Christ's death and resurrection is the foundation on which the structure is built and is itself allowed to regulate theological thought. It ought to be noted further that we never set out to treat Christ's resurrection as a likely event. Our thesis is different: that Christian faith believes that it is true that Christ rose. If we slip off this rock, *faith* will drown. Without that we should not talk about faith. But that of which faith says that it happened is just as unlikely as that God forgives sins. The same sort of unbelief applies to the resurrection as to forgiveness. The difficulty of faith is thus the same essentially in both cases. The difference between them lies exclusively in the different cultural situation in the twentieth century, which makes it a trivial saying that can be taken for granted that God forgives, but which makes it impossible that God should create life. The cultural situation of the sixteenth century led rather to the opposite valuation of the two questions. The offence of Christian faith can, in different periods, be felt at wholly different points.

future event, is, if not lost, at any rate suppressed. It must be so, for if faith does not essentially rest on *event*, it cannot then be an *expectation* of events. Our justification is, however, not the same as our resurrection; between the two lies time, journeying, hope. Now the law must rule the body, for sin still dwells in us, but when sin is finally destroyed, then something will happen in the realm of bodies, then the rule of law, the old aeon, will cease and the dead will rise. But that is, as we see, no different from the completion of the work of creation. Until then an enemy holds God's created world in thrall. If Christ has not slain the enemy then his tyranny will continue on, even if the Christian religion is embraced by all men, even if the sphere above the natural is unimpaired.[1] To give up Christ's resurrection as an outward event is to give up faith in God's creation of the outward world, and it is to give up the eschatological expectation as an expectation for humanity as it actually is. If the two features in our picture of God, *Creator* and *Conqueror*, are clearly visualized, then the position, taken up in advance, that the resurrection can be thought of apart from the body will come to be regarded as no longer acceptable.

Such a thesis simply means, of course, that the preconception in question is outside the boundaries of Christian faith. The entity which we know as the historic Christian faith has not dismissed the message of the resurrection as a message that is true in the usual sense and, *therefore*, as a message of *redemption*. The personal question if I myself can believe this message is not thereby answered, not even raised. If theology were to declare that the resurrection happened it would be saying something that no science has the right to say.[2] But preaching has a wholly different function from theology, the function of presenting the message, of putting itself at the disposal of the message. For this reason no preacher can avoid the personal question. Preaching lives on the basis of events, not on the basis of conceptions, and Christ's death and resurrection are for preaching the basic events: if they go, preaching goes. It must be strongly emphasized that the personal question that is thereby raised is a question of *faith*.

---

[1] The Easter message about Christ's resurrection is, because it is about a victory, a message about something that is *about* to happen to the world. At Easter the outlook is towards what is yet to be. The first note that is sounded in I Cor. 15.53-58 is about the future.

[2] Theology can only say that the Christian message says so, and that this is the Christian faith. But it can say no less. It cannot declare that it is indifferent from the point of view of faith whether the resurrection took place, or characterize the question itself as a mixture from different realms of knowledge.

4. Preaching the resurrection to the twentieth century

It is easier to visualize the nature of the question of faith if it is altered somewhat. Behind the question of the factuality of Jesus' resurrection lies the question if Jesus is really the Only One. It is here that the major question confronts us. The story of the man sick of the palsy (Luke 5.18 ff.) is illuminating in this respect. The Pharisees experienced a real shock because Jesus forgave the sick man his sins: it was this unheard-of claim that most of all gave rise to their consternation and surprise, for healing miracles had been done by others besides Jesus. No prophet had ever dared to claim for himself the right to forgive sins. In exercising this right Jesus 'blasphemed', set himself in the place of God, though himself a man, and thereby threatened the *law*, the foundation of the universe, to the point of rejecting it.[1] We do not react as the Pharisees did; we do not see an act of violence in a man's setting up as the Only One. That, however, is because twentieth-century thought trifles with sin and guilt: in fact, in and for itself, Jesus' claim to forgive sins is offensive. Modern culture freely allows him this claim because a spiritual revolution of enormous proportions has taken place in which the conception of sin has flown away, so that the offence of the Gospel at this point no longer upsets men. The preacher who preaches the forgiveness of sins through Christ must, however, keep clearly in mind that thereby he is already preaching Christ as the Only One.

Humanity, moreover, has always had its religions; every age has its realms where faith is strong and our age is no exception.[2] On the contrary, we are living in a decidedly religious epoch, where certain matters are charged with faith. The Church may well preach about grace, if only she does not touch on *outward* reality. As soon as she passes over the threshold to the world that modern man calls Reality, with a capital R, the same irritation shows itself as the scribes experienced when Jesus cancelled sins. With every kind of faith too, by which modern men, out of Christ, support themselves a certain need is bound up. If law is the foundation of religion then there is a sense of guilt and longing for forgiveness of sins at the same time. The offence of the Gospel lies at that point where the need of the moment lies, where the necessity for help is felt. So in our day a sense of guilt is not the point at which men

---

[1] See especially Luke 5.21 (Mark 2.7, Matt. 9.3).
[2] Christian faith cannot judge the ineradicable need for a 'philosophy of life' otherwise than as a sign that the thraldom of the whole race of man is a fact. Were it only a Christian invention men would be able to live without believing in anything.

most realize their need. They do not seek for forgiveness, but for 'meaning', for 'real life', because by their own reason and intellectual conscience they are made aware of that Reality that is given in space and time, in which no will is at the helm and no harbour is in view.[1] For the intellectual conscience is just as deaf as the conscience of the man sick of the palsy in the Gospel story—or as Luther's conscience, which did not provide the least opening into the locked room of his guilt. The conscience that is burdened with guilt does not give up its grip because of forgiveness, nor does the intellectual conscience give up its grip because of the resurrection.

It is easy in theological work to visualize the religious question as it presented itself to a past age, e.g. the Reformation, and thereby to lose the ability to see the religious features of our own time. When today, by the use of scientific conceptions, the story of the resurrection is avoided, a wholly other interest than a scientific one is at work, an interest clearly springing from a *philosophy of life*. Science works at the side of such problems without need to seek them out. The question of factuality cannot be treated superciliously, as though it were a scientific problem that has gone off the rails, but it must rather be confronted by a simple faith. To say that it is a wrong question to ask is to mistake the element of faith involved in it.[2] The question of unbelief is never foreign to the viewpoint of faith. On the contrary, it is always right up faith's street. The guilt-laden conscience which refuses to allow forgiveness in is a conscience of unbelief—and just for that reason it raises questions to which faith must reply. The intellectual conscience is a comparable religious entity; for that reason the term 'conscience' always turns up

---

[1] We may ask ourselves if, in certain respects, our own time does not stand closer to the Ancient Church than to the sixteenth century. In the theology of the Church Fathers the incarnation and the resurrection took the central place that the sixteenth century accorded to forgiveness and justification. In both cases it was basically a matter of the same thing—the Gospel, Christ's breaking into the prison in which man was incarcerated. Either the Gospel is without significance or it meets the actual needs of the time. It cannot be demanded that the age shall first of all provide for itself a suitable need. If Christ is truly preached then the other aspects of the Gospel will acquire meaning, then the depth of thraldom will be seen. 'Forgiveness' cannot for long remain an empty word.

[2] It also means to give way to the element of faith in it, or rather—from the point of view of Christian faith—to the element of unbelief in it, for it means allowing Christian faith to give up the outward, the body, that Christ in his resurrection won for himself and to betake oneself to the disembodied sphere which today's gods regard as a chimera and which the priests may, therefore, be allowed to have for themselves. It is an irony of fate that those who dismiss the question of factuality as a wrong question fall victim to the basic view of the other side—instead of, as they had hoped, keeping themselves unspotted by it.

in such a connexion, a conscience of *unbelief*, whose questions cannot be brushed aside as mistaken.

Moreover, just as it can never be known where faith is concealed when unbelief speaks, so it is the case here. The old saying that longing for faith is itself faith, formulated in an age of conflict against the law, is still correct, even in an age of 'meaninglessness'. In the most frenzied attack on the message of Christ's resurrection there may be concealed the cry, 'I believe, help thou mine unbelief!'—or, in any case, a contradictory wish to be able to discover an outcropping of faith of some sort. The Church has always had to make known its message about Christ in such a paradoxical atmosphere of longing and opposition; for her work these conditions are normal, and to them she must grow accustomed. She cannot make Christ's resurrection credible, for example, by calling in the aid of natural science, any more than she can make forgiveness of sins credible by calling in the aid of something else than God. To proceed in that manner would only be to preach other words than the Words of Christ and his Father. Preaching has one presupposition— that Christ is the *Only One*, that only in Christ *he* stands forth who *created* the world and now *is victorious* against the destruction of life. If Christ's resurrection is impossible then it is also impossible that God created the world and it is also impossible that such a God should be able to redeem us. There is no difference in 'possibility' here.[1] The personal problem of the preacher's faith is equally involved in each case. If in the case of the resurrection the problem is specially acute, the preacher is face to face with the major decision: 'Can I truly preach the lordship of Christ?'

The right reply to such a personal problem can only be given by him who *sends* the messengers forth. For the preacher to lean on the Church, on ordination, or on succession is, when it is a matter of what is most central, just as impossible as to lean on his own feelings and his conversion. Instead, the question must be changed to this: 'What claim has Christ over me?' Then we catch sight of the foundation that is sufficient to support preaching: Christ's claim to rule over me is but a moment in his rule over the world, and even that is something of which at the same

---

[1] When the conquest took place that restored all mankind's fallen estate, an external miracle took place. To strengthen *a priori* the reality of, for example, a healing miracle would be to mutilate the significance of *redemption* itself. It is a totally different matter that where Christ, who has this power, is active in the world legends grow around him. It is just where there is something extraordinary afoot that the flower of legend begins to grow. Signs of that are present in the New Testament, which is a human document about the Christ who died and rose again.

time I can be personally *certain*. The preacher is one among others in a
whole people of priests. His certainty is not primarily a certainty about
himself but a certainty about the claim of Christ, the lordship of Christ,
about Christ as the Only One.[1] To be doubtful of *his* right to be preached
is to be sure of *one's own* right to push him aside and to be lord oneself.
In the congregation where this certainty of Christ's lordship dwells
the ministry of the Word is committed to certain people, just as other
callings and services are shared out. The ministry of the Word takes its
place in subjection to the authority that the Word in itself possesses,
and which is the power over the world and all races. To the individual
charged with that ministry there is given through ordination the *task* of
preaching this eternal Word and to that end a blessing on his gifts for
the work. Such a public *commissioning* to go forth into the world of men
the Only One alone can provide.

[1] Usually, as soon as question of certainty of any sort comes to light egocentricity comes to light as well. Genuine certainty is never certainty of one's
own ego's religious situation but is always certainty of Christ's authority—then
one's own ego mingles in the company under his authority in the congregation,
without need of knowing more than that Christ comes in the Word, comes in
the sacraments.

XI

THE LAW AND THE GOSPEL

1. 'Law and grace' is 'death and resurrection'

CHRIST'S death and resurrection have taken place for us so that we might be freed from the power of the enemy. When the *kerygma* sets forth the death and resurrection as outward events, happening to the body of Christ, that implies very far-reaching consequences.

Let us consider, first of all, the question of the law and the Gospel. The distinction between the law on the one hand and grace, the Gospel, on the other is integral both to the Early Christian faith and to Lutheran theology. But the technical expression 'law and Gospel' was minted in the Lutheran Reformation.[1] Since we are dealing here with that subject, let us begin, in the first instance, by using the terms of speech of the sixteenth century, though material from other sources will, now and then, be introduced.

The concept of the Gospel is familiar to us from the foregoing treatment of the subject: it is the message of Christ's death and resurrection and the promise of the future based on the conquest Christ thereby achieved, a future towards which we ourselves approach by our death and resurrection. Faith, which receives the message about what has taken place, receives at the same time the promise about what has not yet taken place, the future, and when it comes faith will enter willingly into that event, which in renewing power will break in from above. Faith is very ready to die, but unbelief very unready. If man were wholly left to himself such processes as conflict with his own self-will would never really begin.[2] For until his bodily death man remains, even

---

[1] Without doubt, Luther, in using this expression, hit on a central New Testament reality. But in the New Testament other terms are often employed to express the tension between the old and the new: works and faith, law and Christ, law and Spirit, law and grace.

[2] That means that in such a case baptism would never succeed in its work, for the work of baptism in us is our death and resurrection. Cf. Luther, 'A Sermon on the Sacrament of Baptism' (1519) in *WA* 2, 734.14-24: 'It follows, then, that baptism makes all suffering and especially death useful and helpful, so that they are simply compelled to serve the purposes of baptism, that is, to destroy sin, for it cannot now be otherwise than that he who will satisfy baptism

at the same time as he is justified, a sinner—*simul justus et peccator*.
The duality that is in man, the struggle of the flesh against the spirit
(Gal. 5.17), is a part of the great opposition between God and Satan,
the same opposition in which Christ stood. Because Satan possessed the
power Christ had to be put on the cross and—on the other hand—
because Christ conquered and rose again there is redemption for mankind. When Christ with his death and resurrection takes the field of
humanity the man of sin is choked and crucified and the new man arises
and is sustained, man freed from the enemy. The Gospels describe the
events of the death and the resurrection as past, offer man today the life
that has in that way been won for him, and promise for the future the
total downfall of Satan and the resurrection of the dead.[1] The Gospel
and faith look forward towards that which no eye hath seen.

Till the world is born anew, till then the conflict rages. So long is
faith without sight. So long sin remains a power that the law must con-
demn and fight. A sentence that is continually cropping up in Luther's
writings says that the law must be imposed upon the old Adam and
discipline him, crucify him. It is important to observe at what point the
law comes in alongside the Gospel. Already the Gospel has brought to
us Christ's cross and resurrection and has brought us under Christ's
authority. His death and resurrection are to become our death and
resurrection. The law does not split up the message of the Gospel in
such a way that when the law begins to speak we have two messages;
rather, the law combines with it and carries out something of the work
of death and resurrection, that is, it kills.[2] There are other aspects of

---

and will be free of sin must die, but sin does not willingly die and it therefore
makes death bitter and loathsome. But God is gracious and powerful, so that
sin, which has brought death, is driven out by its own work (death). People
there are who wish to live so that they may be religious and who say they would
like to be religious. Now, there is no shorter road and no easier manner than by
baptism and the work of baptism, which is suffering and death. That they do not
wish for that is a sign that they neither rightly know how, nor intend, to be
religious.'

[1] Cf. Luther: 'The meaning, that sin shall die or drown, is not fully realized
in this life, not until man's body dies and is reduced to dust. So all our life is
nothing but a spiritual baptism continuing unceasingly even to death. So too
the life of a Christian man is nothing else than a beginning of a holy death,
from baptism even to the grave. For God will make him anew at the last day'
(*WA* 2, 728.10-29).

[2] The work of baptism is being accomplished when man is engaged on the
tasks that the law, in the form of secular authority, lays upon him that he may
die and rise again. See Luther, *WA* 2, 734.24-28: 'For this reason God has set
up many institutions that man may learn to be active and to suffer, some to do
with marriage, some with spiritual affairs, and others with ruling; and he orders
all to exercise care and labour that the flesh be destroyed and accustomed to
death.'

the law, but for us, who have approached the problem of the law and the Gospel from the point of view of the content of the Early Christian *kerygma* about Christ's death and resurrection, the factor we have mentioned is the first that must be stated; if law and Gospel are placed side by side that must not be taken to mean that by the side of the Gospel another *kerygma* is placed. There is but one *kerygma*, the Gospel of death and resurrection. The law, in exercising its function, is not at strife with the *kerygma* but in its service. When the law is at work that which the Gospel promises can fully be accomplished; man can die and rise again, thanks to the double action on which the law and the Gospel co-operate. Why then is the law needed? Why does the law not disappear when the Gospel, after Christ's resurrection, goes forth by the messengers who are sent?

Christ came to a world where the law was already in existence and was ruler; he was 'born of a woman, born under the law' (Gal. 4.4). 'For the law was given through Moses; grace and truth came through Jesus Christ' (John 1.17). Jesus' birth in Bethlehem, his struggles, death, and resurrection, all took place in the world created by God, which had been upset by sin and held together by the law. It is the divine creative will that expresses itself as law, force, and wrath when sin stands over against it. Sin and law stand opposed to each other; the law lets go its hold only when sin dies and is destroyed. So the following three things belong together. (1) Christ's death and resurrection, the battle against, and the conquest over, Satan and sin, signify the 'end of the law', for now the Gospel has burst forth. (2) The death of the old man, which is also an attack on the kingdom of Satan, signifies also the end of the law—to the new man the law does not apply. (3) Satan's final fall in the last times is also the end of all accusations, and the end too of all secular authority that demands obedience—as Luther said, 'the law will not rule above'. Each of these three 'ends' for the law signifies a step from 'earth' to 'heaven', a transfer, a 'transition' from the old aeon, which is directed by the law, to the new aeon, established by the victory of Christ. It is typical that the term *transitus* (transition) in Luther's commentary on Hebrews contains exactly these three things: (1) Jesus' transition from death to life, i.e. Jesus' resurrection; (2) the transition from the old man to the new in our present faith; (3) the future transition from death to life through our bodily death and the resurrection of the dead. And, as we have often argued, the three are one and the same reality. Christ died and rose so that the same shall take place in all men. The going forth of the Word among humanity is Christ's own going forth. By this means his death and resurrection extend even to us, as the Word reaches us and awakens our faith. They will have attained their objective when death has laid even the ancient enemy himself low and when all his prisoners emerge from his foreign dominion at the last day. All that is simply Christ's resurrection, whose power cannot be exhausted but out of which life springs up even to the end of time.

That law is done away with when the Gospel is preached is bound up with two realities with which we are well acquainted, conflict and time. We still await the annihilation of sin and the time of waiting is the time of conflict. Sin existed before the birth of Christ in Bethlehem, just as conflict existed and law existed. The one thing that was wanting was *conquest*, and therefore the *Gospel* was also wanting in the strict sense of the word—news of victory. The Gospel was given in the form of a promise, not in the form of a herald's cry about events that had taken place, about a conqueror who had appeared, an oppressor who had been beaten.[1] Only when Christ had passed through his death and resurrection did the *sending forth* to all peoples take place, and the world-mission begin. The Gospel is the new thing, the only new thing, that the messenger brings. The law is old; it existed before. The law ruled not only in Israel, but it rules in all nations under the sun, for they all have rulers and laws, which regulate their affairs in community living. The Galatians came to the Gospel from heathenism, but their later conversion to Judaism would have meant a return to the same 'elemental spirits' that ruled them before (Gal. 4.9 f.). The superior authorities among all peoples are the servants of God in an age of wrath, force and judgement (Rom. 13.1-7). Secular authority, which everywhere exists, is God's law. The Gospel always breaks into a world that has already got law, and for which law is not news, not a novelty. The preacher can make the law plain, can clarify it, and awaken the conscience of the people. However intensively that may be done, the work of the Church is not thereby carried out. Christ's Word remains in every age first and last the Gospel, the Word of resurrection, the Word of forgiveness, which is not intended to improve the earth but to open heaven.

[1] The Old Testament contains not only the law but also the Gospel, for it contains promises. But the promise was first fulfilled in Christ, and so comes the new covenant, freedom. See Irenaeus, *Adv. haer.*, IV.56.1 [34.2].

2. The law and secular authority in Luther and today

In modern theology some difficulty is felt in understanding how
Luther, and with him most of the Fathers, could so easily and immediately make the transition in thought from God's law to the actual ruler
of the day. One cannot avoid the suspicion that the difficulty we find in
understanding that is bound up with the fact that in the last few hundred
years we have been accustomed to dissociating the body from its relation
to God. The same fact makes understanding of the sacraments difficult
for us. Before belief in creation slipped away from us a few centuries
ago, the word of the law had its place in the society where men dwelt,
in the same simple way as the word of the Gospel had its place in the
Church in which baptism was administered and the bread and wine of
the Supper were received. This union of the Word and what is outward
is possible only on the basis of belief in creation and belief in the
resurrection together. So far as the doctrine of law and government is
concerned in detail, it is important to keep two Biblical conceptions,
clear, namely, that of the work of creation and that of one's neighbour.

The world was not created once and for all, but it is being created by
the God who lives today. 'To create is continually to make new' says
Luther; and in another place he says, 'To create is to order'.[1] God
creates now by giving his orders through his law and demanding that
duties be performed. Men stand under the law and are driven from
morning to night by the law, from which all the work of this world
originates, for the law points to one's neighbour, relates all my actions
to my neighbour and forces me to order my life as a servant of others.
When Luther made the law issue in love for one's neighbour he followed
Paul. The saying in the Synoptics that the law is summed up in two
commandments about love, the commandment about loving God and
the commandment about loving one's neighbour, has not in Luther the
same theological significance as has the Pauline *précis*. In Paul the exact
statement is: 'The whole law is fulfilled in one word, even this, "You
shall love your neighbour as yourself" ' (Gal. 5.14); and further: 'He
who loves his neighbour has fulfilled the law' (Rom. 13.8). Such words
of Paul contribute to the tendency found in Luther to ally the law with
the earth and one's neighbour, and the Gospel, on the other hand, with
heaven and God. The work of creation and law are, in this way, brought
very close to each other. By making use of the command of the law God
turns man towards his neighbour and directs what he does towards an

[1] *WA* 1, 563.8; *WA* 12, 328.16.

object lying outside himself, his neighbour's welfare. All that comes into existence on earth by human labour, and upholds our life, comes from God the Creator, the Lord and Ruler in all occupations and classes of society.

From one point of view the kernel of the doctrine of secular authority is that God's law is present with us in the world because our neighbour is. As soon as a fellow-man comes on the scene, law comes on the scene: an order is heard, the Creator of the world speaks and gives commands. We who live in the aftermath of the abandonment of belief in creation find it difficult to understand with what directness and immediacy a Lutheran of the sixteenth century heard the law. The idea, therefore, might easily slip in that technical and social developments make any such concrete concept of the law impossible today. But, in this respect, the technical and social developments mean nothing at all; it is the *theological* revolution, the victory of the spiritualizing tendency in the last two centuries, which deprived us of our ability to hear. In the modern planned democratic state one's neighbour is just as much present and the Creator just as active as in the Wittenburg of those years.[1]

All our work and all the demands that society makes on us spring from the needs of others, of our neighbours. When we are occupied with them and willing to bear our share of the burden we serve our neighbour—that is to say, God's law is in action, the work of moulding society is going on, and life is growing on the earth. And in that work of God we stand not just with our soul, but with our whole being, with all our bodily powers, our tools, our machines, our factories, with all that can uphold life and serve our neighbour. For Luther it was natural to describe all that as 'secular authority' and see it culminating in 'rulers' as in a point. For us, who have spread constituted authority out among the people through popular franchise, and who most readily look on 'authority' as something that comes down in a general election, the way

---

[1] Luther's gift of being able to talk about God's activity so that it was felt as something taking place contemporaneously has its drawbacks. It fills up his writings with noblemen, burghers, tradesmen, mechanics and other groups now no more. If Luther had been born in 1883 instead of 1483, in his books and writings motorists and machinists, factory workers, members of parliament and conscripts, strikers and strike breakers, etc., would have jostled one another. It is a sign of our generation's spiritual impotence that we are not able to combine what the Bible says about God with the realities reported in the daily press. We ought definitely to stop putting the blame for this on the quite blameless technical discoveries, which have nothing to do with unbelief and lack of love and which among freed men should only be looked on as blessings. If our modern society is less capable of endurance than the sixteenth century, that certainly is not the consequence of technics or the like, but is due to the fact that there is less faith now than then.

the reformers spoke can sometimes hinder us in our efforts to understand what the *matter* really was they were talking about, that which continues to be the same through the centuries: that which has to do with our *neighbour*, the embodiment of the law in our actual society.[1]

In our day it is better to choose the idea of vocation than of authority if we want to apply the Lutheran view of faith to the life of society. The term 'vocation' is less bound up with a definite class in society than the term 'authority'. At the same time the idea of vocation is but a corollary of the doctrine of 'authority', a particular form that the concept of authority assumes.

3. Luther's doctrine of man under the law

Luther's description of law as ruling the body is bound up with the emergence of law in the form of secular authority, outward, visible tasks of work. While the law rules the body, the conscience is free through the Gospel. The hands labour, but the heart is at rest in God's forgiveness, without putting any confidence in the labour of the hands. In the conscience the Risen Christ rules; the conscience is already in heaven, in the world of the resurrection, thanks alone to the Gospel, to the Word. The distinction between the body and the conscience is not the difference between the senses and the spirit, between material and idea, as if it were a matter of two entities different in value and fixed in their positions without regard to time, but rather that the body represents the old aeon, the conscience the new: time is integral to the distinction. *The body has not yet risen.* Through death it will attain to the resurrection on the last day, and thus it will come to where the conscience already is through the Gospel,[2] for the Gospel advances from Christ's resurrection and wherever it goes in the world of men it brings the

---

[1] There is no discussion in Luther about how the true state should be established; instead he starts with the actual state in which he lives. The organization of society is not a task for him who preaches; on the contrary, obedience to the demands of the state is a subject for Luther, the preacher, and one to which he often returns. Because of this essential freedom in relation to the form of a state, Lutheranism should be more adaptable than most other confessions. Certain elements in the theological development in Lutheranism after Luther have, instead, caused it to be possibly the most bound of confessions.

[2] Cf. Luther on the Sermon on the Mount (1532) in *WA* 32, 391.23-28: 'From this learn the difference between the two persons that a Christian man must be while he is on earth, because he lives among other people and must use the material of the world and of the Emperor, as much as any heathen. He has just the same blood and body, which he must sustain not from the spiritual authority but from the soil and the land that belongs to the Emperor, etc., until he departs bodily from this life for another.'

heaven of the resurrection with it, and translates the conscience into that heaven, while the body is put to death through the discipline of the law and all the wear and tear of the earth. The cross and the resurrection belong together. If we do not die we do not rise. Still more obvious does the inner relation become when Luther drops the distinction between the body and the conscience, and talks instead about the old and the new man. Not only *time* but also *conflict* comes into the picture then: death and resurrection's mighty process of conflict is being carried on in the new man to whom, as he journeys between Easter and the *Parousia*, the Word has come down. And yet we must retain the distinction between the body and the conscience, must make it part of the distinction between the old man and the new. Otherwise the latter distinction is spiritualized immediately, the sins of the old man are intellectualized into incorrect ideas about God, and the new man's life is rarefied into a friendly disposition. But the old man ravages in our body —that is, in our common life with one another; he splits society asunder. The new man is the first fruits of the resurrection of the dead, the victor over the world and the freshness of the whole life of man.

The process by which the old man is crucified and the new man is born is sanctification. Sanctification cannot be made to take place in sectarian and pietistic circles instead of in the world; in that case it would simply cease, would come to a standstill. The fellowship of a sect is an attempt to bring down the coming age into the old, so that one avoids *moving* towards the new and instead holds the new in his own safe keeping. Seen from another angle, this attempt stands revealed as an effort to eliminate our abiding sinfulness, to transfer the old man to the Gospel, so that one avoids having to *put him to death* and instead allows him to become religious. But the old man remains a child of earth as long as we live, and in the world he must remain; there is no other place where he can really be bound, gagged, mocked and die; if one establishes spiritual circles, there he only becomes the object of care and affection.[1] It is significant that Luther only knows two uses of the law—the civil, which forces us to labour on earth and the theological, which torments man in his conscience. When the Christian stands under the law, he stands as a sinner among other sinners or else he is lifted in faith above all law—one or other, either in death or in resurrection.

---

[1] 'Those are the true mortifications, which are not made in desert places away from the society of men but in economic and political matters' (*WA* 43, 214.3-5; cf. *WA* 18, 65.9-66.20). When Luther describes the fitting lot of the old man, every detail has its counterpart in Christ's suffering: scorn, blows, mockery, buffeting, the crown of thorns, the cross, and the grave. Cf. *WA* 1, 337.16-37.

The third use of the law, which was afterwards cultivated, gave an authority to the law even where there was no sin, and thereby the new age was brought under the rule of the old. If this third use is viewed from another angle, one may say that the Christian, in becoming obedient to the law, betakes himself out of the world, where its civil use is in force, to a reborn group where the taskmaster of the old aeon no longer puts to death but rather gives life, a sort of surrogate life instead of the life of the Gospel, which is the life of forgiveness and resurrection: the whole field of the world is made religious and levelled with piety. But our life on earth becomes fusty when it is made religious. It should be what it is, hard painful work, a journey towards the vale of death, listening all the time to the Word, a passage forwards through the actual rugged wilderness of life with the forgiveness of sins our only piety and the last day our only real hope for the future.

The well-known picture of man as a 'pipe' or 'canal' for God's love does not for a moment imply for Luther man's passivity; he is no dead instrument, a thing in God's hand, but he is man and uses all his reason and all his powers. In responding to God whose voice is heard in the Word and who does not come closer to man than in this way, and in responding to one's neighbour, who remains another, one in a certain sense alien—in this double response, man is a 'canal'. God does not enter as a substance at the top end of the pipe, indeed his voice is heard only in the Word. Man would like to draw closer to the divine, but that cannot be: the deepest and inmost that exists is listening to the Word, that dry, outward thing. Nor does there seem anything divine in commerce with one's neighbour where the lower end of the pipe is laid, but it remains the same, human, everyday affair, in itself without holiness or glory. Man would like to draw closer than that to his fellow, but that cannot be: the deepest and inmost intimacy attainable is the common, unadorned community life, one life beside another. There man is a 'canal'. He listens to the Word and he possesses God; he works at his vocation and possesses his neighbour. His life is a life in both these, in God and in his neighbour, and he is willing that it should remain that till death—waiting for but one change: the resurrection of the dead, sight.

That a life so constituted can be a 'canal' depends on the image in which it was created, upon its driving force, its Master. God's dwelling in Christ during his earthly life did not make an end of his humanity. Christ was a tempted man, a man who had solidarity with the human race, one who listened to his Father. His divinity did not drive out his

K

humanity, but the divine was outpoured on humanity, thanks to the unsullied manhood of Jesus. The resurrection occurred on the third day, because death, involving destitution for the sake of the world, had occurred on Good Friday. The whole divinity of Christ in the Gospel is always like that: we possess God and yet we *listen* as men on earth. The resurrection is ours because death is. To taste the Gospel in our conscience is to experience the rule of the law over our old man. Fellowship with Christ is fellowship with one's neighbour because Christ is risen and the Church is his body. Our actions in the world are human, but with their humanity the divine is united when we perform them in listening to the Word, for faith is the divinity of our actions, outpoured in our actions as Christ's was outpoured in his humanity.

To preach only the Gospel and not the law would be to act as though the Gospel implied sight, the final end of the old aeon, the *Parousia*. Between Christ's resurrection and our own resurrection on the last day the Gospel marches on, but it first reaches its goal when all humanity shall have been incorporated into Christ, for then Satan's power will have fallen for ever. The time between Easter and the *Parousia* is the time for preaching. To believe we can skip this time, to identify the present of the Gospel with the final ending of the age, is to skip *preaching itself*, to cut away the *kerygma* and to supplant preaching by seeing— *theoria* in the strictest meaning of that word—so that the hearer sees (has a theory of) Christ, instead of dying and rising again. Eliminate law and you eliminate the Gospel, for preaching and the Gospel are one, a *kerygma*, a message, a herald's call. The law binds us to the earth, to conflict and to time; it makes us realize the voyaging risk of our situation, that 'not yet' that differentiates faith from sight. The proclamation of the law is not something added to the proclamation of Christ, as though the latter were given in the Gospel alone and the law introduced for pedagogical reasons to make the Christocentric content of the Gospel understandable. The proclamation of the law, on the contrary, is itself the proclamation of Christ, his death, his humanity, his temptation. We should omit something, leave something in the possession of the enemy, if we did not preach the law. We should step rashly into the new aeon in thought and idea without having the body with us there—because the body only rises at the last day—without even having a *hope* for the body, just being resigned about what is outward and contenting ourselves with 'the concept of reconciliation'. But Christ rose bodily from the grave, as he was nailed fast in body to the cross, so that we might be born anew to a living hope, the hope of resurrection.

The dominion of the law over the body in this age is a witness to the
width and richness of the promise, a sign of the Creator's trustworthi-
ness in relation to his work, a support for our hope in God's perfect
conquest which leaves no remainder: nothing God has made will be
left to the tyrant to control. The Creator is Victor.[1]

Excursus

EMPHASIS ON THE OUTWARD IN THE NEW TESTAMENT AND IN LUTHER'S THOUGHT

IN speaking here of 'the body' and 'the bodily state' we are, strictly speaking, guilty of superficiality and making concession to the false dualism between material and spirit. What we are really concerned with is *man*, in the
wholeness and unity of his being. The accent on the body would be unnecessary in an environment where false doctrines were absent. But
throughout the course of Church history, and at the present day, there
have been and are many spiritualizers. They split man's unity open, and
hold fast to the inner life only. The emphasis must be placed on what is
'outward', if the true import of the Gospel and the law is not to be ob-
scured. What is essential is that the message that reaches us from the
Bible is the story of *humanity*. The God who chooses Israel from the fallen
mass of humanity is the Creator of the whole world of men. He has taken
Israel in his hands not in order to isolate them by a special Biblical religion from the other peoples, but in order to take action through his
chosen people for all the world, in order to lift mankind out of its perdition
and restore the unspoiled life of creation. In Christ's death and resurrection that action takes place—the Creator's victorious action for the world,
followed immediately by the sending forth of the Word to all nations.

The division of the Word into 'law' and 'Gospel' is a sixteenth-
century variant of the ancient conception which we have met already, and
of which we have often spoken. We have seen that the Bible has its central
message at the end, in the New Testament *kerygma* of Christ's conquest,
but that this *evangelion* constitutes the inmost meaning and climax of the

---

[1] If faith in the factuality of the resurrection is let slip, it may well be found
very difficult to hold fast the connexion between God's law for the body and,
therefore, to maintain the actual existence of the authority of law in society. In
that case law would become an aspect from which the Christian can view his life
in the world—and which can be abandoned when by chance he does not wish to
view it in that way. Law is one aspect: the Gospel is another. But if we begin
with the conviction that the foundation of everything is that Christ has really
died and risen again, the Christian man's death and resurrection is bound up
with outward events, with his membership of society, with his baptism. One is
under law and the Gospel by the very fact that he is alive, for Christ has come
into humanity and has sojourned where we sojourn to redeem us from the power
of the enemy, to create and to conquer.

proclamation of all Scripture, even if the authors belong to the Old Testament and are engaged on Israel's conflict,—for the account of a conflict reaches its climax in the news of victory. Talk about conflict belongs to the news of victory, in the same unique way as the law belongs to the Gospel without entirely comprehending it. Since some know nothing of any conflict, the law must be proclaimed. But since the conflict between God and Satan lies at the foundation of all human existence, even if some do not know this, victory is the only new item in the news that the messengers have to bring.[1]

Luther's separation of law and Gospel adds nothing essentially new to the picture of the Biblical Word that we have already tried to define. Through the Reformation the New Testament's message sounds forth anew, but certain of its characteristics have been made more definite and others have receded into the background. What is surprising is that *both* the uniqueness of the Gospel as over against the preaching of the law, *and* its insight into what is wrong with us—its insight into our alienation, our need—have been sharpened. Its character as revelation is sharper. Its hidden character is sharper, too. Law and Gospel are *two* and will remain so till death. They are united in God, but not here below on the field of battle; they will be united at Satan's destruction and the resurrection of the body, but not now while faith waits for heaven. The Gospel gains in clarity by being accompanied by the law, and faith at the same time is faced with an opaque hiddenness, against which it has to strain when God's Word is both wrath and love. One characteristic that too easily slips into the background is the relationship between the Gospel and the body. When law and Gospel are divided so sharply as in Luther's thought, the law seizes upon the earth and the body, while the Gospel holds fast to the conscience. Guilt was the only really terrible suffering which Luther knew. In the stories of the Gospel however, a connection exists between Jesus and man's healing that does not really find a place in either of Luther's divisions of 'law' or 'Gospel' alone. Jesus is the Life, which goes forth into the world of death. With Luther it is Forgiveness, which goes forth into the world of sin; the distance between the Church's present situation and the resurrection of the body in the future *Parousia* has been made longer than it was for the evangelists and the Church Fathers. If one is to be true to Luther—that is, to judge him according to the Scriptures, which he himself wished to place 'upon the candlestick'—one must be quite clear that in this matter his teaching is one-sided and defective, and not normative for us.[2]

---

[1] If, with Barth, we change law and Gospel into 'Gospel and law'—in that order—something of the Bible's own content disappears.

[2] For this reason it is very difficult to fit the diaconate into Luther's view. In the Early Church, the Gospel and the body were linked together in the same way as we find in Jesus' healings. Of Luther it could be said that secular authority is the only allowable diaconate, at work in all occupations and callings, but at the same time the Church, as Church, is pretty well unconcerned about the body. The Early Christian Communion was, on the contrary, at once a means of grace in our meaning, a coming of Christ, and a meal by which physical hunger was satisfied.

Above all, in interpreting Luther historically one ought to take suffi-cient account of all in his work that is calculated to counteract such one-sidedness. In Luther's teaching as a whole, only such proclamation of the law as speaks of our actions, of what is 'outward', can subdue—that is to say, can unveil—man's 'inner' unbelief, which is guilt. Judgement falls on man's actions, and yet also manages to penetrate to the depths and point to unbelief as the source of these evil actions.

The best proof of the connection in Luther's thought between 'outward' works and 'inner' guilt is provided by the numerous references to Christ's reconciling death. Christ bears the law, the wrath and all the transgressions that have been committed 'on the plane of works'. The following state-ment of Luther is characteristic: 'Since the merciful Father saw us op-pressed by the law and held under the curse, without any possibility of freeing ourselves from it, he sent his Son into the world, laid all men's sins on him and said to him, "Be Peter, the denier; be Paul, the persecutor, the blasphemer and the violent man; be David, the marriage breaker; be the sinner who ate the apple in Paradise; be the thief on the cross; in a word, be the person of all men who committed the sins of men, and see to it that you pay and make recompense for them." Then comes the law and says, "I find that this sinner has taken upon himself the sins of all men and I see no sin that is not his. So shall he die on the cross." '[1]

It would be Docetism to describe Christ's reconciliation exclusively as God's gift of justification. The dominion of the law cannot be done away unless Christ, as a tormented and a tempted man, fulfils the law in a struggle against God and his wrath, and not simply against humanity and its tyrant Satan. The Ancient Church, with its strong accent on death as a corrupting power and its relatively weak stress on guilt, felt a certain in-clination to regard Christ's work of reconciliation as consisting in his struggle against, and victory over, the devil, the Lord of death. It is the weak point in Irenaeus that to such a slight extent he saw Christ as fighting against God's wrath and against the law. But just as Christ really died, although Docetism taught the opposite, so he also has borne guilt and been a sinner (II Cor. 5. 21; Rom. 8. 3)—although the modern Docetism teaches the contrary.[2] The words 'for us' ought not to be taken to imply any diminution of the full reality. Christ died 'for us'—but that took away nothing from the death. So he was also a sinner 'for us'—but that took away nothing from the sin.

Death and sin are both enemies of Christ. They are conquered only in that Christ rose again from the grave, and as the Risen One forgives sin through the Gospel until that day when he shall have completed his re-demptive work fully and the accuser shall be cast down. The forgiveness of sins and the resurrection of the dead are both included in Satan's fall.

[1] *WA* 40(I), 437.20-438.13.
[2] 'But we ought to bring Christ right in and thus recognize that as he was flesh and blood, so too he was subject to sin, death, and all torments. If I deny the sinner, I deny also the crucified. It is no less absurd to say that he was slain by death than that he was made a sinner by God' (Larger Commentary on Galatians (Rörer MS), 1531. These somewhat strong and daring sentences are modified in the printed text of 1535, *WA* 40(I), 434.7-10.)

XII

BAPTISM AND THE LORD'S SUPPER

1. The place of baptism in the Gospel

SURPRISING though it may seem, many of the lines of thought that we have been pursuing lead straight to the sacraments—especially to baptism, but also to the Lord's Supper. We discover continually that we are within the framework of death and resurrection, and we come to realize anew that redemption includes the *whole* man. Creator and Victor meet us here as well.

One basic thesis to which we have often returned in the preceding chapters has been that Israel was called so that humanity might be redeemed. In Israel a conflict was carried on for the sake of the whole world. When Israel's destiny is realized, the redemption of all the world will be in sight. God's actions by which Israel becomes Israel are actions purifying all that goes by the name of man. Now, among these divine actions of election there is one which is in a class by itself, the Exodus from Egypt through the Red Sea. There God's people received their 'baptism'; there they were born, and there began their history (Ex. 13-15). 'Our fathers were all under the cloud, and all passed through the sea, and all were baptized into Moses in the cloud and in the sea' (I Cor. 10.1-2). But it belonged to the fulfilment of Israel's task for all mankind that Israel as a people should be crushed. Only when, as a corn of wheat, it falls into the ground and dies, can it bear fruit. Only when it loses its power and glory and becomes the Suffering Servant of Yahweh can it spread abroad in the world and become a light to the nations (Isa. 53). That event, the event of death and resurrection, can be hinted at and foreshadowed in the old covenant but it cannot *take place* unless the old departs and the new arrives. When that has taken place the new covenant will have arrived. In Jesus' death and resurrection this took place; therefore that happened which is 'baptism', 'the crossing over', 'the passing through', the forward march, transit through the swelling waters, through death and hell, and so the stepping ashore on the strand of the new age, while the enemy is drowned in the depths.

Jesus says, when he faces his suffering (Luke 12.50): 'But I have a *baptism* to be baptized with; and how I am constrained until it is accomplished!' At another time, too (Mark 10.38), he asks his disciples: 'Are you able to drink the cup that I drink, or to be baptized with the *baptism* with which I am baptized?' When they reply that they can, he promises them—it is James and John, the sons of Zebedee, who are concerned—future martyrdom (Mark 10.39). He also promises them life, though without any promise of special places in the world to come. To pass through baptism is to die and rise again.

Up to now we have discussed baptism without touching on ritual baptism. At the beginning of the old covenant was the event at the Red Sea, and at the beginning of the new covenant the event on Golgotha. Both events are called 'baptism'. In both cases it is a question of defeat and fear which result in redemption and life and in the conclusion of a covenant—just as at the great flood of Noah's day, the origin of all 'redemption by water' (I Peter 3.20 f.). When we are talking about baptism there is no reason why we should not have in mind the flood, the Red Sea, and Jesus' death and resurrection, all at the same time. Were it a question of association of different literary *loci classici* then the possibilities might well be limited, so that by chance *one* passage might be thought of, and not the others. But if, on the contrary, it is the case that everywhere God is taking action for the fallen race in judgement and restoration, by killing and giving life, then 'baptism' is basically the same in all cases: baptism is death and life, to be baptized is to be taken into the hands of God and rescued from corruption. Before Christ, all baptism in Israel was a beginning of Jesus' death and resurrection; after Christ, all baptisms in which his Word is present are divine actions of the covenant. Little by little they draw the world of men into Jesus' death and resurrection—the destruction of the world and its rebirth.

This way of regarding redemption has deep roots in the history of religion. Ideas and conceptions outside the Bible certainly exercised an influence both in Old Testament and New Testament times. Nature's own growth between death and the awakening life is the first source. The corn of wheat really 'died' and 'bore much fruit' long before anyone spoke of it, or gave it a spiritual interpretation. Those who take seriously the first article of the Creed will scarcely be disturbed in their faith in the second and the third by such parallels to Jesus' death and resurrection and to baptism (or the Lord's Supper). It is really the same God who gives a resurrection to a corn of wheat in nature and to his people in Jesus Christ. The creative power of the living God is the origin of (false) belief in fertility gods (cf. Rom. 1.18-25). On the contrary, other forms of religion are not the origin of Jesus' death and resurrection or of baptism; they are rather anticipations and prophecies of these. It is one thing to read from the events of nature an ideology of death as the fountain of life—quite another to give one's life, the only life one has, as 'an offering for sin' (Isa. 53.10), really to cast one's life away 'as a lamb that is led to the slaughter' (Isa. 53.7). That was Israel's task; for that reason it was chosen. At one point in Old Testament history the meaning of this death clearly came in sight—in the Servant Songs. It is a fact of great significance that the story of Jesus' baptism in the Jordan according to the Synoptics shows clearly that Jesus was baptized that he might be the Servant of the Lord, that is, baptized for his substitutionary death.

Only now have we come to ritual baptism. It is important to emphasize that in that we are not dealing with a concept of baptism that is different in any essential way. It is the basic mistake of our theology of the sacraments that the whole world and the life of man is visualized as a profane area which stands in no relation to God, not even under his wrath and judgement, but which has as its very characteristics profaneness, immanence and sheer naturalness. By the side of this profane life the sacraments are set as some sort of holy substances, and we get lost in unending questions about how we are to fit divine activity into the normal life of man. This whole way of looking at things is hopeless. What is decidedly wrong in that whole line of thought is to be found— as is usual in such cases—just before the beginning of the line of thought, in the conception of a sacrament itself. In the case of baptism we must free ourselves of the inclination to begin with the ritual baptism of the Church. We must begin with the actual death and the actual resurrection of Jesus, begin with the event that constitutes the centre of the Biblical *kerygma*. Then the world and the life of man are there from the beginning, and there is no problem of how they are to be fitted in. When we speak of Jesus' death, we are already talking about baptism itself, the baptism of which he spoke and from which he recoiled. Since Christ was baptized, we are also baptized by those whom he has sent (cf. Matt. 28.19, Mark 16.15 f.). And since Christ's work was to undergo baptism, death and resurrection, he stepped down into Jordan as a sinner.

The voice from heaven proclaims that Jesus is the Servant of God. 'Thou are my beloved Son, with thee I am well pleased' (Mark 1.11;

cf. Matt. 3.17 and Luke 3.22). The reference is to Isa. 42.1, the verse introducing the Servant Songs: 'Behold my servant, whom I uphold, my chosen in whom my soul delights; I have put my spirit upon him.' As the quotation clearly shows, the coming of the Spirit on the chosen one was what constituted his appointment as the Servant, and all the accounts of the baptism culminate in what is said about the overshadowing of Jesus by the Spirit when he had been baptized (see especially John 1.32-34). Baptism is thus the entry of Jesus on his task as the Suffering Servant. The Gospel of John brings the Baptist's saying about Jesus, 'Behold, the Lamb of God, who takes away the sin of the world!' (John 1.29) into direct relation with the story of his baptism. The Lamb who bears sin and punishment is a symbol of the Servant who is beaten and slain (Isa. 53.7). For this reason Jesus undergoes baptism in Jordan, which is a baptism for the *remission of sins* (Mark 1.4 f.; Luke 3.3; cf. Matt. 3.6). Just because Jesus assumes a solidarity with all sinners and undergoes baptism—that is, death and resurrection—he 'fulfils all righteousness' (Matt. 3.15), and thereby forgiveness of sins is offered to all. So it is no specially Pauline speculation that forms the background for Rom. 6.2 ff., where baptism is placed alongside death and resurrection —for Paul's line of thought is but a variant of the view of baptism common to the Early Christians. He who is baptized dies with Christ and is raised with him. Christ's death and resurrection did not take place that Christ might be unique in these respects but, on the contrary, they took place that all who belong to him might share in the same experiences and so gather around him, the firstborn of many brethren (Rom. 8.29; Col. 1.18; Rev. 1.5 f.). Christ's flock is gathered when the messengers go out into all the world to baptize and to preach. He who is baptized becomes one with Christ; he shares in his death and resurrection. Baptism binds man and Christ together, and by itself makes the last day and the resurrection of the dead the goal of man's life. By really dying, 'hating his life in this world' (John 12.24 f.), man attains the fulness of his baptism in the work of his earthly calling and at the last in bodily death, the transformation of the corn of wheat into true life.

Our baptism, then, is at one and the same time the death and resurrection of Jesus and our own journey through death to life, the death of the old man and the birth of the new man with all that implies of personal conflict. For Jesus' death and resurrection are not complete until his body dies and rises again, and we, his Church, are his body. The Church lies between Easter and the *Parousia*, the time of the *kerygma*, during which baptism comes to one nation after another in its journey 'to the close of the age' (Matt. 28.19 f. and Acts 1.5-8). The enslaved men burst forth from their thraldom and go through the Red Sea into the age to come, while the oppressors, Satan and his band, are destroyed and shall never recover. Baptism is the action by which God lifts us out of the power of darkness. In every baptism there is a *victory* over the Devil, in every baptism the power of the resurrection comes into the world of men and the morning of the last day draws nigh. Man who is created in the image of God, and who in the resurrection of the body shall become what he was destined by God to be (Phil. 3.21), is sealed by baptism with death and resurrection—that is to say, with Christ's image (cf. Rom. 6.5 with 8.29), with that image which is three things in one: the intention of creation, the future goal of the last day, and the fate that Jesus experienced in the ordinary, outward world of history.

Preaching has, therefore, as its task the provision of an 'image of Christ', the relating of what the Gospel says. Because it possesses 'the image' the *kerygma* is the creative Word, filled with what is first and original but lost, filled with what is last and inconceivable, what can only be waited for and believed in—what can only be 'seen with the ears', as Luther puts it, what must be grasped by hope. Even more is this duality true of baptism, where faith possesses something that is more than the Word, where the body is included in the sacrament, but where listening to the Word is still the only possible way of holding fast to what has happened. Faith hangs on to the Word, and the water gives faith a foothold saying, 'The Word's promises apply to *you*, for *you* are baptized, touched with water, named by name.'

2. The Lord's Supper: 'the real presence is heard'

In passing on now to the Lord's Supper, we are not entering on a new circle of thought from that in which we have just been moving, but we find ourselves within the same unique Biblical scheme of thought. 'This cup is the new covenant in my blood' (I Cor. 11.25). If it is asked where in the Old Testament a 'cup' is mentioned in connexion with the suffering and death of the Mediator sent by God, we are brought once more to the Servant of the Lord and to him alone: in him the 'covenant of the people' is fulfilled. He is to be 'a light to the nations, to open the eyes that are blind, to bring out the prisoners from the dungeon, from the prison those who sit in darkness' (Isa. 42.6 f.; cf. 49.8). His blood is poured out 'for many' and it is poured out 'for the forgiveness of sins'

(Matt. 26.28; cf. Mark 14.24), for delivery from thraldom to sin and destruction. The 'many' are not a limited flock but an unlimited, 'all men of all nations' (Schniewind), the flock who are met with in the journeying of the Gospel over the world till the *Parousia*, to the ends of the earth and till the end of time. Just as Jesus emerged as the Suffering Servant of the Lord when he was baptized in the Jordan, so he did again when he held his Last Supper. In both cases it is one and the same reality that is placed in the centre: Jesus' death, along with what is to follow death. In both cases there is fulfilment of that for which Israel was called: Israel's death for the world, for mankind, out of which that people was once selected so that in it all nations on earth might be blessed (Gen. 12.3).

When a person is baptized he is baptized that he may die and rise again and thereby be delivered out of the power of Satan, become a healthy man, redeemed for that life for which man was destined and for the realization of which Israel was chosen. In his own person he experiences the history of humanity, which Israel passed through and whose end is the resurrection of Christ, so far as we are concerned the resurrection of the dead, that future towards which we are on the way. Christ passed through baptism himself, through the Red Sea, when he died and rose again. We leave Egypt and are redeemed by water when we are baptized. For that reason, like Israel we receive food and drink as we journey on. The food of the Lord's Supper is food for the desert journey, manna from the ground and water out of a rock (I Cor. 10.1-4). Just as the Creator conquered at the Red Sea and in the death and resurrection of Jesus, so it was also the Creator who gave life to Israel on the journey through the desert. Our baptism is a part of the conflict which the God who created us and the whole world wages. In the same way, every celebration of the Lord's Supper is a meeting with the Father who causes seed and vines to grow and ripen and who cares for the well-being of his children. Only when faith in creation takes firm hold in our celebration of the Lord's Supper does the eschatological hope get firm footing in the meal—for then time, the history of redemption, comes to be a constitutive and inescapable element of the action of the sacrament. When bread and wine mean something for the body, the first article of the Creed becomes real in the Eucharist, and at the same time so does the second article, expectation of the resurrection of the body. The beginning of time and the last day come together around a centre, around the axle of all things, Jesus' historical death and his resurrection in human form—the second article. Nothing succeeds in

making so manifest and explicit the bond that unites what has taken
place with what will take, the event of the third day in Jerusalem and
that of the last day. In the Lord's Supper man is sealed with 'the image'
just as in baptism. And the power of the image comes from the Word,
as in baptism. Man receives the gifts and listens to the words, 'for thee',
'for you'—Christ's words, Christ's presence. The real presence is heard.

3. Word and sacraments in the Church

On the last day, however, the real presence will be seen. That is the
inner core of the *Parousia*, Christ's real presence in visible form; herein
eternity differs from the time of the Word, the time of the *kerygma*.
'Every eye will see him' (Rev. 1.7). Then there will take place in heaven
the great supper that is a fruit of preaching's onward march to all
corners of the earth in the days of waiting. 'And men will come from
east and west, and from north and south, and sit at table in the kingdom
of God' (Luke 13.29). Christ is just as much present in the Lord's
Supper now as he will be in the heavenly supper, but his real presence
now is in accordance with the phase of the history of redemption in
which we stand—the phase between Easter and the *Parousia*, faith's
phase, not sight's. Baptism and the Lord's Supper are bound up with
the Word, and their time is the time of the Word—the time of journeying, of listening.

This interim period is where the Church fits into the history of
redemption. The Word and the sacraments are, accordingly, constitutive
for the Church. Through his grace Christ collects his flock before the
judgement—that is, while preaching is going on. In the Lord's Supper
there is 'proclamation', just as in baptism and in preaching generally,
of 'the Lord's death until he comes' (I Cor. 11.26). Preaching, baptism,
and the Lord's Supper have their place in the midst of the conflict in
which many go down without attaining the goal. It is Paul's main concern in I Cor. 10.1-33 to stress the danger of that. Many of the people
of Israel who were delivered from Egypt fell in the wilderness journey,
and the same can happen to the new Israel—to those who have been
baptized into the Church and have shared in the Lord's Supper. 'Therefore let anyone who thinks that he stands take heed lest he fall' (I Cor.
10.12). In true preaching about Christ—a real *kerygma*, where death and
resurrection are the centre—baptism and the Lord's Supper are *always*
given their place, even if they are never mentioned. Mechanically drag-
ging them in can often befog the listener more than simply suggesting

them. When it is self-evident that baptism and the Lord's Supper are deeply rooted in life, then they rightfully assume their central place in the Church, and at the same time the great perspective into the future is held open so that men understand that they are on a journey and not yet at its end.

4. Word and sacraments in human life

When we thus set both baptism and the Lord's Supper in the perspective of the future, we also forge a strong bond between the sacraments and *the body*. After Jesus' resurrection and before our own eventual resurrection, we are baptized, we eat bread and drink wine, waiting for the transformation of the world, for a new heaven and a new earth. If hope and future outlook exist at all in our worship, it is unthinkable that the body should be excluded from that hope. That the sacraments have a relation to the body is not peculiar to them: the Gospel, too, holds out hope for the body. Moreover, there is no thought of magic power in this relation.

We are here face to face with the fact of the history of redemption, the fundamental significance of time in God's action: if the sacraments are not to possess a promise that points to the future, then faith will be smashed to bits—its spiritual content will be broken up and become nothing in empty and superficial talk about aspects where time has no place. If we let go time, the body and conflict, *journeying*—all these belong together—then the Supper becomes something profane, which 'Christianity' regards in a certain way, or for which it finds a place in its concept of redemption, a concept which in itself is unconnected with baptism and the Lord's Supper and which can equally well express itself in other well-known Christian forms. Just as 'law' is an aspect which we need not apply if we do not wish to, so, for such a theology, 'the Gospel' is a purely spiritual aspect. But in society law is actually imposed on the body, and that is a promise of the Creator's decision to deliver the creation out of the sphere of Satan's power. The Gospel does include the body in baptism, and feeds the body in the Lord's Supper as a promise of the resurrection of the dead. The promise is founded on a rock, on what has actually *happened* to the Lord of baptism and of the Supper, who is also the superior of the law, for it is founded on Christ's actual death and resurrection. The starting point for faith is not a document about religion, but a message about an event that has taken place. The sacraments do not consist of examples of the same

religious *motif* as is found in faith in the resurrection, but rather the
resurrection on the third day is an advent which unrolls before us a road
for us to travel; the resurrection is the first baptism's culmination, which
afterwards is followed by ever new baptisms, new events, a new succession of men who celebrate the Lord's Supper, struggle and die.[1]

We do not deny that the sacraments are expressions of God's grace,
of God's love, just as Christ's resurrection is. All the great Christian
beliefs may be brought together and the same meaning, the same *motif*
found to be behind them all. Since baptism and the Lord's Supper are
observed today, it is of first-rate importance that they should constantly
be linked with a true conception of grace. But, as against that, such a
conception of grace by itself provides no reason why baptism and the
Lord's Supper *ought* to be observed today. There are hundreds of ways
in which God's grace may be expressed that are not sacraments; that
are not indispensable to the existence of the Church as a Church; and
that are not, therefore, the mark of *every* Christian congregation.

We are here faced with essentially the same question as we met when
dealing with the reason for preaching today. The reason we preach is
that we have been sent, have been ordered, to preach—in the final
analysis, that Christ actually died and rose again.[2] So, in the same way
the reason for the sacraments is their *institution*, Christ's historical
action. In this connexion it is not essential that we should be able to
find a definite point in Jesus' life when he instituted the sacrament, and
ordered that in future it should be repeated among his disciples (although even in this matter of the time of the institution there is good
reason to entertain greater confidence about the New Testament sources
than has generally been believed in recent times). What is essential is
that Jesus regarded his death as the way to a new covenant, that he
expected and requested his disciples to share what he himself passed

---

[1] The question what the sacraments give over and above the Word often
springs from a religion of works. The secret presupposition is: if it cannot be
shown that there is some special advantage with the sacraments there is no point
in making use of them, we should rather content ourselves with the Word. If,
however, we start with the conviction that it is hard to believe and easy to fall
as we journey, then the means of grace do bring grace, are gifts: then we receive
them all with gladness when they all give us the same thing.

[2] God's grace meets us just in that outward form that God has appointed.
That we have been ordered does not make it opposed to God's grace, but brings
it into its service. We are never so free from the conception of merit as when we
know that we are plainly commanded by God, never so abandoned to attack by
egoistic religion as when we enter on a course of action without being clearly
ordered to do so. Preaching, faith, prayer, baptism, the Lord's Supper, are all
full of promises and have been commanded by God; the more clearly one sees
the *mandatum Dei* behind them, so much the more purely does his grace emerge.

through and won (indeed, he promised them that they would); further, that he experienced baptism that he might die as the Servant of the Lord; together with the fact—and this is basic—that he *really did die and really did rise again*. This last is and must remain the kernel of preaching, as of sacramental life. Christ has died and risen again so that we may die and rise again. His own baptism and his own celebration of the Supper included, even then, his own death and resurrection; our baptism and our celebration of the Lord's Supper include, even now, our death and resurrection, for they include his death and resurrection —which have taken place already, which in the advance of the Word spread out into humanity in its journey to the *Parousia*, and which are now with *us* and bring us redemption. If Christ is not risen 'then our preaching is vain' (I Cor. 15.14); then is our Lord's Supper also vain, our baptism as well—just a religious rite like so many others in the history of religion. Then neither their basic *motif*, nor their institution at a definite point of time by the deceased, can give life to dead bones.

Since death and resurrection are the content of baptism and the Lord's Supper, they have the same place in the history of redemption as the *kerygma* of Christ's death and resurrection. This *kerygma* went out into the world *after* Christ's death and resurrection, not before. Then began the time for preaching. That historically we come across Christian baptism after Jesus' death is exactly what we should have expected—keeping in mind the meaning of baptism, if that, like the Lord's Supper, had its basis in Jesus' own decision. We have so long neglected to think in terms of the history of redemption that now we are hardly able to do so. Baptism and the Lord's Supper have their place in time, and their time is the time of the Word; their function is like the Word's—to throw a bridge between what has taken place and what is still awaited, between Christ's resurrection and the last day. This time is just the time in which man is created and develops, as God carries on the conflict with Satan. The creative Word makes man man when it offers him forgiveness of sins. The resurrection body is not supernatural, but the freed body, man in his purity. So the water of baptism and the bread and wine of the Lord's Supper are no supernatural substances—if they were how could they bring us redemption? —but they are water, bread and wine with the power of the Word, the power to expel unbelief and the Devil, the power to create human life afresh. We hear Christ in the Lord's Supper and in baptism and we receive his 'image' in faith—that is to say, in death and resurrection. This at the same time is God's image in which we were created, from which we fell and towards which we journey when we go towards our death that we may rise again, for Christ is God's image and the source of man's life. Man comes to exist, he is created, in baptism and the Lord's Supper; he receives his life from the source—or better, to use the language of the New Testament, from the Rock. 'They drank from the supernatural Rock which followed them, and the Rock was Christ' (I Cor. 10.4).

The Lord's Supper is repeated, for it is the food and drink of the desert journey. But baptism is not repeated, for it is the crossing of the Red Sea, which only took place once for all. Through baptism a person enters the Church, and afterwards grows within the Church towards his full stature. Through baptism a person is delivered from the land of slavery and then begins his journey to heaven: the Lord's Supper is 'the food of travellers'. Paul makes the rock in the desert into a rock that journeyed, so that what is said of the water of Meribah (Ex. 17.6 f., Num. 20.2-13) may agree with what is said about the manna (Ex. 16.9-21), the food that was continually being given. Deepest of all, certainly, lies the thought of birth in baptism; birth into life takes place once only. Thereafter one lives the life into which one was born—lives by receiving food. Birth takes place in baptism, which is undergone once for all; food for the journey is offered to man repeatedly in the Lord's Supper. The concept of conflict may well be brought in at this point: just as baptism is delivery from the land of darkness, so the life that follows is a continual conflict against sin, a conflict that is made possible because man has been freed from slavery and has been given weapons (Eph. 6.10-17). As Luther said: 'Through baptism we are born anew. But we retain the old skin in our flesh and blood; the Devil and the world so hinder and tempt us that we often grow weary and tired and at times stumble. Wherefore the Lord's Supper is given to us for our daily need and nourishment, so that faith may be strengthened and refreshed, and that we may not fall back in such struggles, but ever increase in strength. For the new life in us is to be so constituted that it shall ever increase and continue.'[1]

Both in the case of birth (baptism) and in the life that follows (the Lord's Supper), it is the *Word* that accomplishes the task. From creation's morn till the last day, life comes from God's Word—that Word which in Christ became flesh and in the sacraments continues to clothe itself in bodily form, but is and must remain the Word, conversation.

The Creator steps forth in the sacraments as the Conqueror. He

[1] *WA* 30(I), 225.8-15.

carries through his creative work and drives the enemy back. The Christian's struggle ends in bodily death, and in resurrection to which that same death is the gate. The life of the resurrection is the goal to which man is led by the sacraments; both baptism and the Lord's Supper have that forward-looking character. When the resurrection takes place, then will be complete the creative moulding of man that God has had in hand ever since the beginning of time. The Word's series of events will be at an end when man stands forth free of the enemy, without sin, and without death. To say that the sacraments have the eschatological fulfilment in mind is the same as to say that man comes into existence through them. What is called 'ethics' is the life of action that is born in baptism, gets its nourishment from the Lord's Supper, and is completed in the resurrection of the dead. The Spirit is the power of the new life, and the Spirit is the power of the resurrection. The Spirit struggles against sin in the ethical struggle, winning it at the last after many trials and reverses. Thus man goes through the passage of death—baptism is at an end, and man rises from the dead. The sacraments do not bring into being a supernatural life but just human life, and even if, as we have said, that undamaged human life is fully created only at the last day, yet even in this life it rises every day above its hindrances and its imprisonment, struggling all the time; in the fellowship of the Christian congregation the new and pure humanity that belongs to the future and to our expectation takes shape. The sacraments are God's work, but still not specially religious entities, side by side with the 'profane' life, for God is Creator and where his work is, there, quite simply, is life.[1] Apart from God's Word and a congregation of Christ, a human life cannot be lived, for there hell and destruction of human life hold sway. We never need to face the problem as to how the power of the sacraments is to 'come alive in human life' (in that case the 'normal' life of man is looked on as untouched by God's gift), for human life is enslaved and its freedom from that slavery is the object of our hope. We journey towards human life when we journey in baptism, and when we join in the fellowship of the Lord's Supper—listening to the Word, killing our own will, filled with hope for that future that will destroy our own sin and all the power of the enemy. That means living in death and resurrection, living in Christ.

[1] In the Ancient Church, where the Lord's Supper was at one and the same time a service of worship and a meeting of hungry men, that relation between the sacraments and human life was easier to see and to hold on to. Nowadays we have fashioned liturgical forms and regulations that are a direct cause of our difficulties in perceiving that inner connexion: when one sees a wafer one does not think of daily bread.

Throughout the ages there has scarcely been any preacher of the
Christian message who has emphasized so strongly as Luther the unity
of human life and the sacraments. Nor does the human thus come into
opposition to the divine. It is *God* who is in baptism and the Lord's
Supper, and he is there to give and to be received; he is there to create,
which means life, human life, for the man who receives. Accordingly,
baptism comes alive in one's earthly calling with all its troubles and
conflicts. It is just in the life *of society* that baptism is actualized.[1] The
Lord's Supper, too, in a corresponding manner, sets a man in a fellowship with those who celebrate it. Christ is changed into us and we, as
Luther says, 'are changed into one another', enclosed in one another by
love.[2] When Christ approaches, our neighbour approaches as well, for
humanity is something that Christ in his incarnation became. Therefore
—again—the exclusion of the body from the work of baptism and the
Lord's Supper is an impossibility. Even here in time the body is drawn
into the life of baptism, for secular authority lays burdens on us, which
discipline our sinful bodies, and which bring a foretaste of the fact that
the work of baptism, death and resurrection, will at last be achieved also
in our bodies. In like manner the Lord's Supper establishes a fellowship
between us and our neighbours—people who can be seen and touched—
here in this earthly life. But the sacraments have their goal in that life
where sin is no more. In that life, for which we wait, the body also will
have part. That the sacraments are linked to the body means above all
that we have this hope for the body.[3] That it is the *Word* that is at
work in the sacraments as well—that, in spite of the fully visible nature

---

[1] *WA* 2, 734.14-33.   [2] *WA* 2, 748.6-26.
[3] 'Not only are you baptized, have the Gospel preached to you, and are blessed
through it, but it has to do with your body; not only to your mind in the sacrament of the altar are body and blood given to you, but to your body as well.
That is not to be left out. It is to be a spiritual body as Christ's was in the
resurrection' (*WA* 36, 666.11-667.2; Rörer MS). But we may ask if the unity of
the Lord's Supper and the social community of men in general would not have
found fuller expression if the emphasis on the concept of sacrifice in the sacrifice
of the Mass had not made Luther so excessively scared of the very mention of
sacrifice. In the Anglican Church, since the first Prayer Book of 1549, self-
dedication takes a central place in the liturgy of the Lord's supper, shortly after
the words of institution. The point of departure is Rom. 12.1, where Paul speaks
about the presentation of our bodies as a living sacrifice. The union of the
liturgical and the social within Anglican piety is bound up with this, and must
be regarded as a legacy from the Early Church that we Lutherans have unfortunately lost. Cf. A. G. Hebert, *Liturgy and Society* (1935). If the Lord's
Supper and baptism could be regarded once more today as God's creative acts
in the world of men, that would of itself lead gradually to a more realistic
ordering of both—even liturgically, so that the Lord's Supper should become
a meal where bread is broken and shared out, and baptism a bath and not just
a mere moistening of the head. The forms now in use invite spiritualizing
interpretations.

of baptism and the Lord's Supper, in both the real content is *heard* and not seen—is emphasized in a unique manner by their character of expectancy and future reference. For the Word is the divine reality in the form it assumes before the *Parousia*. The Word always moves towards the visibility that is not yet—moves towards the world and towards the last day at one and the same time—moves towards the resurrection of the dead.[1] In thus stretching forward, the Word shows itself as the creative Word from the beginning. What the Word says comes to be when its voice goes forth. For that reason, faith when it is tried can lean entirely on the Word, as the most dependable thing in all the world.

[1] The continuation of the quotation we have just made from Luther is striking. 'For we do not immediately become spiritual by baptism so that sight might be ours, but in order that we might believe. For if I accept baptism and the Lord's Supper I receive eternal baptism and eternal food in the same life. In the flesh I believe, I was baptized' (*WA* 36, 667.5-8). The duality of the Word and the *Parousia*, of faith and sight, shapes the line of thought.

XIII

THE DOWNFALL OF SATAN

1. Conflict with Satan is vital to preaching

It is important that we should adopt a sufficiently radical view of preaching, the *kerygma*, and keep clearly in mind the wide embrace of the history of redemption. Preaching is the link between Christ's resurrection and our own. 'Man after preaching' is, accordingly, the man of the last day, not just the man who goes home with new resolutions after Sunday's worship. The latter is always in need of fresh preaching, both of the law and the Gospel, but the former is at last beyond the double Word; he has attained to sight. He alone it is who, in the exact meaning of the word, lives the life of the restored man, for he alone definitely lives after the fall of Satan, the final event with which the end of preaching is bound up. Till then the battle continues, till then preaching goes on.

The double sentence that 'Satan has been conquered and will be conquered' has, in its essential meaning, far-reaching significance. The sentence is not really in the least paradoxical. Only he who believes that conflict is just picture language and not actuality, and who argues that time must be left out of consideration, talks about 'paradox' in the case of such two-sided statements as we have just now made. If one is aware what conflict is, and what time is, one perceives that the inner unity between the two parts of the double sentence is ordinary and simple: the enemy is struck down by concentrations of forces with pauses between —the certainty that he shall be destroyed is founded on the message that he has been struck down. But so far as man is concerned, the two-sided sentence must imply that he already possesses something, since the victory *has been* won, but also that he is still lacking something, since the victory *will be* won. Briefly, what has already been accomplished and what is still awaited may be summed up thus: in the Word the forgiveness of sins is bestowed, but the resurrection from the dead belongs to the future. Forgiveness and the resurrection belong together, both are moments in Satan's downfall and in the restoration of the life of man.

We shall come back presently to the inner connexion between these moments. Here our first concern is to stress the fact that the background to both these ideas, and indeed to the whole faith of the early Church without exception, is a deep-rooted certainty that the whole world of men lies in the hands of an enemy of humanity. Jesus shared this view of life; so, too, did the first preachers, and the Church of the early centuries. In the sixteenth century, as soon as the content of the Scriptures was able to push aside the philosophy that stood in its way and stifled its voice, the same view of life as 'antagonism' emerged from the Biblical texts, and taught the men of that time to recognize once more the marks of the opposing powers in the conflict of which the Bible spoke. It would be totally impossible to revive the message of the Scriptures at all—for any generation in any century—if first of all it was desired to cut away belief in conflict, in demons, and in victory as too 'primitive' and 'superstitious'. It is only the perspective that opens out when one penetrates deeply into what is involved in the conflict that gives definite meaning to talk about Christ and his work for man's redemption. Until then it is rather inevitable that we should slip into talking about 'Christianity' and its 'major significance'.[1] About this latter the Bible does not concern itself, nor had the Reformers any primary interest in that question.

The theme of conflict, which we have stressed on many occasions, runs like a scarlet thread through the Bible. Recent study especially has urged upon us the role of the 'enemies' in Israel's view of life and has brought belief in creation, the cult, and messianism into relationship with that. The work of creation is carried through in struggle against the powers that promote chaos and death.[2] The final execution of God's creative work takes place in Christ; around Christ, therefore, opposition gathers. In Christ's death Satanic power puts forth, as never before in the history of the world, a supreme effort and there results, therefore,

---

[1] It is distressing how often the modern preacher begins by talking about 'Christianity' instead of about God, the Word, faith, unbelief, sin, etc. The term 'Christianity' is totally unkerygmatic in substance, and we might risk putting forward the somewhat rash thesis that it has nothing to do with the pulpit. Its rightful place is in an academic lecture or an educational talk. Preaching must be the voice of the Scriptural passage, not above it, not setting out to make analysis beyond what the passage has to say.

[2] It is of great significance theologically that the story of creation in Genesis has *nothing* at all to say about the powers of chaos being overcome by the creation of the Word itself. Instead God's *Word* is the sovereign Word, which creates and establishes all things. Even the beings who afterwards fall into sin are created by God through his Word. It is striking that Barth regards sin as a chaos-power that was in existence even before the Fall, and showed itself even at the creation of the world.

an exhaustion of the enemy's resources and—since this Chosen One holds his ground and cuts his way through—a wound that cannot be healed is inflicted on the body of him who is beaten, which is a sentence of death on the evil will. We can sin still, even after Christ's resurrection, but sin is without hope of success. The evil opposition that surrounds Jesus is the same as that which through all its history was opposed to Israel and whose ultimate intention remained the same from beginning to end: the bringing to nought of God's redemptive plan for the race of man as a whole. The inner unity of the enemy powers that is described in the Bible is a direct result of faith in Christ as the Saviour of the *world* and cannot be detached from that faith in Christ, cannot be a peripheral appendix to Christian faith. If the redemptive power is universal, so also is the corrupting power universal. God and Satan are both present, both active, in Adam's creation, in his temptation and fall, just as they are right through Israel's outward and inward history till the cross and the resurrection of Christ. They are both present and both active in the present-day life of every man on earth. They will both still be active in the time of agony, which is the end of world history. But at that point comes the end of their shared activity. After that the Devil's time is over and God becomes 'all in all' (I Cor. 15.28). Therewith sin and death are driven out of the creation.

2. Preaching is the restoration of nature

The idea of conflict with Satan is something that is pretty familiar from our foregoing discussion. So too, at an earlier stage, we have often emphasized that Christ's work restores creation to its original purity. Corruption came with the entry of the hostile element: victory over the hostile element is redemption and, as such, redemption is the free forward surge of the pure and fresh work of creation. Since we said just now that Christ's victory has both taken place and will take place, we can only affirm that it is a process now going on, a movement that has begun, with the future as its goal. The race of man is rising from the mud; on the last day what still remains of redemption will be ours. Then we shall have reached a point which will be beyond the position we held when first created. For apart from sin—whose gradual expulsion involves a wider prospect for the future—creation in its beginning, though, of course, pure, had in addition its own settled destiny, a divine command to become something more, something different from what it already was. That follows from the description of God as the One who continually creates anew, as the active and living God, the God of the long series of historical acts. That conviction has left its stamp on the accounts in the first chapters of Genesis as they now stand: each sentence bears witness that what is described is regarded as a beginning, a start, meant from the first to become more, to grow.

In Jesus, 'primeval time' and 'Paradise' advance. That is expressed in literary forms in many ways, for the New Testament Scriptures are rich in parallels between the event of Christ and the first creation. Not only the eschatological future, but that which has taken place and is taking place provides parallels indicating a return to the time before Adam's sin. Even now Christ is the unsullied presence of the original life. If the Old Testament is compared on this point with the New, the contrast will be found striking. The New Testament knows that it is living in the time of fulfilment and the fulfilment is the 'rule' or 'kingdom', that is to say, the downfall and break-up of the evil power—the journey of the world of man back to its primeval purity, or its journey forward to the coming and eternal purity, whichever we will. One thing that could and actually did happen in the days of the original purity cannot happen in the time of eternal purity—the fall of man. They who are saved from Satan are saved for all eternity. They have definitely attained the goal that God in the beginning set for the first man, life without disobedience and without corruption. Christ's ministry is to restore, within the framework of this incomplete human life, the race of man to its innocence, and to cancel the fall and guilt. He discharged that ministry by living a human life; he discharges it now by dwelling in the Word. Daily he enters the human conflict by speaking and by making himself heard by human ears.

Some of the New Testament examples of the concept of restoration deserve to be more fully quoted. It may well be that there is a definite theological idea behind the order in which the material in Matthew, Mark, and Luke is arranged, according to which at the very beginning of his ministry Jesus was subjected to temptation. That temptation must be seen in the context of the history of redemption as an example of the Devil's attack on God's plan to save the world and humanity. Other Satanic attempts to overthrow God's plan will follow in later chapters of the Gospels—for example, Peter's inclination to protect Jesus from suffering (Mark 8.33). Just before and during the crucifixion the tempter put forth his utmost efforts but, as in the desert, was repulsed. What was at stake in this conflict was the destiny of all mankind: through the fall the Devil had brought man into his control. Jesus' birth and ministry

were in themselves a threat to that unnatural order, for they meant the
return of the pure creation and as such were the object for attack and
had to take place in the face of continual difficulty, disturbances and
opposition. In the stories of Jesus' childhood opposition plays an essential role; at the same time, however, opposition to Jesus leads to the
fulfilment of God's will (Matt. 2), just as later in the case of his death
on the cross (see Acts 4.27 f.). As for the temptation in the wilderness,
the central fact there is that Jesus was the Victor in his temptation.
Therein lies the contrast to what happened to Adam, who, on the
contrary, was conquered in his temptation. The fundamental Biblical
contrast between Adam and Christ (e.g. Rom. 5.12-21) lies hidden in
the stories of how Jesus was tempted in the wilderness and emerged
victorious. Goppelt[1] attaches a certain significance to the special way in
which Luke links the genealogical table (Luke 3.23-38) with the story of
the temptation (Luke 4.1-13). The genealogical table leads us right back
to 'Adam who was the son of God' (Luke 3.38); then immediately it is
said that Jesus was led out into the wilderness to be tempted (Luke 4.1).
That Jesus accomplishes redemption by conquering in temptation is a
common thought in the New Testament (see Heb. 2.10-18; cf. 'obedience' in Rom. 5.19; Phil. 2.8; Heb. 5.8 f.). It is not specifically Pauline
to think of redemption in the category 'Adam-Christ', but is fairly
general within the Early Church. The victory of Christ in his temptations is the downfall of Satan and *eo ipso* the restoration of the life of
man, that is to say, its redemption, its salvation.

Further, a concrete example of a similar line of thought may now be
followed out at length—that is, the passage about the so-called 'miracle
of tongues' in Acts 2.1-42. The preaching at Pentecost is typical *kerygma*:
it concerns 'God's mighty acts' (Acts 2.11). The kernel of the story is
that all who hear, from whichever of earth's many nations they come,
understand the message.[2] This is a miracle, and the miracle is identical
with the fact of Pentecost—that is to say, that Christ has died and risen
again (that Easter has taken place) and that the *Spirit* has come. When
Christ underwent baptism and conquered, something happened that
touches all men and not just the Jews. The time for preaching, the time
for mission, must, accordingly, begin. So the time of the Spirit has
come. The Spirit and the Gospel belong indissolubly together, and their
times are identical. In the outgoing missionary preaching, which reaches

[1] L. Goppelt, *Typos*, 1939, pp. 140 f.
[2] The account in Acts is of an entirely different phenomenon from that of the
'speaking with tongues' that Paul mentions in I Cor. 14.2 ff. The latter is not
speech directed to man, and is not understood without being specially interpreted.

the nations and is understood by them, the Spirit is present. And where the Spirit is, there the last days have begun.[1] Preaching constitutes a link in the chain of events whose end and meaning is the resurrection of the dead. Pentecost is the bursting of Israel's small frame, which must take place since Christ has risen again. Preaching is the expansion towards the *Parousia*, which is approaching *via* the onward-marching *kerygma*. Preaching is the return of 'primeval history', the history of humanity; therefore all races suddenly understand the Word.[2] For long had Satan been unconquered, and the creative Word locked up in one single little nation, which had once been chosen for the salvation of mankind. But now the conquest has been won and the fetters of the Word have been cut away in an uncontrollable act of expansion, 'a sound like the rush of a mighty wind' (Acts 2.2). Soon sin will be wholly abolished, soon hate between the nations will be blown away and the fractures in the world of men healed. In the miracle of Pentecost the confusion of tongues after the tower of Babel begins to lose its power. Christ leads men back to their first purity, before the entry of sin. His new humanity has not yet fully attained to the health of creation; there remains much conflict and self-denial before the goal is reached, before the final 'miracle of tongues' happens. For the final miracle is the song of the company 'from every nation, from all tribes and peoples and tongues' (Rev. 7.9). When that song is sung, the poison of sin will have been expelled out of God's creation. Satan's fall means the restoration of the life of man.

We shall only refer to one further example here; it has a certain interest because Luther's ideas on 'growth' easily fit into this setting. Now that Christ has risen from the dead, the world of men is to partake in his victory and, therefore, the *kerygma* goes forth and preachers are sent out. This emerges not only from the Lucan account in Acts, with which we have just dealt, but also from what corresponds to this in St John's Gospel (John 20.19-23). Jesus bestows the Spirit and sends forth his envoys, who have power to loose and bind, with the Word. The Spirit is given by Jesus' breathing upon his disciples, as the Creator gave life to Adam by breathing into his nostrils the breath of life (Gen. 2.7). The parallel is conscious: through Christ the new creation takes place.

---

[1] After the death of the prophets Israel no longer has the Spirit. Judaism looked forward towards the messianic age as the time when the Spirit would be given anew. When Christ gives the Spirit, that means that the last times have broken in.

[2] Possibly faith in a coming common speech (a cancellation of the confusion of tongues after the fall of the tower of Babel in Gen. 11.1-9) was even in the days of Israel a part of the expectation of the future kingdom of peace.

The Word and the Spirit always constitute a unity in Biblical thought. In the most primitive parts this unity is thought of as both coming out of the mouth at the same time—when anyone speaks breath streams out along with the words. In the New Testament, however, this unity is due to the fact that the Spirit from God and Christ is at work wherever the Gospel is heard and received in faith. Luther's conviction that the Spirit is the Spirit of the Scriptures and is not given apart from the Scriptures is, indeed, a manifestation of a genuinely Biblical—one is tempted to say: unalloyed Semitic—line of thought. He who attends to the outward Word in faith, listens to that which sounds from the mouth of God, has also the Spirit. He who departs from the Word to burrow into his own soul's 'experiences' goes away from the Spirit. When, in Genesis, it is sometimes said that God creates through his Word, sometimes that he creates by breathing in the breath of life, both expressions mean basically the same thing: man owes his life to that which comes from the mouth of God (Deut. 8.3; Matt. 4.4). When, in the New Testament, it is sometimes said that preaching, that is to say, the Word, began at Pentecost and sometimes that the Spirit was given at Pentecost, both expressions mean basically the same thing: both imply that creative work has begun anew and is spreading among the prisoners, among men who are waiting.[1] If these two basic facts of Early Christian experience—the clear call and challenge of the *kerygma* on the one side, and the outpouring of the Spirit on the congregations, which were growing more numerous, on the other—are too rigidly separated from each other, then the *kerygma* is intellectualized and the Spirit is sentimentalized. The creative power in the Word and the Spirit is drained away. Because it is filled with the Spirit the Word has a determination in itself, an inner impulse to go out into the world and to refashion the world. From that comes missionary power. After Satan's fall in Christ's death and resurrection, the *kerygma* must go out for the restoration of the life of man.

3. The forgiveness of sins and the resurrection of the dead

The part of the New Testament that comes to mind most readily when one thinks about the 'breathing in' of the breath of life in Gen. 2.7 is, however, not John 20.22, but, of course, I Cor. 15.45-47, about the

---

[1] Even when Jesus spoke, before his death, the Spirit was there (see Luke 4.18-21; John 6.63). But the sending forth to the nations of the world took place only after Christ's death and resurrection, for only then was the troubler and corrupter of those same peoples beaten down.

first Adam as a 'living being' and the last Adam as a 'life-giving Spirit'. There again we have the creative character of Christ: he makes alive, from him goes forth the life-giving Spirit. What is decisive for Paul and what he stresses is, however, the *difference* between Adam and Christ, between the man with a soul and the man with the Spirit. 'But it is not the spiritual which is first but the physical, and then the spiritual. The first man was from the earth, a man of dust: the second man is from heaven.' What takes place in Christ corresponds to what took place in Adam, but at the same time it implies a heightening and an enhancement. Christ does not simply restore what Adam lost, but gives something that did not exist in the first and original creation, not even in its unbeflecked purity. Luther, moreover, in his exegesis of the passage, points out, often in wholly different contexts, that the enhancement, 'the growth', with which we are concerned here, has not to do with the fact that Adam was sinful while Christ was righteous.[1]

In the stories of the temptations and in Rom. 5.13-21, a direct contrast between Adam and Christ is referred to. The former brought sin and death into the world of men, the latter righteousness and life. Since a contrast does exist between Adam and Christ, it is possible to regard Christ's work as simply a return to the original situation: when a stain has been removed completely what has thus been cleaned is exactly what it was at the first. But to think like this is to leave out the active God who creates and remoulds. Luther holds that time—'the history of redemption'—and enhancement belong to God's purpose from the beginning, since God is what he is. Man is destined to grow, to develop, by receiving without intermission from the hands of God. Adam, had he not fallen, would have developed more and more and at last would have received the heavenly life in the Spirit. But now, in addition, there is the fact that Adam was overthrown by Satan and that Christ's conquest, which casts down the corrupting power, only little by little and in stages gains control in man. So then conflict and the growth that belonged even to creation in its purity are intertwined. Man looks forward in hope to the restored human life of the last day which, when it arrives, will be richer than it ever was.

And yet it will be the same as it was from the beginning, for even then it was a growing life, destined to journey forward in the power of the Creator. So long as sin remains in man and conflict against it exists, so long will an element ravage within him that is destructive of human life and he will remain in a state foreign to humanity. Even the presence

[1] *WA* 36, 665.5-11, 666.8-10, 671.7-11; 42, 49.8-13; Rörer MS.

of death in its outward form is a sign that something is lacking in the restoration of the life of man. This last enemy too must be deprived of its power (in the resurrection of the dead) before the creation can be regarded as fully whole. Faith is, accordingly, the beginning of man's attainment of manhood's estate, for faith means that Satan is giving ground in his heart. The Word penetrates, nourishes faith, and puts the enemy to flight. Grace does not raise man above nature, but grace is the forgiveness of sins. We might without any hesitation replace the difference between 'the natural' and 'the supernatural' by a difference of intention between 'nature' (God's undamaged work in his creation) and 'the unnatural' (the Devil's work in God's creation) and say, as a consequence, that grace restores nature and brings the unnatural to nought. As far as terminology goes, however, we should not in that case have the support of Luther, for he, unfortunately, continued to use a terminology that is misleading by describing the *sinful* man as the 'natural' man. We are abandoning this conventional and somewhat questionable usage, so that we may be free to take a truly radical view of sin and not fall into a superficial and optimistic 'first-article religion' along the lines of the Enlightenment. Only the man who rises at the last day is wholly natural and pure. By *dying*, and not just by going out into the life of the world, he reaches that point. The dominion of the enemy is so firmly imposed on us that the one enemy must attack the other and drown him before we can be fully freed from the hold of them both.[1] Death and sin are both God's opponents—but one of them, sin, which is first and the cause of death, is attacked first, and is struck down partly with the help of the other, death. For the killing of the old man is, in reality, not death but life, a real giving of life *sub contraria specie* which goes on till bodily death, that is, in the time of the cross on earth. After that God's other opponent, death, shall be destroyed too and life will spring up in the *Parousia*. Therewith Satan's whole tyranny shall be broken, and man shall be free.[2]

In what we have just said the theological relation between the two

---

[1] It should be noted that it is *man* who is evil. The creation apart from man has been cursed for man's sake (Gen. 3.17 ff. and Rom. 8.19 ff.), but it has not fallen. The creation has been destined to be the servant of man, but is now purer than man is. Sin strikes man when he turns inward to his own heart, not first of all when he moves outward towards things (cf. Mark 7.15-23).

[2] *Vis à vis* the creation apart from man, the consummation implies at one and the same time restoration and elevation. Man will then rule over all the other creatures as Adam was ordered to do (Gen. 1.26, 28), but that too will be enhanced. 'Then it shall be that all the other creatures will be *more* subject to us than they were in Paradise to Adam' (Luther, *WA* 42, 48.30-31). From such thoughts sprang the concept of chiliasm in the Early Church.

items that are brought together in the third article of the Apostles'
Creed, the forgiveness of sins and the resurrection of the dead, stands
out clearly. For later theology it would scarcely have seemed so self-
evident that the forgiveness of sins should come at the end of a creed
and in such obviously eschatological surroundings, where all has its
climax in the concept of 'eternal life'. In the Early Church, on the contrary, such a position was readily acceptable. The two divisions in the
Satanic kingdom were sin and death. Sin—transgression, defeat in temptation—was what was primary, and on that followed death (Gen. 2.17;
Rom. 5.12). When Satan's fall comes, and man is again released, the
order is the same. So first of all the bond of sin around man is cut away
and then the bond of death. The former takes place in the forgiveness
of sins, the latter in the resurrection of the dead. When that has taken
place, the healthy life of creation will have returned and cannot again
be damaged, for it will have returned as life eternal. When seen in this
perspective of redemptive history, the forgiveness of sins and the resurrection of the dead are both actions in the conflict, grapplings with an
antagonist. While they are concerned with human beings they are also
divine blows against the enemy, who is God's enemy and man's enemy
at the same time. Otherwise we easily slip into the way of making a
contrast between God and man in thinking of such matters, so that
these two alone stand over against each other as if there were no enemy
dominion. In that case forgiveness brings consolation to man in his
guilt, the resurrection adds a miraculous supernatural addition to the
ordinary life of man. But in fact, forgiveness destroys the tyrant who
causes the guilt—the Accuser, Satan, the Devil—and hunts him out of
the conscience, cleanses man's conscience from the army of evil spirits;
and the resurrection drives out the same usurper from the body. Life
now, and the life of the resurrection, are in every way *the same life*—
just as life before and after forgiveness is one and the same human life:
in the first case it is life lived with a tyrant, in the second without him.
Oppression, then, is rendered void by degrees, in stages, in a history
that takes time. So Christian life maintains a faith in something that
happened, and a hope of something that has yet to happen.

But forgiveness is not simply an act of war with one objective; it
cannot be understood if it is viewed only as an attack on the kingdom of
Satan. Forgiveness of sins is the removal of guilt, and guilt has its roots
in God's judgement and wrath. There is a unique inner unity between
the dominion of the Devil and God's wrath. The law is God's law, and
yet it holds man accusingly in the power of God's enemy. 'The sting of

death is sin, and the power of sin is the law' (I Cor. 15.56). Satan and
the law accompany one another in attack and accusation, in the conscience as well as at the last day. For this reason the work of Jesus is
not simply directed against man's enemy, but at the same time against
God himself—in his agony in Gethsemane, as in his heavenly intercession (Rom. 8.34; Heb. 7.25 and 9.24; I John 2.1). Since guilt, even
under the old covenant, was recognized as the inmost point in Israel's
corruption, the prophets recognized forgiveness as the only possible
starting point and foundation for redemption. Forgiveness is the threshold of the new day 'in which the creation returns to its origin', the day
of redemption, the messianic age (Hos. 14.5-8; Isa. 53.4 f.; Jer. 31.34;
Ezek. 36.25-30). When Jesus came and with power and humility bestowed forgiveness, which until then no prophet dared to do, or was
able to do, that unheard-of claim was felt as somehow blasphemous:
the dominion of the law had fallen and was shivered in pieces in forgiveness, that is, in Christ (see, e.g., Luke 5.21).

At this point we ought to summarize the general view of the Spirit
in the New Testament. In the Gospel and in faith the Spirit is given as
a 'first fruits', a 'pledge' of something that will be given later (II Cor.
1.22 and 5.5). What will be bestowed later is the rescue of the *body*.
'And not only the creation, but we ourselves, who have the first fruits
of the Spirit, groan inwardly as we wait for adoption as sons, the
redemption of our bodies' (Rom. 8.23). Even now the Spirit struggles
against the enemy who still dwells within us (Gal. 5.17), but the Spirit
will eventually conquer, and conquest in the ethical struggle is the
resurrection of the dead. Then the Spirit will have control, and from
faith and conscience where he formerly was and ruled he will have
penetrated to the body, into the limbs, where the law of sin formerly
ruled (Rom. 7.22-25). Then all, the whole man, will be dominated by
the Spirit, who will drive out his enemies, sin and death, from the
human field, so that only life will remain and the resurrection thus
become accomplished fact (Rom. 8.11; cf. I Cor. 15.44).

Luther in his teaching about the law and the Gospel brings out this
Early Christian view of the history of redemption in an unusual manner,
by making a distinction between the conscience and the body.[1] In the
time of faith the Gospel rules in the conscience, while the body, bound
by the law, sojourns in the world of toil and the cross. Forgiveness has
taken place and takes place daily, but the resurrection has not yet taken
place; the old Adam still awaits his death and must be disciplined, must

[1] E.g. *WA* 40(I), 213.30-214.21, and 469.23-27.

taste wrath. But in the resurrection the body will experience what the conscience can experience in forgiveness. Foreign dominion will be broken even in the limbs of man for all to see. Then we shall not need to restrict ourselves to believing and to hearing Christ's dominion, but there he will be King before our eyes. For then the Satanic power will be at an end, and man will be free. But until then man, to be man, must live by listening to the Word of the kingdom—or, in other words, he must live in the Church.

XIV

THE COMMUNION OF SAINTS

1. Christian fellowship is natural fellowship

HERE we are quite definitely taking up our stand in the situation that exists *before* the consummation. We are not fixing our attention on the last day, but instead we are going right down into the conflict that is taking place in this earthly life. There is, however, one bond of union between the section that is now beginning and that just ended: they both concern the restoration of man. The fellowship of the Church is the fellowship of the natural life—is, it might be said, the healthiness of the life of man.[1] The communion of saints pulsates and expresses itself in the neighbourly relations that arise, and are called for, in our worldly callings. The attempt to set a low value on these bonds of fellowship, which are imposed by the Creator, in favour of others in which 'spirituality' becomes visible unfailingly leads away from the fellowship of the Church to that of a sect. In that case a claim is made to sight, which means that *hearing* is done away, that 'journeying' and 'listening' are not regarded as constitutive of Christian life. The central place, on the contrary, is taken by 'having' and 'knowing'—a certainty has crept in that is not the certainty of the Word but of religious experience. Immediately this latter certainty holds the field, the communion of saints is broken up and the fellowship of the group replaces that of the Church. In what remains of this chapter we shall turn our attention to the firm bond between the communion of saints and the Word.

Ebeling points out that it was a wholly new feature in the tradition of the interpretation of the Gospels when Luther, preaching on the story of the lame man, interpreted the words, 'Rise, take up your bed and go home' (Matt. 9.6), to mean that the man who was healed, his sins being forgiven, was sent back to the tasks of his job, his calling. The individual Christian is hidden in the commonplace tasks of his work, which are

---

[1] For this reason Christian fellowship is without a programme and is hidden in the commonplace. Christian fellowship cannot become a 'movement' marked off from others by the distinction between those who are members and those who are not.

without the sheen of holiness or glory.[1] In this way God's children until the end of the world have their battlefield—where the conflict is neither 'watched' nor 'seen', but has got to be *fought through*, as just something human and without glory. They meet for worship and there receive the Gospel, the Word of forgiveness, but disperse afterwards to many tasks, and out there in all sorts of places each has to take his stand and hold himself in readiness for temptation. And when they are thus sent out to their different occupations it is God's orders which thus send them out: 'Rise . . . and go home.'[2]

If those who believe were only to be brought together and formed into a group, that would mean giving up all those battlefield positions out in God's created world and would involve an egocentric concentration on the saving of their own souls. Then creation and redemption would not be one work but two, and two entirely different from each other. Then the world would never be born anew, but redemption would be redemption out of the world, out of the profane sphere, and this latter would be unredeemed, corrupted and given up by all the pious to become a haunt of the ungodly.

Jesus' action in sending the man whom he had healed back home fits into a larger New Testament setting which is possibly more easily des-

---

[1] Cf. Luther in 1528: 'When he has healed him what does he order him to do? He does not tell him to go into a cell or to flee the society of men. But he orders him to do those tasks that a holy man won't look at. . . . The tasks that Christians do have no glory. Who could not arise, take up his bed and go home? Dogs can get up, horses can carry men. But he does this very thing that men might truly know the glory of their tasks. Perhaps he was a father of a family. So he says to him, "It is not for you to fast; go home, see to your affairs and think what task is to be done." Thus servants and maids, if they do what they have to do, do the best thing they can. But the world does not believe that, but says "We take a poor view of that . . . if anything is very special, *that* is valuable. It isn't of any importance to be a prince, or a father of a family, for there is no glory there." But those are wise Christians who know it is of no importance what glory tasks have' (*WA* 27, 381.7-19 (Rörer MS).

[2] Luther continues: ' "Here you have heaven and eternal life through me, because I forgive your sins. Go away, do good, but first believe, be of good cheer, your sins are forgiven you, then take your bed, go to your house and do what you did before." He does not tell him to go into the desert nor does he impose any other tasks on him but says, "Go home and do what is to be done at home." . . . So let me do what my ministry lays upon me. My tasks fall to me there as to that paralytic to whom God said "Arise . . ." No one believes that he has been told by God to do such things. It comes into his mind "I should be holy", and he seeks other tasks. So he fasts and goes away from home, looks for other tasks and thinks thereby to become holy. We ought to give thanks that we have attained to this light that before faith and the forgiveness of sins all works are right out of the question, but that afterwards it is "Go home to your house"—that is, when you have been justified and believe in Christ, remain in that station in which you were before.' The last sentence refers to I Cor. 7.20 as the starting point for a doctrine of vocation.

M

cribed in negative than in positive categories.[1] All of us, who have been
brought up in the religious individualism of the last centuries, often fail
to observe one characteristic feature of the Gospels: we never hear how
it afterwards befell all those men with whom Jesus met and dealt or to
whom he spoke. Every man who has breathed ever so little the atmosphere of romanticism and revivalism carries about with him an almost
ineradicable need to regard his relation to God as 'the history of the
soul'—a religious development of at least a few stages, either as a slow
emancipation as a personality is shaped, or as an act of grace effected by
the Church. Of this there is not a trace in the New Testament. Certainly
Jesus said to some, 'Follow me' (e.g. Mark 1.17; 2.14; John 1.43; 21.19 f.);
some were thus taken away from the circles in which they had worked
until then and became, in a special way, disciples and apostles with tasks
unique to them. But not even in their case is there a trace of 'the story
of their souls'. If something is told of them it is because some action or
other of theirs was important for the Church. Not even the deaths of
the leaders are regularly recorded. What biographical *lacunae* there are!
Life's scroll is unrolled before our eyes, but we stand there with our
questions about 'what followed'—and time and again the sources are
silent when we expect them to speak. The silence of the New Testament
is a witness that points in the same direction as the word to the lame
man: 'Rise . . . go home.'

In an anti-liberal epoch which sets out to campaign against the nineteenth-century cult of personality there is a certain temptation to make
something anti-human out of this feature of the New Testament that we
have mentioned, by taking it as the starting point for a general denigra-
tion of man and, with a sort of brutal joy, expatiating on man's insignifi-
cance in the eyes of God. But such slandering of man certainly finds no
place at all in the New Testament. Man is precious and sought for by
God. For the redemption of humanity God's only Son is given and
sacrificed (John 3.16). The sinner is plainly called a sinner, but he sins
because he corrupts his human life instead of living it. Redeemed life is
human life, restored and healthy. Modern theological perversions of the
concept of redemption make it possible to talk pathetically about 'redemption' and in the same breath to talk bitterly and negatively about
man as man—redemption belongs only to God and the divine does not

---

[1] In the stories of other miracles of healing, there are to be found what correspond to Jesus' words to the lame man, e.g. Mark 5.18 f.; 5.34; 8.26; Matt. 8.13
among others. The most expressive among them is the saying about the bringing
to life of the son of the widow of Nain: ' . . . and he gave him to his mother'
(Luke 7.15; cf. I Kings 17.23). See also Mark 1.44.

affect the human. Docetism's ancient chasm blocks the way. Such a combination of ideas bears the marks of the nineteenth century. It is certainly not Early Christian in origin, just as little as it is Reformed. But if man in the New Testament is the object of God's care and of the work of Christ, how does it come about that what happens to him after meeting with Christ leaves no traces in the stories of the Gospels? Why the same invariable phenomenon that men are healed and then disappear into the crowd? Had it been the intention of Jesus to gather a group about him, its origin, its meeting together, and its growth would be an important part of the report in the Gospels of his work, and in every case the silence about 'what followed', as well as the fact that he sent home those who had been healed, would be somewhat difficult to explain.

Behind these peculiarities of the New Testament, however, there may be an important and simple conviction, which is not only to be found in the Early Church but belongs to the Bible as a whole, though missing in all the religious 'movements' that the last few centuries in Europe have thrown up—the conviction that *life as life* is the creation of God. That spiritual life is an ongoing work of God is stressed by many, has indeed become almost a slogan, but man is thought to have the ordinary outward life in himself; it is a raw material, which, as such, is undetermined and empty, but *out of which* something can be made if it is fashioned aright. Where such a conviction prevails there are only two forms of spiritual fellowship that can be envisaged—the sect and the authoritarian church. In the sect those who have common experiences in life are united, and in the fellowship of the sect, which is built up from below, their souls are moulded into the pattern approved by the fellowship. In the shelter of the authoritarian church, too, those are gathered together who do not wish to build up a fellowship from below but regard that life alone as right that is guided and directed from above by the ecclesiastical institution acting with the authority attaching to its office. Neither of these two spiritual types takes the idea seriously that the life of man itself has any meaning. In both cases they want to take life in hand, to take the raw material in hand and make something of it. For that reason *law* rules in both: religion puts pressure on the created world.[1] But the Gospel's inmost presupposition is that life is a work of

[1] If life is regarded as raw material and 'Christianity' as shaping the raw material, then all is under *law*. We must sometimes wonder if law has not too strong a hold even on the men of our day, indeed, if much of the hatred of Christianity is not the result of the tyranny of law in men's consciences. Luther, who himself was brought up at a time that led him to regard his life as material

God before man makes anything out of it and that therefore, because it is created, because it issues from God's hands, it *has* meaning. Sin and death are a disturbance of life's original meaning. Christ's Word, Christ's healing of sickness, Christ's death and resurrection, destroy the disturber and thereby the original meaning is restored. Nothing needs to be made *out of* him who is healed—he is, indeed, healed, healthy; he has already got his place and his station where meaning lies waiting for him. So: 'Rise . . . and go home.'

What the New Testament says of man's transformation into the image of Christ must not be confused with the tendency to which we have just referred, to regard man's life as raw material which has got to be given a form by Spirit. The latter viewpoint, which has its origins in Scholastic thought and, further back, in Greek philosophy, is based on the conviction that opposition exists between matter and spirit, and that they are different in value. The New Testament, on the contrary, reckons on a conflict between God, the Spirit, and a power that twists both matter *and* spirit, body *and* soul—that is, the whole man. This hostile power is not moulded at all by God but is destroyed and cast into the burning pit (Rev. 20.10, 14). When that happens man will definitively be *free*. The whole emphasis is laid on freedom. He who is free through forgiveness 'grows' certainly, journeys to 'God's image', that is, he is moulded—but it is just into *man* that he is moulded. To be born, to be baptized, to believe, to confess, to work, to die, to rise again, all these belong together. All the time *man* is coming into existence. The chasm between spiritual and profane that marks both the Roman Church and the sects cannot appear here. What is sinful still exists—and the root of that is always in men's hearts and not in what lies without—but there is nothing that is profane. The whole concept of the profane is unchristian and misleading. Out of that springs the ecclesiastical bullying of human life, that unjustified pressure that claims the right to mould men, which without the least doubt is one of the greatest hindrances to the Gospel in the present situation of the West.

2. The Christian mission involves an open Church

What we have just said has the most far-reaching consequences for

to be shaped by religion, found release in *faith* from the foolish and false question about the right way to shape it, the right 'works'. This is why he could say, for example, of a child that had been baptized that it had *faith*. Put concisely: the child has faith for the child does not ask why he exists—only in baptism can Christ come freely as he wishes.

the concept of the Church and for our view of fellowship. We have
already seen how baptism and the Lord's Supper set man in social
fellowship with his neighbour, with his fellow-men. Just as Christ is
changed into us in the Lord's Supper, so we are changed into one
another. We are the recipients of each other's burdens and love, of each
other's sins and forgiveness; we become one body in him who was made
a sinner for us. The fellowship of the Lord's Supper is also a fellowship
of every day and of the body. The same also applies to baptism, whose
work takes place in the troubles of our calling, which bring about the
death of the old man as we listen to the life-giving Word. Those who
think that sanctification is something on its own, the work of one's
calling something else (which *also* has significance), ought not to claim
that they share Luther's view of vocation. The ecclesiastical revivalistic
movements in Scandinavia, which are characterized by a 'way-of-sal-
vation' mentality, have generally stressed the importance of fidelity in
one's calling, but this calling has no place in the 'order of grace'. One's
calling has one's *neighbour* in mind, while the 'order of grace' is concerned in principle with a man's *own* redemption and holiness. Luther's
conception of vocation breaks up the 'order of grace'. For Luther,
consequently, sanctification takes place *within* the work of one's calling;
an isolated 'special' sanctification, side by side with one's calling, is a
humbug, where it is nothing even worse.[1] The communion of saints
cannot be described in any other way than by describing a fellowship
where men, in the light of the Word, help each other to live the life of
man, which is one unified life, a life on earth even while journeying to
heaven. Where there is a wish to suppress and dub 'profane' those forms
of fellowship that lack connexion with the church building or the hour
of prayer, there the communion of saints is upset and harmed. He who
listens to the Word goes in the Word wherever he goes; he hears it
everywhere—just as he finds the enemy everywhere. The holy and the
evil have no defined boundaries; God and Satan do not live in different
spheres, but are in conflict—that is to say, they meet and clash in the
field of man's life. It is impossible for man in the days of faith, of the
Church, to have to do with God without at the same time, in some way,
having to do with the Devil.[2] These two, moreover, fill all existence.

[1] The search for an ethic that shall possess 'something special' outside one's
calling implies *opposition* to the love of one's neighbour, for it contains within
itself a wish for separation—that is, it has approved a certain religiosified egoism.
The man who succeeds ethically by travelling on that road becomes unclean;
they who fall and fail to succeed may, thanks to that, remain, to some extent,
healthy.

[2] Of the call and the cries of the Spirit in the heart Luther says: 'You are not,

But neither of them is profane. Neither allows anything to be profane, but all is qualified and is good or bad.

The life of man does not acquire a supernatural nature through the Church, but in the Church the life of man comes into being in the struggle of the Spirit against the powers that destroy it. The Christian congregation is the new *humanity*, whose life is the original life of creation and, as a consequence, the life of the resurrection that is drawing near. Where the Word is at work the end of the Creator's chain of events approaches, redemptive history widens out to take in the nations of the earth, who on the last day will stand waiting before Christ. It is important to determine here what is the right direction in which to move. Men should not be pressed to submit to an authoritarian church nor should they join a Christian sect. Rather is the Church to be looked on as an achievement of the *Word*, the creative Word which has been sent forth and is on the march. And this Word, the *kerygma*, moves towards humanity; mission is the unique event that is the distinguishing mark of the time of the Church. The Church's men are continually on the way towards the world's men. The congregation is humanity coming into existence; it exists for those who are without, just as Christ came into the world and died for the world. Thus it approaches the *Parousia*, the kingdom of God. The Church, regarded as a body of men, is to lose its life and thereby really *preach* as the *dying* Servant of the Lord. The Word reaches out as the congregation moves outwards and is ready to die in order to reach out.[1]

From this it is clear that mission is not to be regarded as a special piece of work supported by what Christians collect for it, a piece of work in a far-away land. In that case the 'friends of missions' can go about as strangers in their own town and there among the children of this world, with whom they have no fellowship and want none, earn money which they then give willingly to missions. That is a wrong

however, to expect that these cries should be quite alone and quite pure in you; a cry of murder will be there as well, for you experience that as others have done. Your sin will also cry out—that is, it will produce a sharp pain in your conscience. But the Spirit of Christ will and must cry louder than that cry—that is, he will give you comfort beyond your pain' (*WA* 10(I.1), 373.4-9).

[1] Israel began to realize its significance for the nations around through its exile and defeat, when it suffered and became 'a light to the Gentiles' as the Servant of the Lord. In Christ that is continued and fulfilled and the work still goes on; the absence of honour and glory (Isa. 53) in the Church of today could help the Word to advance if it were accepted with gladness and an end were made of looking for signs of coming success and of admiring Rome. According to Roman ideology the Church ought to have secular power. An evangelical Church that in its suffering looks admiringly towards Rome blocks up the sources of its own life.

meaning of mission. Missionary work is, of course, also to go on in far-off lands, but *all* mission must be rooted in the full responsibility of the Church for the world, conscious of being bound up with *every* heathen one meets. The Church lives at present in a phase of redemptive history that will pass away; she lives in order that the next phase, the consummation of all things, may come. The life of the Church is a movement towards humanity and therefore a movement forward in time. It is not her task to analyse the state of culture and to search for signs of a movement from without towards herself but her task is to *go* —to journey, to make a move herself from within outwards towards the world, towards the last day.

That involves, in turn, decisive consequences for determining the concept of one's *neighbour*. If one's neighbour is reckoned to be the Christian brother or the Christian sister, then faith in the presence of the creative God in the Word is cut short. Then love circulates within the Church body (*ecclesiola*). It is no longer of the very nature of the believing circle that it exists for the sake of the world. In that situation no missionary collections will succeed in avoiding the disjunction of such a congregation from the redemptive history of the living God: its members turn on principle in on themselves and not outwards towards mankind. Our neighbour is the man we meet and especially the man who needs our help—this simple definition must not be given up. One main object in such a definition is to hold the *Church open* and be an obstacle to any policy of shutting the door: *it is not intended* that we should be able to say who 'belongs to' the Church. Even if we were to succeed in tying them all up in a sack and counting those inside as saved we should also thereby—this we must recognize—succeed in silencing the Word of the living God, which is the basis of the Church.[1] A church with a membership is not a Church of the Word, even if within it Bible study is enthusiastically carried on and many sermons rich in Biblical language are to be heard and even if its membership increases every day. It is another principle than the Word on which, in that case, the church is built: the church is here basically regarded as a sect, perhaps a very strong sect with ninety-five per cent of the population within its walls, but still a sect with all the marks of a sect.

[1] It is an entirely different matter that, for example, not every one should have the right to vote in a Church election. That is a practical matter; the conditions for that can be laid down in the laws and orders relating to such an election. But it has nothing to do with the being and concept of the Church. There God's work through Word and sacrament must go forward, without being confused with the question of membership, which in this connexion is poisonous in its effect.

The conviction that we have a 'neighbour' would never have opportunity to arise in a Church so built up. Now, in the Bible one's neighbour is spoken of and, therefore, he is, of course, spoken of within the sectarian forms of Christianity (which are often very 'high Church')· But the full meaning of the word 'neighbour' can only become clear when the full meaning of God's work as Creator becomes clear.

The work of the Creator is not first of all God's work through the outward orders in the life of man, that is, through secular authority; although that divine work must certainly be borne in mind when we are talking about our neighbour. It is, rather, a matter of God's creative work through the Word, the Gospel—that Gospel which nourishes the Church, gives her life and lets her expand and grow. The Church can acquire stability and firmness through union with Christ, the Head, the Source of growth (Eph. 4.15 f.)—that is to say, the Church can acquire stability and growth through the Word and the sacraments, for therein lie the energies that build up, nourish and guide the Church. For this reason there is a *ministry* of the Word and Sacraments, whose duty it is to keep watch and to work in this matter. But the Church is *not* to have the stability and firmness that belongs to an association, nor has she ever had it in her best days. She is to be bound fast to the Word and the sacraments—and here the ministry of the Church has its responsibility —but outwards towards the world of men she is to be open. It is no part of the duty of a priest to know how many of his congregation are true Christians. If he is seized with curiosity about such matters he must immediately suppress the thought as a temptation. A congregation receives a deadly wound the moment it acquires the stability and firmness of an association. Without establishing boundaries with humanity the new humanity (the Church) journeys towards the last day and, therefore, towards 'the nations', towards 'the heathen'. Openness belongs to true firmness in this that the Word lives and creates, journeys in the direction of the consummation.[1] When the last day comes the Christians will not be found in one place, but where they work, where they live together with unbelievers (Matt. 24.40 f.). The Lord himself will separate them

---

[1] That the Early Church was a 'gathered church' is now very seldom argued. It is still customary to assert that the congregations on the mission field are normally of that nature. This argument should not be accepted until a searching investigation has been made of the relations between the modern missionary movement and Pietism, in order to discover the motivating ideas. If every conception of 'mission' has been shaped by people who even in their homelands were supporters of Congregationalism (*ecclesiola*), the argument loses its force. There is every reason to doubt that the congregations in the missionary areas of the Ancient Church were of a 'gathered' character.

out; in the time of the Church, of the Word, no separation takes place (Matt. 13.24-30, 37-43, 47-50).

3. The boundaries of the Church cannot be determined

Fellowship during the Church's time cannot be isolated from this secular and human fellowship of one's *calling*. The Church, if enquiry is made about her number, is hidden in the troubles of every day, in all occupations and concerns that must be carried on so that the life of man may continue. The calling that each man follows is the concrete form in which the law makes contact with his old man to discipline him. The time of the Church, too, is the time of *conflict*, which does not allow of any flight from the discipline of the law. Breaking away from one's earthly calling for self-chosen forms of fellowship that involve setting aside the relationships that bind men together, given in creation and continually renewed through the course of life, is a course always fraught with danger for the fellowship of the Church. The fellowship of a sect lifts men out of their setting and then cultivates an intense feeling of solidarity distinct from the contacts between men that the day's work brings. The fellowship of a sect empties normal life of content, but provides as a recompense a much richer solidarity within the group. The Church, on the contrary, has an essentially opposite intention: she possesses the divine Word and that is her sole holiness—but the Word cannot be locked up; its power must out, for it is the Word which created the world, the world now in thrall. This longing for what lies without is itself a demand to be allowed to journey towards sight, towards the *Parousia*, towards the inclusion of the body in the kingdom of the Spirit. For this reason the Church sends men *away from it*—'Rise . . . and go home'—sends them out to many occupations in the power of the forgiveness of sins, so that the life of man itself may grow healthy, so that the contacts between men out there in secular relationships may be between members of the same body, of Christ, members who serve one another (I Cor. 12.12). Throughout the Bible it is love for one's neighbour, uprightness in all one's dealings, that is the kernel of the message. No proposal for any social reform, or for any new type of society, is ever put forward. The very conception of ethical improvement, of improvement of life, apart from man's obedience to God's will in his own concrete relations with his neighbour is entirely absent. Out there in everyday intercourse between men lies the possibility of renewal of life.

If we stand elsewhere, we stand outside the possibility of being able to contribute towards the renewal of human society. Where his calling is shall each remain. There he stands beside his *neighbour*. 'Programmes' avail nothing if this place is abandoned. Satan keeps a grip on us till our last breath is drawn, but limits can be set to his progress if each one stands out there where he can alone be truly sanctified in the sanctification of every day by the Word, which passes over into our bodily death and eternal life, that is, into the downfall of Satan. The sect shuts its eyes to the fact that the Devil lives in us. It believes that he only lives in certain worldly men—another proof that the sect regards the end of redemptive history as already reached. The Church has not reached the point of Satan's downfall, but is on the way thither: so her life streams out to the peripheries of society, out to the many limbs, out to the centres of conflict. *Out there* everyone is to 'take up his cross' and follow Christ through death and resurrection (Mark 8.34). The cross is not a deduction of faith. The cross is found *out there*, just as one's neighbour is found out there. 'Each man will have to bear his own load' (Gal. 6.5). The question is not what my cross is, but—quite clearly—the question is whether I will take up my cross and bear it, or not. The question is not who my neighbour is, but—again quite clearly—whether I will bear his burdens, or not. When it is a matter of what is to be done, I am always referred to the world without, to what is insignificant. Christian fellowship must be open, must include our fellow-men, without questions of membership being raised or—as they now appear in all cases to be raised by some foolishly zealous person—without being answered.[1] Thus the fellowship is the fellowship of the *Church*, the fellowship of the Church of Christ in its forward march towards the last day.

This theological basis constitutes the inmost meaning of the conception of a *parish church*. Those who insist on talking about membership understand by the term 'parish church' that all who live within the confines of a parish belong to the church of that area. That means retaining a sectarian point of view but employing it quantitatively. In that

---

[1] It is of the utmost importance that they should really be left unanswered. No such answer 'Everybody' or 'All who are baptized' or 'All on the roll', etc., should be made. It is easy to be pressed into giving such answers in these days, which are dominated by the conception of membership. If such a reply is made, he who makes it shows himself to be of a sect, even if a lax one which makes few demands. The Church must, instead, be regarded as a work of the Christ who by the Word and sacraments marches forward in the world of men. It is necessary to drop this question of membership if the Word's creative and progressive character is not to be suppressed. The introduction of the question of membership implies that the Church is *static* in the world of men and, therefore, no longer the Church, but is departing from her task of being a 'phase' in redemptive history and of moving out towards the world. Thus she becomes authoritative, timeless, demanding and dead.

case the whole discussion about the Church becomes a discussion about *how many* belong to it. The question about the boundaries of the Church within the nation is, however, a question that takes us right away from the one point from which it may be discovered what the Church is— the Word. The Church of the Word is in a land when the occupants of the preaching ministry proclaim the Word in all its parishes, and it is a Church with local congregations. The local congregation is but an expression of the demand of the Word to have opportunity to *go forth*, of the intention of the Word to go to 'the nation'. The local congregation is no reply to the question about membership; it is rather the elimination of such a question. Here are the Word and sacraments; there lies the village with its people, a bit of the world, a bit of humanity—Christ must go through this whole village if he is to reach his goal, the *Parousia*. All in the village need not be true Christians for this goal to be reached. To make visible success belong to the forward march of the Word is foreign to the belief of the Early Church. What is important is that the Word should actually be proclaimed. The flock will be divided on the last day before the Throne, but it is only then that the division will become visible, not now in the day of the Word, of invisibility, of hearing: now the separation is in hearts and consciences into which no clerical eye can penetrate.

No objection can be raised against the idea of the parish church on the grounds that men themselves fix a boundary to the fellowship of the Church by not entering by baptism into its fellowship. It cannot be said that while its arms are open for all, a fixed boundary is still set by the presence of unbaptized people within the parish. The Word reaches forward in one way or another—further than is contemplated when opponents think about controlling its advance; and the Word cannot reach anyone without something happening. Those who try to retain the idea of membership, which has been taken over from the 'gathered' churches, pick on baptism, since anyone's baptism is something that can be controlled and the fact that it has taken place can be noted in a book: the baptized can be counted. But we must look to the Word and the sacraments themselves, and regard them as the mouth and hands of Christ through which he advances, speaks and acts. He who thus regards the Church is driven by inner necessity to the idea of the parish church. It is indifferent, in this connexion, whether the Church is linked with the state or not. Even if the Swedish Church became a Free Church she would be forced, because of the Gospel, to carry on with the idea of the parish church.

If we maintain a clear and firm grasp of the idea of the open Church we are still free to draw very definite boundaries for *practical* purposes. The drawing of boundaries must not, however, be extended beyond the concrete cases it applies to, so as to enter into the definition of the Church, the Church thereby becoming the sum of those individuals who are within certain boundaries. Into this category fall, for example, book-keeping questions, questions about the right to vote at church elections and of eligibility, as well as about questions of church discipline. It may help us in keeping distinctions clear if now and then we think of certain other situations in life where we have to fix boundaries continually without their having anything essentially to do with the meaning of the concept. Health is something that cannot be achieved in any other way than by living creatures being healthy. Counting the number of healthy people in an attempt to describe what health is would be a complete distortion. Health must be defined otherwise—and it is hardly ever found, moreover, except by contrast with its opposite. But in certain situations people obtain a certificate of fitness, something which other people in the same position cannot obtain. In view of these practical instances there is no reason to make the question of membership into an important question which needs to be answered generically. The same is true in the world of science. Science is a function, just as health is, and is found only where men are engaged upon it. Now and then, for practical reasons, we have got to say that so and so is engaged upon scientific work and, accordingly, is within certain suddenly drawn boundaries, while another person is outside them. But, in reality, the world of science is not a total of individuals: the membership question is not only unnecessary but is actually misleading if it is extended beyond the practical situation to cover the question what science essentially is.

The Church is, of course, a body of people in quite another way than that in which these other two, health and science, are. But she is a body of people whose nature is wrongly described if boundaries, the problem of membership, are dragged into the definition of what the Church essentially is. It can belong to the very essence of something—that is shown in the two examples—that it includes people and functions only in people. Concrete situations can make it necessary that the question of membership, so far as certain matters are concerned, should be raised. Yet in describing the reality in question *function*, activity, must be the guiding principle, and the idea of a *number* of people must be put aside as soon as it arises. That applies most of all in the case of the Church. Her own history also shows that she has been aware of the necessity of refraining from raising the question of membership, and that this question came to the fore first in times when the Word lost its central place and the varied reception of the Word claimed all the attention instead.[1]

It will perhaps be most evident how the Church that is grounded in the Word resolves itself into local churches and lives in them, if it is compared with the Church that is built up on its ministry. Where the concept of the Church is orientated from the concept of the ministry, priests are readily thought of when the word 'Church' is heard. From priests thought moves over to bishops who bestow the office. One of the most important tasks of the episcopate is to defend the Church's rights and the Church's interests over against the world, over against the state. In these days of state absolutism it is easy to become somewhat disturbed about the question whether this episcopal task is receiving sufficient attention. But if, on the contrary, we start out from the *Word*, then the stream of life flows into the body of the Church and runs in the very opposite direction. If one thinks of a priest one thinks immediately of his congregation as well. For the priest exists that the Word and sacraments may move outwards. Out there in many parishes, in homes, in places of work the conflict between God and Satan is being decided. To these places the Word must go. Even the bishop himself exists, first of all, for the *congregations*—just as the other ecclesiastical organizations and authorities are servants of the congregations, servants of the remote places, of the peripheries, which are growing centres of life and fields of conflict. Afterwards the consequences of all the hidden decisions will follow. They follow in the Church Assembly or in Parliament. But these latter bodies have no primary significance for the Church. The life of the Church is not lived in them, does not pulsate in them, is not decided there—just as little as when the bishops assemble as an official body. *Life is the Word*, and the Word moves out to the parishes where men go about their vocations and bear their burdens. Only there can the Word restore the life of man. Only there can fellowship become the fellowship of men's own lives. For the Church's first duty towards the world is not to maintain its own interests against the world, but to go into it with the

[1] When the question of the reception of the Word becomes a major concern in the matter now before us (the discussion of the Church's basis and nature), a question of the last day has become the main concern a phase too soon in redemptive history; what belongs to the harvest has crept into the time of sowing. The sect, the 'churchy' group (*ecclesiola*), always involves the loss of redemptive history, the inability to wait, forestalling sight (II Cor. 5.7). The sect breaks with faith. Where faith is absent there men feel themselves free to do the work that, if only they could wait, God and his angels would do (Matt. 13.41, 49). So the whole task must be done over again at its own time (Mark 10.31).

Word of life.[1] Her conquest is not to be justified over against those who
are without, but to *be lost in* those without, to pass over into humanity.[2]
Her own stability and security is the stability and security of the Word;
if she turns herself into a collective power against the world she loses
her backbone. But if the naked Word presses forward to 'the people',
to the 'uttermost part of the earth', then the kingdom will come.[3]

[1] Otherwise the Church will come to be set over against the world as national
Judaism set itself over against the heathen. It was this self-righteous opposition
which was the object of the criticism of the prophets. It existed for humanity
and this, its true task, could well have been accomplished through events that
outwardly meant Israel's downfall. The same is true of the Church today: the
Word can reach out through the fall of the Church as an institution. God himself can be directly at work in the attack on the Church, which does not for that
reason become good, just as the evil deeds of the Assyrians did not become good
by being the instruments whereby God punished Israel (see Isa. 10.5-12).

[2] The New Testament command to pray for our enemies ought not to be
regarded as envisaging only individual enemies. Intercession was the usual
attitude of the Early Church towards persecuting world powers:' Pray for those
who persecute you' (Matt. 5.44). Our task as preachers in relation to the world
is a direct consequence of this.

[3] It must be stressed that this wide and open fellowship whose life runs along
the naturally-provided human relationships is the communion of *saints*, nothing
less. Openness does not put an end to holiness; it remains and moves outward.
See on this I Cor. 7.14-16, where a picture is given of the Christian Church in
action. The communion of saints is mission by being everyday life.

XV

GOD SPEAKS—MAN LISTENS

1. The Christian week and the Christian year

As a consequence of our approach to the subject we have arrived at the concept of the Church through a door that is seldom used. Usually treatment of the incarnate life of Christ leads straight to the concept of the Church. In that way it is easy to be misled into giving the Church a position that rightly belongs to the next phase in redemptive history, the resurrection of the dead. The Church is falsely described if she is taken as the consummation. She is the road to it, the movement to it, the journey to it and, therefore, she is the movement and the journey of the Word out to the world. In this book we have not passed on from the finished work of Christ on the third day to the Church—but, first of all, as it were, hopped over that and drawn a line from Christ's resurrection right to the consummation. The long chain of divine actions only reaches its objective in the total downfall of Satan. Then will be revealed the full significance of the conquest that is the decisive point in the chain of actions, Christ's death and resurrection. The Church is wrongly understood if she is not understood from the final dominion that lies beyond us, beyond the Church. First we must think of the kingdom. There sight shall prevail. After that we can pass on to the Church, and do so fully conscious of what she cannot offer. Otherwise we readily make sight belong to the Church's day. But it is hearing and listening to the Word that dominate the Church's day. We *hear* even in baptism, even in the Lord's Supper, just as in the days of Christ's earthly life they listened to him, if they were his disciples—they listened even when they saw him. For they who did not take his word to themselves were far away from him even if they saw the outward signs.

We propose now to give further consideration to this Church that listens to the Word—to the Word in which the life of man is on a journey towards a goal, and in which man can journey, thanks to the fact that he hears a voice that leads him on. It here becomes plain why we preach from a passage of Scripture—why, indeed, we preach at all, in contrast to lecturing or expounding. The voice must be heard, and it is a man on a journey who must hear it—hear a bit of the Word at a time. If preaching makes the passage speak, then the living God speaks, and there is forward movement towards the goal of the great chain of actions, and man, as he listens, is led on his way towards life. What the significance of preaching from a passage is can best be perceived by analysing the content of the Christian year. We might say that the Christian year is, in a compressed form, God's long chain of actions. For this reason, too, the Christian year has its obvious centre in the feast of the cross and the resurrection. Redemptive history and the Christian year have the same turning point, the same outcome, Easter and the last day. When redemptive history is preached, the Christian year advances. It is useful at this point to establish certain facts about the origin of the Christian year.

The first Christians neither lived nor thought in terms of a year; they lived in terms of a week and they thought of the work of redemption in terms of a week. In this way concentration on the cross and the resurrection was even more marked than it has ever since succeeded in being. Where the Early Church made a new beginning from the point of view of the calendar was the keeping of *Sunday*, the first day of the week, the day following the Sabbath. Sunday was a day of gladness, because Christ rose at dawn on that day, the first working day of the Jewish week (Mark 16.1 f.). Every week the earliest Christian congregations met for an Easter festival. Continually, with the interval of only a few days, Easter returned anew. The Spirit was poured out, too, and preaching began, on a Sunday, on the fiftieth day after the first Sunday.[1] But the six days that lay between were not just empty days of waiting. So it might have been had the resurrection not been preceded by death, but in the faith of the Early Church the resurrection is linked with the cross and with death. Therefore the suffering of Christ was given a place in the weekdays and the Christian community early in its history came to regard Wednesday and Friday as two 'station days' in his suffering. Wednesday was the day of the betrayal, Friday the day of the death. Accordingly, the *Didache* and *Hermas* (beginning of the second century) speak of the keeping of these two days. In this way the whole week is devoted to Christ's death and resurrection. Station days are the feast of the cross, Sunday is the feast of the resurrection. On station days the rule was to bow down and bend the knee, on Sunday to stand up and

---

[1] Hence the name 'Pentecost' (Acts 2.1). John saw his visions on a Sunday, 'the Lord's day' (Rev. 1.10) and was, therefore, as it is expressed, 'in the Spirit'.

look towards heaven, in free and erect position, singing praise. Thus the week takes primacy altogether over the year and in the course of the week the primitive *kerygma* is heard: Christ has died and is risen again.

Later *yearly* feasts developed. In this case too, Easter was first and gave rise to the rest. Christmas was not celebrated before the fourth century. That provides pretty strong proof that the Incarnation by itself did not stand at the centre of the Early Church's belief. The Incarnation was the presupposition of Christ's conflict and victory, but the *kerygma* dealt with Christ's conflict and victory themselves—that is, with the cross and the resurrection. When, at length, Christmas came it was in order to replace a feast of the sun, whose date was fixed (25th December). Accordingly, it was tied to a date and without connexion with Sunday. The original yearly festivals were two: Easter and Whit. They always go together, the second rests on the first.[1] The Jewish origins of Easter, as well as of Whit, are evident. What matters is that both, in the early days of the Ancient Church, were filled with a content wholly un-Jewish and set on a foundation wholly un-Jewish—Sunday. That Jesus of Nazareth was the one who had been anointed with the Spirit, whose Gospel was to be preached to all peoples, involved a major stumbling-block for any faithful Jew, and the stumbling-block was already inherent in Sunday. It was Sunday which from the very beginning burst the old bottles; in other words, it was Christ's resurrection. When later the yearly Easter and Whit were brought in, they both became *Sunday festivals*—after disputes, of course. The famous Easter controversy of the second century was over the problem whether the Sunday should be victorious over the 14th Nisan. From our point of view it is most interesting that it was Asia Minor that stood out in isolation, holding to the 14th Nisan (whatever day of the week), and that it was the Sunday Easter—and, therefore, of course, Sunday Whit—that was victorious. So the same process was at work in the case of the year as had quickly shown evidence of itself a century or so earlier in the case of the week. The New Testament *kerygma* made its way into the course of the year as it had formerly leavened the week.

Not only the resurrection, but the cross and death as well play their part even in this matter. Just as the suffering of Christ, in the form of station days, took its place in the week alongside the joy and light of Sunday, so the year also was coloured by the Easter of the cross. This is partly due to the fact that the Easter of the Ancient Church was strongly

[1] It cannot be proved that Whit was an independent feast before the third century.

N

characterized by what was later separated off from it and became Good
Friday and partly also to the fact that at quite an early date—as early as
the yearly Easter and Whit—another yearly element was brought in,
which more or less corresponded to the weekly station days, *the days of
the martyrs*.[1] The days of the martyrs were not primarily festivals of
commemoration, but they preached about death as the covering that
conceals life for all those who are in the Body of Christ. The secret of
martyrdom is no other than the secret of Christ's death: it is Christ's
own presence in his Church. For this reason it is a fact of the utmost
importance that the foundation stones of the Christian year in the second
century were partly the Sunday feasts of Easter and Whit, and partly
the days of the week.[2] The year thus appears as an extension of the week
with its basic elements, Sundays and station days. In both cases it is the
kerygma that dominates, for the centre of the *kerygma* is death and
resurrection.

Afterwards the Christian year was built out both backwards and forwards from its centre, Easter. Jesus' birth and the story of his childhood
were filled in. Times of preparation and follow-up of feasts were fitted
into the spaces between, etc. This later liturgical history is of less
interest to us. What matter are the significant beginnings in the second
century. It is worth pointing out, however, that the part of the Christian
year that was later called 'The Year of the Lord'—that is, the time
between Christmas and Ascension Day—has the same proportions as a
Synoptic Gospel: the story of the sufferings receives proportionately
greater space. It is the story of *Christ* alone that provides the framework
for the Christian year—not the whole redemptive history from, and
including, the creation and the fall. It is the Gospel, the message of
victory, that is clearly the main element in the Christian year, just as it
must be the main element in preaching, the herald's call. Redemptive
history is compressed into the Christian year. It quite clearly shows
where the centre of gravity of the message lies. In the part after Whit
no sequence of events can be discerned: between the Ascension and the
Parousia is the time when it is quite simply a matter of preaching and

---

[1] Among the earliest of the days of the martyrs was the death of Polycarp.
It began to be celebrated immediately, that is from A.D. 156. We have no certain
evidence of an annual Easter earlier than about this time.

[2] That Epiphany was celebrated as a Church feast in the first half of the
fourth century is as far as the evidence goes. Earlier, possibly even in the second
century, Epiphany was known as a feast of the Gnostic sects, for the divine
Christ, according to the followers of Basilides, did not emerge at Jesus' birth, but
came down at Jesus' baptism. Jesus' baptism was, therefore, the subject of the
celebration of the Gnostic Epiphany.

that is the content of the chain of events there. But in Advent the congregation is reminded again and again of the goal towards which all preaching moves. The concentration of attention on the last day is certainly a valuable element in the last part of the Christian year, by which the parallel between the Christian year and the history of redemption is emphasized anew.

2. Preaching's exposition of the Christian year

In the Middle Ages the Christian year grew fast, thanks to the saints whose number increased on all sides and whose days began to jostle one another for place. At the same time theology underwent a structural change. The concept of merit was cultivated. The latter was bound up with the former. The *kerygma*, both in preaching and in the Christian year, found itself accompanied by an alien element. If the measure is to be the original Christian year that was built up around the work of Christ, then Luther's reduction of the Christian year did not imply its destruction but its restoration—for it was the alien element, the cult of the saints, that was washed out. 'The Year of the Lord' stood out *more clearly*. At the same time preaching was filled with the genuine *kerygma*. The Gospel *pericopes* were 'served out' in the service of worship, and they were 'served out' in the speech of the people. In this way every Sunday came to have its own distinctive character. Faith itself in the Word, as the bearer of Christ's presence and of the action of the living God, became more important still. The feasts of the Christian year denoted God's actions with the congregation. Time no longer stood in opposition to God's world and eternity but the passage of time was charged with God's activity. Where the Word is given life and voice, men are given life and voice as well; the congregation becomes active in psalm-singing, a new, continually-changing element in the Christian year, which began to give different tones to different parts of the year.

This entity which we, following tradition, have been calling the Christian year, but whose kernel and meaning is 'The Lord's Year', in a certain sense regulated preaching at the time of the Reformation. It is typical that Lizell, when he examines Olavus Petri from 'the point of view of homiletics', cannot find more than one item beyond the simple exposition of the Scriptures and this one item is the concept of the Christian year. Certainly Lutheran reformers were compelled to emphasize that in all such matters we are *free*—free in the matter of all feasts, free in the matter of Sunday (which in no way is the Sabbath so far as meaning is concerned); we might choose any day at all for worship and rest. But, Luther says, the different parts of Christ's work for us must, nevertheless, if they are not to be forgotten, be continually preached; hence the feasts on special days of the year, set apart in order that in preaching these parts may be treated one after another. When 'parts' are mentioned here the reference is to the items in the second article of the Apostles' Creed: conception, birth, crucifixion, death, burial, resurrection, ascension, return—items which in their unity are, in Luther's phrase, like a 'calendar of the whole year in which we celebrate all the feasts of the Lord'. That the Gospel is spread out over the year in this way, and fills all the time with its content, is bound up essentially with what lies in the background—the basic concept of redemption as something still going on, not yet completed, present in the Word, moving towards the rebirth of the world. There exists a striking structural likeness between the Christian year and the parish church. Both bear witness to the fact that the Word moves, goes forward, and, therefore, outward, to the outskirts—'to the end of time' and 'to the end of the world'. When the Word so comes, it is Christ himself who comes. Because he comes as the living One redemptive history is not complete. He who has caught sight of the living Word of the age of the Reformation will not expect to discover in the theology of such an age the elements of the later 'order of grace'. Possibly all the terms of the 'order of salvation scheme' are there, but the search for the *thing itself* is in vain. If Christ has not finished his work and fully completed it, if he is still actively engaged on it, then his *coming* is our life, and movement is located in the *Word* itself and not in 'application' of the Word.

For this reason it is characteristic that when 'the order of grace' begins to take shape, indifference towards the Christian year begins to show. It is a movement, a process, that is the commanding factor in pietistic preaching, but the movement is no longer the course of events in Christ's life, not the long series of actions of redemptive history. The work of redemption is already *accomplished*. To use exact terms, it lies far in the past, objective and stationary. Now the question is how this fully completed work is to lead to holiness. The *individual* must inevitably become the centre of attention. If the movement is Christ's own movement out towards us in the Word, then the *congregation* is the point where life springs up, and it is enough for the individual to be in the congregation —under the Word, in baptism and the Lord's Supper. Christ is with us till the last day. But if Christ's work is done, then the Church is only a place where it is described and set forth in clear statements, and it is another question if *I* have clearly understood this objective fact. 'Holiness' is something off in another direction, in the direction of the future, and everyone approaches it alone. It looks somewhat like trifling with what is serious to introduce the congregation at this point, for it is no longer *Christ* who advances towards his visible kingdom by means of the advancing Word; it is not he who is in conflict in the Word and makes his way forwards as a Conqueror, for he has already conquered—completely—now the conflict has passed to another field: the individual is on his way through the obstacles to holiness. The objective is eschatological and future, just as in the first centuries and in Luther, but the term 'kingdom' does not suit as well and it becomes 'holiness'. In the kingdom the individual is lost in the haze just as much as he is in the Church, but in holiness the individual can remain an individual even after he has attained his goal.

But it is wise for those who polemize against 'the order of salvation' scheme to beware of the danger that they run because of the polemic itself. It is quite clear that the scheme we have been discussing arose at a time when *man* began to take a central position in the spiritual life and that the scheme itself is a product of the general culture of the day, though it might be described as a self-critical product, which was conscious of its own weakness and taintedness, and, for that reason, somewhat nervously introduced a theocentric corrective to give balance. The polemic against the pietistic tendency to talk at every opportunity about how a man becomes a Christian—that is, about man instead of about Christ—can result in a theocentricity against man as man. Such theocentricity is not healthy but poisonous; its usefulness as a corrective in an unhealthy situation does not alter that in the least. The Word is the *creative* Word. That is an insight we must never let slip. Its significance is that when the Word comes, man lives. The human comes into being when God speaks, when Christ advances. The Word's advance towards the *Parousia* does not exclude *our* journeying. On the contrary, it is the case that we stand still and die when the Word is absent. The right order of salvation consists in this that *Christ* does what he does. That is the right thing to say and it must be asserted in face of every attempt to ascribe redemption to human effort. The first step in the order of grace is that Christ was born; then follow his temptations, his sufferings, death and ascension. If indeed it is permissible to talk at all about grace and redemption having an 'order', a sequence, this is it, a series of actions in which Christ is at work and advances and whose outcome is

Whit, preaching, and the last day.[1] But all that takes place with *men*; they are present from the beginning; we are there in all Christ does. But we are present in that series of actions *now*, for they did not just take place in the past, but are now taking place since the Word comes to us and brings everything with it. Christ is in the Word, and approaches us in preaching with his work, just in that regular preaching that treats one 'part' after another. If we carry this argument to its logical conclusion, we may say that the *Christian year*, 'the Year of the Lord', is the only true order of salvation, the order of redemption in which we live, breathe, and have our being, as we live in the congregation. To be a member of a congregation anywhere and to hear the readings as they come is to have share in the works of the living God—is to journey, listening all the while to the Voice.

The Christian year is an order of salvation that does not lead men to any other stage than to that of the parish church. We must often reflect that before the eighteenth century the piety of the people was, in a sense, anonymous and without contours. After that, movements and parties stood apart from each other and it belongs to the very nature of a spiritual movement to have a 'programme', and thereby it separates itself off from the given relationship. He who lives in the Christian year, on the contrary, cannot create for himself any other spiritual home than the congregation in which he lives. Christian faith of that type has long existed in such a land as Sweden, both before these movements and alongside them till the present day, though it is seldom documented by historians enquiring about pietistic movements. The fellowship of such faith is usually the fellowship of vocation and the fellowship of a parish church. Of this Christian faith the words of Luther might well be employed: it 'falls from heaven like rain, which makes the earth fruitful'.[2] Rain is soon lost to sight, but growth is healthy where rain falls—though the rain itself loses its life, as the corn of wheat must lose its life when it falls in the earth and dies. In the Christianity of the Christian year, of the parish church, and of the work of every day, about which we are speaking here, there is a certain readiness to die and disappear in what is always an unprogrammatic and anonymous relation to one's *neighbour*. That readiness arises from the fact that it is in an unusually pure form a Christianity of the *Word*.

[1] When it is a question of that event, it is easy to see in the New Testament the marks of a time sequence. Indeed it belongs to the very nature of Early Christianity to regard redemption as something that has thus been realized in time. See the treatment of this in O. Cullmann, *Christ and Time* (ET, 1951).

[2] *WA* 40(I), 51.21-23.

That we now find ourselves in a hard and almost unendurable opposition between Church and people in our country is due to many causes
none of which can be dismissed. One of them, however, deserves special
mention: this Christianity of the Word has not been appreciated, often
not even recognized, for it lives half-hidden in the very human, very
local relationships of villages, while what is sought after and eagerly
desired are all sorts of revivals, which are of questionable value, nearly
always give rise to sects, or are destined gradually to choose for themselves what has in all ages been the unacknowledged motto of the self-
established fellowship: 'I will save my life, not lose it.'[1] Where this desire
to live and to hold one's ground is dominant the life of man withers
away on all sides. Where rain falls, readily runs down into the earth and
disappears, life springs forth and there is growth. That is the meaning
and desire of the Word: to be able to go out and create new life among
men who believe in the Word but not in the fellowship that they themselves would create. Fellowship belongs to that place where I meet my
neighbour: it does not need to be sought out, for I stand there already.
In that same place, too, the Word dwells; it comes in the course of the
year itself. The forward march of the Word to Advent will continue
until the life of man is free and restored in the Consummation. To break
away from the outward fellowship in which everyone is involved would
mean that we believed we had already attained, or, at any rate, were in
advance of some others. But to abide in the fellowship that God has
established is to let judgement wait until the future, and for the present
to maintain our hope—that is to say, to understand that so long as God's
actions are incomplete so long the chain of events goes on. It suffices to
hear the Gospel, and then carry on with one's calling.

3. Divisions of the text and of the congregation

The doctrine of the 'order of holiness', as it was developed in Lutheran
orthodoxy and Pietism, has had direct results in preaching, in so far as
it drove out the 'three stages' (*tritomi*), the threefold application. Earlier
Lutherans were familiar with a fivefold application, *usus quintuplex*. A
preacher had to find in every passage five applications: doctrine, refu-

---

[1] Thus cleavages must appear, and mission—that is, movement outward—
be rendered impossible. Mission in such cases becomes a special piece of work
and then it belongs to the very nature of mission to be carried on hundreds of
miles away from the congregation engaged on it. But there is a mission that is
wholly in line with the outward movement of the work of one's calling and the
parish church. World mission can be seen as the continuation of the local congregation: the Word goes out to the ends of the earth.

tation, nourishment, punishment, and consolation. In Sweden this five-fold application played a very small part in preaching. Such a procedure was, of course, stereotyped and clumsy. But it is to be noted that the preacher who adopted this scheme of a fivefold application did not thereby come under the control of a dogma of a developing process in which men supposedly have their place. In applying the passage the preacher did not address different groups of men whose positions were set out at different stages along a line. When the *usus quintuplex* was changed by Rambach to a threefold scheme, the 'order of grace' was introduced into homiletic theory. Three groups were then addressed—unsaved, repentant and saved. In Germany, where it was constructed, this scheme of preaching remained in fashion for a short time, but in Sweden, where it was adopted by specially outstanding and influential preachers, it set its stamp on preaching for a couple of hundred years. Even today in Sweden, conservative ecclesiastical preaching proceeds in this way.

The risk is that it is primarily *men* who are divided and not the Word. Movement and life and forward march are on man's side. There are men asleep in their security who have not yet begun to think. Those who are aroused have advanced somewhat farther but they are not yet in grace. Most difficult of all is it to fit in 'those in grace'; theoretically they should be put in front of 'those who are awakened', but in that case as one well knows, the *theologia gloriae* opens like a chasm at our very feet. A much felt need to be able to devalue progress on man's side manifests itself in a general unwillingness to make a division at all between 'those who are awakened' and 'those in grace'. By such correctives we in no way got rid of the major risks and dangers in the scheme of preaching and the care of souls that we have been considering. The 'division' of the living Word is not what comes uppermost, for in the first instance it is to *men* that the division applies; they must be divided *so that* then, in the second place, the Word may be divided.

Luther's 'division' is primarily the division of the Word; further, it is a division of it into *two*. Both these facts are important. Those in the congregation are all one; every one of them is *simul justus et peccator*, the preacher himself included. But the *Word* divides itself: it is law and Gospel. The law belabours the old man, the Gospel nourishes the new man. *Both* parts essentially concern *every* man. Of course, the hearers can be grouped from different points of view, but how the division is made depends upon the particular point of view that is adopted: at one time there may be two groups, at another five, three, six, etc. Two things must always be avoided: making a *principle* out of any grouping, whatever it may be, and allowing any grouping to be based on progress in the appropriation of redemption. Progress that leads a man downwards and backwards is just as risky, just as new-fangled, as the superficial, perfectionist progress.

But if we only say that Luther divides the Word and not men, and that the division is a twofold one into law and Gospel, we have not touched on what, in this connexion, is the vital point. If we only say this, the usual intellectualizing of law and Gospel can continue unhindered. The intellectualizing referred to could be described—in schematic form —in this way. The preacher thinks, 'The Word in this passage is law, therefore I ought to preach the law', or 'This is the Gospel, therefore I ought to preach the Gospel.' Here, then, we have fixed concepts, 'law' and 'Gospel'. It is really the preacher who produces and employs these two. The passage gives occasion to produce them—now the one, now the other. If Luther's sermons be examined from this point of view, they appear confused, unclear, disordered, carelessly arranged. Time and again we stand perplexed and can only say, 'This is neither law nor Gospel; this is only textual exposition, repetition of the passage.' But when Luther preached, he did what he did after having given full consideration to the task of the preacher and after having rejected the subtle type of preaching that sets itself *above* the passage. He did not consider that the passage became law and Gospel by being expounded. The expositor is only to provide mouth and lips for the passage itself so that the Word may advance and then the Word becomes law and Gospel in the heart of the listener. That is something wholly different from the practice of the priest sometimes preaching the law and sometimes the Gospel.

'There is no man on earth who can separate law and Gospel', says Luther at one point in his Table Talk. 'We often think to ourselves as we listen to a sermon that we understand it, but much is lacking. *Only the Holy Spirit knows the art.* Not even the Man Christ knew it out on the Mount of Olives. So an angel had to strengthen him.'[1] Luther is thinking about Luke's account of Jesus' struggle in Gethsemane: 'And there appeared to him an angel from heaven, strengthening him' (Luke 22.43). Luther is thinking more about the situation where someone is listening to the preached Word, than about the situation where someone preaches the Word to others. The listener hears the Word without knowing if it is law or Gospel he hears. Therefore doubt can arise; he is not

[1] *WA Tischreden*, II, 3.20-4.1 (No. 1234).

able to separate body and conscience, but when the Word comes in judgement it applies not only to the body but presses in upon the conscience and drives out the Gospel. That is what it means to be in Christ, the tempted and the crucified, and in his body, the Church—to engage in conflict with Satan. But this thesis about our inability in practice to make a division between 'law' and 'Gospel'—we can do it very well in theory—applies just as much when we preach the Word to others. And God makes most successful use of his law and Gospel when we, who preach, cannot separate them and cannot push in our concept of the law and our concept of the Gospel between the passage and men. It is the passage that is to be preached and the passage *is* God's Word: if only *it* advances and manages to speak, the Spirit is present, and the Spirit knows well in what hearts judgement is needed and in what hearts mercy is needed. The Spirit is present in the flock that listens when the Word in its simplicity is there, but that means that law and Gospel are separated, for 'the Holy Spirit knows the art'. The preached Word journeys along different roads to different hearers. Of how that comes about the priest needs to know nothing. There is no other reason for poking into the spiritual state of the hearers than clerical inquisitiveness. The ability to avoid such rootling about in souls can only be attained by resting more on the *Word itself* than on its exposition. If we begin to trust in certain methods of exposition we steal faith from the Word and give what we have stolen to a certain way of preaching, that is to say, to a movement, a tendency, that is quite modern. With that subjectivism has got its head.

4. Preaching's exposition of the Bible

The really great preachers—who often provide occasion for the rise of schools where there is more confidence reposed in the 'methods' of these masters than in the Word—are, in fact, only the servants of the Scriptures. When they have spoken for a time the very words of the passage, the quotations from the Bible, come to have such power as if the Word sounded forth for the first time. It gleams within the passage itself and is listened to: the voice makes itself heard. The passage was perhaps read at an earlier point, but it was not heard because of multifarious thoughts in the mind of the listener which got in its way. The preacher has since been at work on these obstructing thoughts, that is, he has been contending against the power of the enemy, and now at last the passage is heard, at last the Word (*verbum*) has broken down argumentation (*ratio*).

The preacher is, therefore, not to set out from a passage and then pursue side issues suggested by the passage, but he must step aside for it, give it a mouth, and remain himself *in subjection* to the Word. The passage itself is the voice, the speech of God; the preacher is the mouth and the lips and the congregation, the company of people there, the ear in which the voice sounds. For only by the Word are we created men, not by the conceptions that arise from the Word. The passage is an act of the living God, who alone can make us men. To listen to the passages as they come *is* to go in 'the order of salvation'—to live in the great chain of events of the Bible, of the Christian year—to be born, to suffer, to die and rise again—to become men, to receive life. For the long road of the Bible is the road of humanity, the road by which humanity becomes healthy and pure and redeemed through Christ's life, death and conquest. We travel along a road by travelling a bit at a time. Preaching that surveys everything—that lectures, rises superior to the passage, and sets forth an all-embracing system of ideas—results in our hearing nothing and in our leaving the road for the dead world of timelessness, where God is dumb and where there is a spurious seeing before the true seeing comes. The Word has *life*; hence there are set passages, there is limitation, 'bits', a calendar, a Christian year.

Hence, too, it is sufficient to *listen* to the Word—not first of all to classify it as law and Gospel and thereby allow conceptions to come in between oneself and the Word and create an obstacle to the Voice so that it is no longer heard. First we must *listen*, let the Word come home to us, leave it to the Spirit to chasten the heart or to comfort, as he will. The Word divides itself when it advances and makes an entry. Only in order that the Word *may* advance—may go out into the world, and force its way through enemy walls to the prisoners within—is preaching necessary.

XVI

THE DIVINE AND THE HUMAN

1. *Luther's understanding of the* communicatio idiomatum

In bringing our study of the essential nature of preaching to a close with an analysis of the Lutheran doctrine of the sharing of Divine and human attributes, the *communicatio idiomatum*, it is not our intention to describe in detail the history of this theme in Luther or in later Lutheranism. Just as in the case of the question of the sacraments, we are limited by the general subject of our study, preaching. Added to that, our concrete reason for turning at this point to a discussion of the *communicatio idiomatum* has the effect of fixing our attention on certain restricted aspects of the subject. In determining the content of the concept 'the Word of God', Barth on many different occasions touches critically and negatively on Luther's beliefs about the relation between the human and the divine in the Incarnation, the Scriptures, the Lord's Supper, preaching, and faith; and we have this Barthian criticism specially in mind.

Idioma means especially that attribute that is essential to something, and that distinguishes one thing from another. The *communicatio* of attributes is a Christological relation that is typical of Luther's theology —a 'sharing' of the attributes of Christ's divinity with those of his humanity, and a corresponding sharing of the attributes of his humanity with those of his divinity. Thus God suffered and died when the Man Jesus suffered and died. On the other hand, man was raised to heaven when Christ sat down on the right hand of the Majesty on high. This doctrine cannot be understood unless it is seen against its background: the attempt, especially from the Reformed side, to make a gulf between the divine and the human. In the controversies about the Lord's Supper especially, there sprang up differences and conflicts about the relation between God and Man in Christ. For Luther, Christ was in the bread and the wine; for the Swiss he was with his divinity in heaven, while the meal proceeded on a human plane. For this reason the doctrine of the Lord's Supper was the point where the two Christologies met and conflicted. That only meant, however, that an inner difference between Reformed and Lutheran doctrine showed itself at this point, not that it originated here. The differences existed from the beginning. They go back ultimately to the Thomistic tradition, in which the Reformed churchmen, and perhaps one might say Calvin in particular, stood, and to the fact that for Luther, who was determined to derive his whole theology from the Scriptures, such a philosophical framework for the Word was alien. Under the Reformed contraposition of divine and human lurked the Greek doctrine of the two worlds, which had countless supporters in the course of European theology and philosophy. Luther was one of the few who was outside this broad stream—which contributed to making him a good expositor of the Bible, for the Bible is also outside it.

Now, the reality expressed in the doctrine of the *communicatio idiomatum* is by no means restricted to Christology. Wherever one turns in Luther's theology, one comes upon the same theme. And the theme in question is nothing other than the Gospel itself. Apart from the Gospel Luther had no concept of God into which he could have fitted the revelation in Christ as a significant modification of our knowledge of God. Rather he starts by knowing nothing of God; then he stands before Christ's cross; and afterwards he seizes upon the words and expresssion that he has been able to find in the Gospel to state the fact that *here*, in this humiliation, *God* dwells. He does not first of all construct a theory about God's honour and majesty and then set the meanness of the cross *over against* God's honour. Rather he begins with the cross and finds majesty there—a majesty, of course, not like our own—so that Christ's kingdom does not need to be a kingdom of this world and he who is truly a bondservant becomes the first of all (Mark 10.42-45). This means that dominion consists in service, and the power of a king in the Gospel, in mercy and in self-giving.

In Reformed thought, on the contrary, God's honour is something that is opposed to forgiveness, opposed to the lowliness of Christ. Barth is strongly influenced by this. His criticism of Luther's thesis about the *communicatio idiomatum* goes back to his conception of God's majesty, and (what follows from that) the opposition between God and man. His intention is to make God holier and more divine by setting him in opposition to man, but, in reality, in this way God becomes very like us in his basic attitude and in his reactions. The Incarnation cannot work a miracle—that of grace and love—in God's being and heart: even in Christ the divine and the human natures stand opposed to each other as 'the high' (*Höhe*) and 'the low' (*Tiefe*). For Luther, it is just *majesty* that is humble. *Majesty* lies in the manger and hangs on the cross, for there, in poverty, is the true Conqueror of Satan. God's honour consists in this, that he redeems, not in thinking about himself. God's majesty is a conquering majesty—the majesty of a conqueror who bleeds on the battlefield, not an unconcerned, far-away, and distinguished majesty on high. Just because God accomplished his purpose in suffering and down-fall he is *fathomless*. If he sat majestically on high he would be easy to understand. We should only need to prolong the measure of our own honour to infinity to have the formula for God's holiness. But now there he is, down in the depths, on Golgotha. Such a God we can never understand; he is hidden in the midst of his revelation. We cannot rise above faith, however long we live. Only by death and resurrection do we attain to sight, full understanding and knowledge (I Cor. 13.12). Faith is not a faith that strives towards the higher stage of knowledge within this earthly life, but a faith that contents itself with being faith until the clear vision of the last day. It is not *fides quaerens intellectum*, but simply *fides*.

If the *communicatio idiomatum* implies a unity between Christ's human and divine natures, and if this unity is an expression of the Gospel itself, it is to be expected that Christ's death and resurrection, the content of the Gospel, will somehow confront us in this relationship. That indeed is the case. Yes, the *communicatio idiomatum* has its roots quite simply in this—that Christ, on the one hand, died in humiliation and, on the other, rose in exaltation. It is the *kerygma* with this double content that comes first. It has to be given expression and the formula *communicatio idiomatum* is an expression of what is real, an attempt to say what happened, happens, and shall yet happen. Luther and his successors refused to systematize the doctrine of the *communicatio idiomatum*; they refused to enumerate attribute after attribute; they refused to speculate, but held firmly to *certain* attributes that were chosen with reference to *redemption* and were thus drawn from the actual *Gospel*. So far as Jesus' human attributes are concerned, all the emphasis lies on the suffering and death. Not only the Man Jesus, but also the divine nature, had part in the event on Calvary. And so far as the divine attributes are concerned, it is the exaltation, the sitting on the right hand of power, that is the main thing. Not only had Christ's divine nature part in the event at Easter and the Ascension but the poor man Jesus is in heaven, which means that we are there. God is in Jesus Christ; therefore we are in God. This is no speculation and gratuitous statement; this is the *kerygma* about his death and resurrection, the Gospel of the acts of the merciful God, set forth in such a way that it can be what it is: the Word was God and became flesh (John 1.1, 14).

Unity between cross and resurrection does not imply that they are the same. Dying is one thing, rising another. But victory is already accomplished on the cross; majesty is there, concealed in death. And in the resurrection humiliation is not cut away but it remains even in the dominion of Christ as the risen One. The unity of, as well as the difference between, the cross and the resurrection is best perceived if attention is directed to the death, the crucifixion, that man experiences and the resurrection that, in like manner, is man's experience today. Christ's death and resurrection do not take place to stand alone, while man remains apart from them; they take place, on the contrary, to implicate us, to kill us, and to raise us up. Accordingly we cannot share his death without sharing also his resurrection, nor his resurrection without his death. We may very well die without rising to salvation and eternal life for we can, of course, be destroyed. But in that case there is a death that has not taken place, the death of the old man, the death of sin. On the contrary, the body of sin takes the tiller and steers the whole man, spreads itself through our heart and conscience, and brings all to death and destruction. In that case it is the real death on the cross that is lacking: the old man has, in that case, never been crucified. If the cross is present, if selfish appetites are curbed and drowned, then it is impossible that *life* should not also be present. There is no ground on which we can stand and let the subjugation take place if *faith* is absent. To accept the heavy strokes of fortune and not to be embittered, but to show them the way to the sinful body, which needs these hard blows, is not only to die, but it is to live, to breathe freely, to have one's head above the surface of the water and to see the shore, to taste the resurrection of the dead. Conversely, to share in the resurrection of the new man is to emerge into that light where we see for the first time the contours of the old man and experience judgement on ourselves as the murderous blows fall on our own body, even as we recognize that these blows are life and salvation, just as health returns when a boil is cut away.

2. *The* communicatio idiomatum *in the Word*

Death and resurrection, about which we are talking here, would never take place if the Word did not reach man. It is the Word that provides the feet on which Christ walks when he makes his approach to us and reaches us. Law subdues what is evil in us and lays us low under its chastening blows when these fall from left and right. The Gospel abolishes sin from our conscience and thereby places us under the kingship of the risen Christ, which at last shall emerge in visible form and towards which the body too is on its way by taking upon itself the burdens of the law, and bearing the cross. The Word is law and Gospel. He who proclaims the Word has to give it voice and utterance; then of itself it will accomplish its double work in the hearts of the listeners. The Spirit is in the Word and knows the art of separating law and Gospel, of apportioning judgement and restoration. The question is, however, if something more cannot be said about the preacher's task in relation to the Scriptures and the hearers—something further on *how* he is to make the voice of the passage heard and understood.

Preaching has but one aim, that Christ may come to those who have assembled to listen. That too is the great object of the passage, since it is a passage from the Scriptures. The Word, the Bible, carries within itself Christ's coming as its general aim, to which all tends. At any particular time, however, it is one particular passage that is its voice; it is a certain 'bit' provided for the journey. When the preacher enquires about the general aim he finds it to be Christ's coming, and when he bows obediently before its words, accommodates himself to the *simplicitas* of a passage, he finds it to be humanity. Even in the passage and even in preaching, the *communicatio idiomatum* holds sway. God's greatness eludes us if we seek to attain it by cutting away what is human, what is poor and mean in the Gospel narratives. It is in the simple words, in what is human in the Bible, that God's power is hidden; divine and human must not be separated. We must beware of attempting to cleave the Word with a daring stroke and with Barth to reckon on two levels in the Word—'high' (*Höhe*) and 'low' (*Tiefe*), 'God's Word' (*Gotteswort*) and man's word (*Menschenwort*). Indeed part of the hiddenness in the revelation consists in the 'worldly nature' of the Word—its humanity, its historicity. The *real* hiddenness consists, however, in this, that the Word, which gives us life, tastes death, bitterness and judgement, and actually conveys death and judgement to us, so that the body of sin may be destroyed and we may live. This hiddenness, too, which is a vertical division of the Word, a duality in the Word's conversation with us, a division into law and Gospel, is lost if the Word is cleft horizontally. In the latter case we become half uninterested in the outward, human Word which is the bottom storey; the whole interest in the Word becomes speculative, centred, as it is, on looking into the upper storey, the superhuman, as if Christ had not been a man come in lowliness. It is just the cleavage of the Word into law and Gospel that holds us back from speculations and reminds us that we are still in the battle, in time, on the journey where death and resurrection happen to us and where the true Christ thus lives in us. Rising from 'the word of man' to 'the Word of God' is rising from redemptive history to sight and the *Parousia*, that is, it is moving to that place where Christ has not yet come. Now he is in the *kerygma*, in the outward Word.

3. The necessary humanity of preaching and the Church

The task of the preacher is to speak this outward Word in such a way that it reaches the man who hears it. It is not possible to say anything further about the entrance of that Word so long as we refuse to particularize about how that Word comes home to anyone. One sure means of obstructing the Word is to regard oneself as within the sacred sphere and the dull listeners without. Understanding the odd secularized life of these people then becomes the main task, and very soon methods become more important than the Word. What belongs to the very nature of secularized man is that he is a sinner and the approach to him ought not to be so impossibly difficult and inconceivable for the preacher, who is secularized in this way himself and will continue to be so till his last breath. He only needs to look honestly within and see how the Word strikes him, how it wounds and upsets him, how he is healed and consoled and restored by it. It is by no means certain that his experience will be shared by his congregation. He is not in the pulpit to turn out his inside but to give voice to the Word. Since he is a man, however, and since all to whom he speaks are also men, he can often let the passage say to them what it has said to him—but all the time, as a protection, he must keep two things in mind: the aim, *scopus*—that Christ may come through the Word; and simplicity, *simplicitas*—that the actual text of the passage must determine what is said. To undertake so dangerous a task as preaching without this dual protection leads to misfortune. Our ability to speculate is too great, and that includes argumentation (*ratio*), which likes to operate on its own against the Word. That is, in the end, to cast the passage aside, so that its voice is not heard and life does not come to the listener.

When, however, the voice penetrates to the conscience there it is both law and Gospel. If the passage has struck the preacher a blow, then it has been both, for the preacher is *simul justus et peccator* just as his

o

hearers are. If he has been struck, if it has come home to him, then already the Word is twofold, even if in analysing its concepts he is not able to say what in it is Gospel and what law. Did he succeed in doing that, it would be almost the same as Barth's splitting of the Word into 'the Word of God' and 'the word of man'; the *communicatio idiomatum* would be lost. Death cannot be isolated from resurrection. Life lies hidden in the bitter, wounding, killing Word. The preacher only knows that he has been gripped, uplifted and held fast by Christ who comes in the passage—now the passage has succeeded in going out with Christ into the congregation and that is preaching. He is thus the living Christ with his cross and resurrection in the preached Word, and therefore God's Word is in the midst of his humanity. Humanity is not something like a vestibule, for *Christ* is man, his divinity has been poured forth in humanity. Nor is judgement, law, something like a vestibule, for death has been united with the resurrection. Christ comes into the heart when judgement is passed on the old man. If human existence stood opposed to divine existence, then the human could never be swept into the divine. Satan and sin it is who stand in conflict with God. For that reason the human cannot constitute a danger for the divine, nor be a lower sphere where God's glory is locked up and diminished. If Christ is not man, man is lost. If, on the other hand, Christ is man, Satan is lost. But *God* is not lost; he retains his glory in the cross and the humiliation. God's glory consists in this, that he redeems. And he does that by coming *sub contraria specie*, clothed in his opposite.

When, thinking specially of the Word in preaching, we speak of 'the human' or of 'humanity', the expression has a very rich content. First and foremost we have Jesus' own humanity in mind, to which the Gospels continually bear witness—his outward poverty, his hunger, his thirst, his lack of knowledge, his anxiety in face of death, his prayers to his Father, and his unity with other men. Preaching cannot flee from that; for that would mean fleeing from the true and living God. In the midst of all this is the divinity of Christ, not above it. Then after that comes the humanity of all Israel and of the Old Testament. That, too, belongs to *Christ's* humanity; it is a life and a struggle that is lived and fought out so that at last *Jesus* may be born, live and struggle, that is to say, that God may save humanity. To make use of an Old Testament saying is to make use of a saying that he read in his uncertainty to reach certainty, or which he used in his weakness to gain strength. It is a historical human saying, with historical human results in him—and therefore a divine saying. Humanity, again, consists in the unique particularity of any passage, its concentration on a concrete event or human situation, as for example, the widow with the two mites, Peter sinking in the sea, the children who are blessed or Zacchaeus. All these are to be found in the lives about us today; they are not figures locked up in the Scriptures, but are sitting in the pews, and they can *listen* just because what is read is so limited and so human: Christ comes now and has to do with all these people once more. The passage read is the work of the living God in them. Those around Jesus who need help are present in the readings, so that *we* may be enabled to be there too and 'to go in the Word' with our whole earthly and sinful existence. Last of all this humanity is the humanity of preaching itself, its search for us where we are in the twentieth century. The *communicatio idiomatum* means that the priest may venture to belong to his own age and mix in the ordinary life of society without thereby losing the divine life. It is this search, this outgoing movement, that is the sign of life in the *kerygma*. The message does not lose its divine content when it moves out, but it loses it when it does not move out, when it keeps within the temple walls and fears being in the world, in the depths, among the doubters, prisoners and sinners. Divinity is not something different from the search, but it is the search itself, self-giving. When preaching willingly concerns itself with the needs and problems of its time, there takes place once more what ought to take place: Christ sits at the table with publicans and sinners, that is, with us. In the human, the divine is present.

For Barth, on the contrary, the human is a smooth, flat surface, from which the divine rebounds. Revelation comes from above, and strikes the surface—but the human point where it strikes does not come into the revelation. That point is a 'sign' that 'points' upwards; the downward movement changes into an upward movement, as when a ball strikes a floor. It may be, again, that the divine is mirrored in the shiny and opaque surface of the human so that an 'image' on the human plane results while the divine reality remains on high. The feeling produced in Barth by Luther's talk of God's entry into the world is, one can believe, almost one of disgust, something like that repugnance awakened by an intimacy that has gone too far. It is quite inconceivable to him that anyone should be able to regard him as too intimate with God. Yet that is just the actual reaction to his theology in Lutheran circles. Barth knows far too much about God; his concept of God has elements that he did not obtain from the revelation of Jesus Christ, but from another source—from some divine region, some 'high place' with which he is familiar and which he can set *against* the revelation in lowliness. Luther is ignorant about God, far from God, unable by speculation to produce a single thought about God: for this reason he has nowhere else he can go but to the humanity of Christ when he wants to seize hold of God. The doctrine of the *communicatio idiomatum* is evidence of Lutheran inability to speculate, that delightful inability that is faith's contentment with the Word. For this reason that same doctrine is the foundation of true preaching, for to stand there with the passage in question, and *not to be able* to speculate, is to understand the presupposition of the possibility of preaching. What destroys the *kerygma* most of all is *gnosis*.

Often before we have had cause to reflect on the place of preaching in redemptive history between Easter and the *Parousia*. The message is the act of the living God by which today he carries forward, to the fulness of health which lies in the future, that long chain of events that had its beginning in the primeval days of creation. The passages of Scripture as they follow each other in temporal succession show the continuing activity of redemptive activity itself. As out of these passages, out of the Word, man drinks life, he lives the true life of man, the life that is destroyed as soon as he turns away from the Word and tries to stand by himself, as if no powerful enemy threatened him. To listen to the divine voice is to live a human life. It is a sort of *communicatio idiomatum* in our life: the divine and the human cannot be separated. Our human existence arises out of the divine action in the Word (cf. Deut. 30.20; 32.47). Christ is the first true man, for he is God, the Conqueror of that power that is hostile to man. The Church is human and should not be disquieted when she observes that side in herself, when she experiences in herself the welling up of fresh human life—human life could not spring up within her were she not divine, the body of Christ, the presence of the Spirit in the age of conflict. Passing from the age of conflict to that of sight does not break up the unity of the divine and the human: the resurrection body is the triumph of the Spirit over the flesh, it is the break-through of Christ, and for that reason the resurrection body is a human body, 'the image of God'. When that point is reached man's creation as a human being as it was intended in Gen. 1.26 will be complete. Conceptions like these were much in evidence in the Ancient Church—for example in Irenaeus. They abounded in Luther, not least in his last major work, the *Commentary on Genesis*. Of their congruity with the Bible there can be no question. Divine and human are intertwined most intricately of all, and are most difficult to disentangle, in the link between God and man, in the Christian life on earth as it is lived in faith's fellowship with God and in love's fellowship with one's

neighbour. If I live in faith in God and in comradeship with my neighbour, responsive to his needs, then it is God who loves my neighbour.
The link between faith and love is the link between the divine and
human natures, for there dwells in faith the Christ who comes down
and is incarnate in the love of one's neighbour, which is born of faith.
Just as Christ took the likeness of a servant when he came the first time
in human form (Phil. 2.6-8), so he continually takes the likeness of a
servant when he comes in human form, that is to say, in acts of service
towards a neighbour, in his body on earth. Christ in the heart is just as
great a miracle as Christ in the bread or Christ in the womb of Mary.
The Word was not just God once upon a time, did not just once upon a
time become flesh (John 1.1, 14), but the Word *is* God and now *becomes*
flesh. It comes with the reading of the passages of Scripture, with the
advance of the *kerygma* as a living Word, with Christ's divinity hidden
in the ordinary human voice that proclaims the Word. It presses home
to the heart by faith and becomes man in actions lacking glitter and
brilliance as the Son becomes man in the stall. There lay God in the
manger, and there is faith down in the depths—out there in our commerce with other men. Christ is changed into us, and therefore we are
changed into each other. At one point after another the *communicatio
idiomatum* takes place: in the Incarnation, in the Word, in the Church,
the sacraments, in faith and love, and in the resurrection. Today, in the
present phase of redemption's long course of divine actions, it is
preaching that is the bearer of this transforming, creative power. Every
passage of Scripture with which preaching deals, and to which it gives
voice, is an action of the living God.

Even the point on which we have just touched shows the usual affinity
between the *communicatio idiomatum* and the double event of death and
resurrection. It is certainly not into a profane and God-abandoned world
that love for one's neighbour comes down, but into one regulated by
God's law, a world of violence and unwilling service. Through love,
which unselfishly flows forth and breaks down violence from within,
which is free 'to do or to leave undone', which reshapes what is there
and masters all laws, the Spirit creates the world anew. For the old man
worldly rule and vocation are oppressive, burdensome, and cramping in
their demand for service to one's neighbour; for the new man, the whole
system of regulations of the outer world is softened, for the new man is
God, and God is love, the Recreator, occupied in the marshalling of his
powers for conflict against the destroyer and enemy of the world. For
Luther, who more than most thought through the problem that is in-

volved in the relation between unforced love for one's neighbour and the law that compels us to serve him, the connexion between freedom and force is itself the main question when we are concerned about the part that the Church should play in world affairs. That interpretation of Luther according to which for him freedom attaches to *certain* acts and force to *others* is by inner necessity incorrect, for force is the coercion, the crucifixion, and the death of the old man, while freedom is the resurrection of the new man, his conquest and life—but death and resurrection cannot be separated. The kingdom of works is at one and the same time the kingdom of law and the kingdom of love. No attempt should be made to determine when it is the one and when it is the other. Both freedom and force are there at the same time, for the Christian is *simil justus et peccator*. The Word gives life when it kills and heals, when it stings and cleanses.

4. Our need of a theology of the Word

The Barthian criticism of the *communicatio idiomatum* is based on a speculative tendency that betrays itself at every point in the dialectical theology, and that makes very difficult the task that same theology sets itself, of making theology a theology of the *Word*. Here the Word is volatilized because the Incarnation has been volatilized. There is no reason why Lutherans should conceal or modify this criticism against the leading theologians of today—so much the less when they themselves are made the butt for an attack in grand style from that very quarter. It chances that the attack is concentrated just now on the Lutheran picture of society and the distinction between law and Gospel. This acute opposition, however, is only one result of the decided antagonism between Barth and Luther on the most central point of theology, Christology, that emerged in the 1920s and has lasted ever since. Should further conflict break out in years to come between the Lutheran and the Barthian outlooks, Lutherans may enter the fray and carry on the conflict with a good conscience, confident that in doing so they are not only on the side of Luther but on the side of the Bible as well. Here the Lutheran theologians—and this applies to us Swedes too—have the advantage of knowing Luther by the research they have done on the primary sources better than their counterparts.

That does not mean that systematic theology within Lutheranism is untouched by speculation and is a pure theology of the Word. Looking at work that has been going on for several decades in Sweden, one is compelled to say that, with us, all becomes *history*, and the task of ascertaining what the Word means today is quite impossible of solution as a scientific task. One must not regard such theology as a theology of the Word. Discussion of what belongs to essence and what to expression is confined to religio-philosophical questions; as soon as it is a question what is the content of the Christian faith the attention is directed away from the present to history, and fastens on what once *was* Christianity, in Luther or Paul. It may be that there is concealed here a fateful legacy of the school of Schleiermacher, for which dogmatics was a *historical* science. The Barthian tendency to combine the *kerygma* with theology makes for strength and not for weakness. The only question is how it is to be done. This much in any case we may say: in the debate about the task and method of systematic theology there is every reason for Swedish theologians not only to ward off the Barthian attack but also to listen and—above all—call in question their own method over again, and direct the hunt for speculative and metaphysical elements into their own domains. The territories of our neighbours have been fine-combed in that sort of game. It is so very difficult to keep free from theological speculation, from a theology of ideas instead of a theology of the Word, that those who exclusively direct their criticisms against others unfailingly end by resembling the man who tries to take the mote out of his brother's eye.

A theology of the Word cannot be chosen in preference to something else chosen by others. On the contrary, we ought to be able to converse with theologians of widely differing viewpoints, on the basis that we have all made the *same* choice and are working towards the same end. The real problem is how that end is to be reached, what hinders and what helps. One thing is certain: the worst of all hindrances is to believe that the end has been reached. A theology that does not criticize itself is not in a position to criticize others. The elements that defile theology are so intimately bound up with the whole cultural situation that no theology of the present day is free from them.

INDEX OF NAMES AND SUBJECTS

INDEX OF BIBLICAL REFERENCES